AUSTRALIA, OCEANIA, and ANTARCTICA

A Continental Overview of Environmental Issues

THE WORLD'S ENVIRONMENTS

KEVIN HILLSTROM AND
LAURIE COLLIER HILLSTROM, SERIES EDITORS

Global warming, rainforest destruction, mass extinction, overpopulation—the environmental problems facing our planet are immense and complex.

ABC-CLIO's series *The World's Environments* offers students and general readers a handle on the key issues, events, and people involved.

The six titles in the series examine the unique—and common—problems facing the environments of every continent on Earth and the ingenious ways in which local people are attempting to address them.
These are the titles in this series:

Africa and the Middle East

Asia

Australia, Oceania, and Antarctica

Europe

Latin America and the Caribbean

North America

AUSTRALIA, OCEANIA,

and

ANTARCTICA

A Continental Overview
of Environmental Issues

KEVIN HILLSTROM
LAURIE COLLIER HILLSTROM

A B C ☙ C L I O
Santa Barbara, California
Denver, Colorado   Oxford, England

Copyright © 2003 by Kevin Hillstrom and Laurie Collier Hillstrom

Library of Congress Cataloging-in-Publication Data

Hillstrom, Kevin, 1963–
  Australia, Oceania, and Antartica : a continental overview of
environmental issues / Kevin Hillstrom, Laurie Collier Hillstrom.
      p. cm. — (The world's environments)
  Includes index.
  ISBN 1-57607-694-6 (hardcover : alk. paper); ISBN 1-57607-695-4 (eBook)
  1. Environmental sciences—Southern Hemisphere. 2.
Australia—Environmental conditions. 3. Oceania—Environmental
conditions. 4. Antarctica—Environmental conditions. I. Hillstrom, Kevin, 1963– .
World's environments.

  GE160.S645H55 2003
    363.7'0099—dc22   2003020748

07 06 05 04 03   10 9 8 7 6 5 4 3 2 1

This book is also available on the World Wide Web as an eBook.
Visit http://www.abc-clio.com for details.

ABC-CLIO, Inc.
130 Cremona Drive, P.O. Box 1911
Santa Barbara, California 93116–1911

This book is printed on acid-free paper ∞.
Manufactured in the United States of America

Contents

List of
Tables and Figures

Tables

Figures

Introduction
THE WORLD'S ENVIRONMENTS

A s the nations of the world enter the twenty-first century, they confront a host of environmental issues that demand attention. Some of these issues—pollution of freshwater and marine resources, degradation of wildlife habitat, escalating human population densities that place crushing demands on finite environmental resources—have troubled the world for generations, and they continue to defy easy solutions. Other issues—global climate change, the potential risks and rewards of genetically modified crops and other organisms, unsustainable consumption of freshwater resources—are of more recent vintage. Together, these issues pose a formidable challenge to our hopes of building a prosperous world community in the new millennium, especially since environmental protection remains a low priority in many countries. But despite an abundance of troubling environmental indicators, positive steps are being taken at the local, regional, national, and international levels to implement new models of environmental stewardship that strike an appropriate balance between economic advancement and resource protection. In some places, these efforts have achieved striking success. There is reason to hope that this new vision of environmental sustainability will take root all around the globe in the coming years.

The World's Environments series is a general reference resource that provides a comprehensive assessment of our progress to date in meeting the numerous environmental challenges of the twenty-first century. It offers detailed, current information on vital environmental trends and issues facing nations around the globe. The series consists of six volumes, each of which addresses conservation issues and the state of the environment in a specific region of the world: individual volumes for *Asia, Europe,* and *North America,* published in spring 2003, will be joined by *Africa and the Middle East; Australia, Oceania, and Antarctica;* and *Latin America and the Caribbean* in the fall of the same year.

Each volume of The World's Environments includes coverage of issues unique to that region of the world in such realms as habitat destruction, water pollution, depletion of natural resources, energy consumption, and development. In addition, each volume provides an overview of the region's response to environmental matters of worldwide concern, such as global warming. Information on these complex issues is presented in a manner that is informative, interesting, and understandable to a general readership. Moreover, each book in the series has been produced with an emphasis on objectivity and utilization of the latest environmental data from government agencies, nongovernmental organizations (NGOs), and international environmental research agencies, such as the various research branches of the United Nations.

Organization

Each of the six volumes of The World's Environments consists of ten chapters devoted to the following major environmental issues:

Population and Land Use. This chapter includes continental population trends, socioeconomic background of the populace, prevailing consumption patterns, and development and sprawl issues.

Biodiversity. This chapter reports on the status of flora and fauna and the habitat upon which they depend for survival. Areas of coverage include the impact of alien species on native plants and animals, the consequences of deforestation and other forms of habitat degradation, and the effects of the international wildlife trade.

Parks, Preserves, and Protected Areas. This chapter describes the size, status, and biological richness of area park systems, preserves, and wilderness areas and their importance to regional biodiversity.

Forests. Issues covered in this chapter include the extent and status of forest resources, the importance of forestland as habitat, and prevailing forest management practices.

Agriculture. This chapter is devoted to dominant farming practices and their impact on local, regional, and national ecosystems. Subjects of special significance in this chapter include levels of freshwater consumption for irrigation, farming policies, reliance on and attitudes toward genetically modified foods, and ranching.

Freshwater. This chapter provides detailed coverage of the ecological health of rivers, lakes, and groundwater resources, extending special attention to pollution and consumption issues.

Oceans and Coastal Areas. This chapter explores the ecological health of continental marine areas. Principal areas of coverage include the current state of (and projected outlook for) area fisheries, coral reef conservation, coastal habitat loss from development and erosion, and water quality trends in estuaries and other coastal regions.

Energy and Transportation. This chapter assesses historic and emerging trends in regional energy use and transportation, with an emphasis on the environmental and economic benefits and drawbacks associated with energy sources ranging from fossil fuels to nuclear power to renewable technologies.

Air Quality and the Atmosphere. This chapter reports on the current state of and future outlook for air quality in the region under discussion. Areas of discussion include emissions responsible for air pollution problems like acid rain and smog, as well as analysis of regional contributions to global warming and ozone loss.

Environmental Activism. This chapter provides a summary of the history of environmental activism in the region under discussion.

In addition, each volume of The World's Environments contains sidebars that provide readers with information on key individuals, organizations, projects, events, and controversies associated with specific environmental issues. By focusing attention on specific environmental "flashpoints"—the status of a single threatened species, the future of a specific wilderness area targeted for oil exploration, the struggles of a single village to adopt environmentally sustainable farming practices—many of these sidebars also shed light on larger environmental issues. The text of each volume is followed by an appendix of environmental and developmental agencies and organizations on the World Wide Web. Finally, each volume includes a general index containing citations to issues, events, and people discussed in the book, as well as supplemental tables, graphs, charts, maps, and photographs.

Coverage by Geographic Region

Each of the six volumes of The World's Environments focuses on a single region of the world: Africa and the Middle East; Asia; Australia, Oceania, and Antarctica; Europe; Latin America and the Caribbean; and North America. In most instances, the arrangement of coverage within these volumes was obvious, in accordance with widely recognized geographic divisions. But placement of a few countries was more problematic. Mexico, for instance, is recognized both as part of North America and as the northernmost state in Latin America.

Moreover, some international environmental research agencies (both governmental and nongovernmental) place data on Mexico under the North American umbrella, while others classify it among Central American and Caribbean nations. We ultimately decided to place Mexico in the Latin America volume, which covers Central and South America, in recognition of its significant social, economic, climatic, and environmental commonalities with those regions.

Similarly, environmental data on the vast Russian Federation, which sprawls over northern reaches of both Europe and Asia, is sometimes found in resources on Asia, and at other times in assessments of Europe's environment. Since most of Russia's population is located in the western end of its territory, we decided to cover the country's environmental issues in The World's Environments Europe volume, though occasional references to environmental conditions in the Russian Far East do appear in the Asia volume.

Finally, we decided to expand coverage in the Africa volume to cover environmental issues of the Middle East—also sometimes known as West Asia. This decision was made partly out of a recognition that the nations of Africa and the Middle East share many of the same environmental challenges—extremely limited freshwater supplies, for instance—and partly because of the space required in the Asia volume to fully explicate the multitude of grave environmental problems confronting Asia's central, southern, and eastern reaches. Coverage of other nations that straddle continental boundaries—such as the countries of the Caucasus region—are also concentrated in one volume, though references to some nations may appear elsewhere in the series.

Following is an internal breakdown of the volume-by-volume coverage for The World's Environments. This is followed in turn by overview maps for the current volume showing country locations and key cities and indicating physical features.

Africa and the Middle East

Middle East and North Africa:

Algeria
Bahrain
Cyprus
Egypt
Gaza
Iraq
Israel
Jordan
Kuwait
Lebanon
Libya
Morocco
Oman
Qatar
Saudi Arabia
Syrian Arab Republic
Tunisia
Turkey
United Arab Emirates
West Bank
Yemen

Sub-Saharan Africa:

Angola
Benin
Botswana
Burkina Faso
Burundi
Cameroon
Central African Republic
Chad
Congo, Democratic Republic of
   (Zaire)
Congo, Republic of the

Côte d'Ivoire
Equatorial Guinea
Eritrea
Ethiopia
Gabon
Gambia
Ghana
Guinea
Guinea-Bissau
Kenya
Lesotho
Liberia
Madagascar
Malawi
Mali
Mauritania
Mozambique
Namibia
Niger
Nigeria
Rwanda
Senegal
Sierra Leone
Somalia
South Africa
Sudan
Tanzania
Togo
Uganda
Zambia
Zimbabwe

Asia

Afghanistan
Armenia
Azerbaijan

Bangladesh

Bhutan

Cambodia

China

Georgia

India

Indonesia

Iran

Japan

Kazakhstan

Korea, Democratic People's
  Republic of (North)

Korea, Republic of (South)

Kyrgyzstan

Lao People's Democratic Republic

Malaysia

Mongolia

Myanmar (Burma)

Nepal

Pakistan

Philippines

Singapore

Sri Lanka

Tajikistan

Thailand

Turkmenistan

Uzbekistan

Vietnam

Australia, Oceania, and Antarctica

Australia

Cook Islands

Fiji

French Polynesia

Guam

Kiribati

Nauru

New Caledonia

Northern Mariana Islands

Marshall Islands

Micronesia, Federated States of

New Guinea

New Zealand

Palau

Papua New Guinea

Pitcairn Island

Samoa

Solomon Islands

Tonga

Tuvalu

Vanuatu

Wallis and Futuna

Various territories

*(Note: Antarctica is discussed in a
  stand-alone chapter)*

Europe

Albania

Austria

Belarus

Belgium

Bosnia and Herzegovina

Bulgaria

Croatia

Czech Republic

Denmark

Estonia

Finland

France

Germany

Greece

Hungary

Iceland
Ireland
Italy
Latvia
Lithuania
Macedonia, Republic of
Moldova
Netherlands
Norway
Poland
Portugal
Romania
Russian Federation
Slovakia
Slovenia
Spain
Sweden
Switzerland
Ukraine
United Kingdom
Yugoslavia

**Latin America
and the Caribbean**
Argentina
Belize
Bolivia

Brazil
Caribbean territories
Chile
Colombia
Costa Rica
Cuba
Dominican Republic
Ecuador
El Salvador
Guatemala
Guyana
Haiti
Honduras
Jamaica
Mexico
Nicaragua
Panama
Paraguay
Peru
Suriname
Trinidad and Tobago
Uruguay
Venezuela

North America
Canada
United States

AUSTRALIA

TASMAN SEA

CORAL SEA

ARAFURA SEA

TIMOR SEA

INDIAN OCEAN

SOUTHERN OCEAN

TASMANIA

QUEENSLAND

NEW SOUTH WALES

Canberra

VICTORIA

NORTHERN TERRITORY

SOUTH AUSTRALIA

WESTERN AUSTRALIA

500 km

0

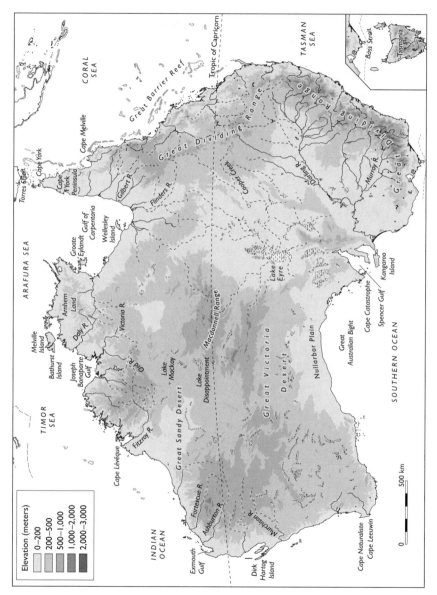

AUSTRALIA

Elevation (meters)
- 0–200
- 200–500
- 500–1,000
- 1,000–2,000
- 2,000–3,000

INDIAN OCEAN

TIMOR SEA

ARAFURA SEA

CORAL SEA

TASMAN SEA

Bass Strait

Tasmania

Torres Strait
Cape York
Cape York Peninsula
Cape Melville
Great Barrier Reef
Tropic of Capricorn

Gilbert R.
Flinders R.
Gulf of Carpentaria
Wellesley Island
Groote Eylandt
Arnhem Land
Melville Island
Bathurst Island
Joseph Bonaparte Gulf
Daly R.
Victoria R.

Great Dividing Range
Great Dividing Range
Cooper Creek
Darling R.
Murray R.

Cape Lévêque
Fitzroy R.
Great Sandy Desert
Ord R.

Lake Mackay
Lake Disappointment
Macdonnell Range
Lake Eyre

Exmouth Gulf
Fortescue R.
Ashburton R.
Murchison R.
Dirk Hartog Island

Great Victoria Desert

Nullarbor Plain
Great Australian Bight
Cape Catastrophe
Spencer Gulf
Kangaroo Island

Cape Naturaliste
Cape Leeuwin

SOUTHERN OCEAN

0   500 km

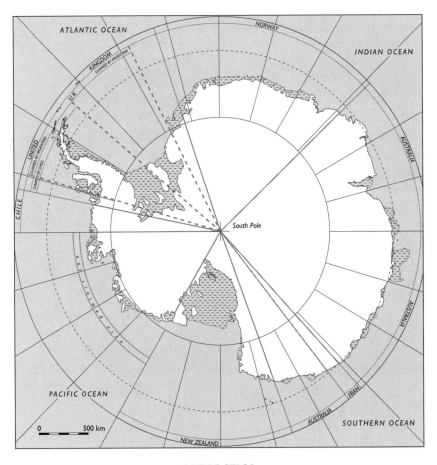

ATLANTIC OCEAN

NORWAY

INDIAN OCEAN

KINGDOM
CLAIMED BY ARGENTINA

UNITED

U.K.

CLAIMED BY ARGENTINA

CLAIMED BY CHILE

CHILE

AUSTRALIA

South Pole

AUSTRALIA

PACIFIC OCEAN

FRANCE

0   500 km

AUSTRALIA

SOUTHERN OCEAN

NEW ZEALAND

ANTARCTICA

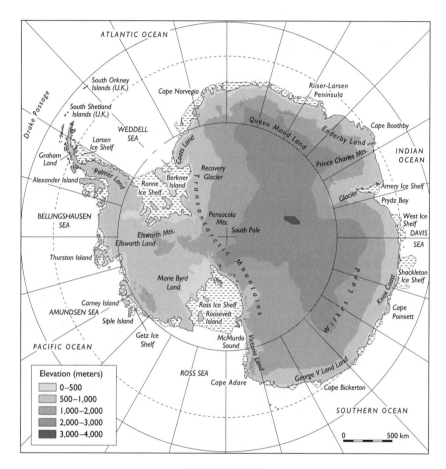

ATLANTIC OCEAN

South Orkney
Islands (U.K.)

Cape Norvegia

Riiser-Larsen
Peninsula

Drake Passage

South Shetland
Islands (U.K.)

WEDDELL
SEA

Queen Maud Land

Enderby Land

Cape Boothby

Larsen
Ice Shelf

Coats Land

Recovery
Glacier

Prince Charles Mts.

INDIAN
OCEAN

Graham
Land

Palmer Land

Berkner
Island

Ronne
Ice Shelf

Glacier

Amery Ice Shelf

Alexander Island

Prydz Bay

BELLINGSHAUSEN
SEA

Pensacola
Mts.

South Pole

West Ice
Shelf

Transantarctic Mountains

Elsworth Mts.
Ellsworth Land

DAVIS
SEA

Thurston Island

Wilkes Land

Shackleton
Ice Shelf

Marie Byrd
Land

Knox Coast

Carney Island

AMUNDSEN SEA

Ross Ice Shelf
Roosevelt
Island

Cape
Poinsett

Siple Island

Getz Ice
Shelf

McMurdo
Sound

Victoria Land

PACIFIC OCEAN

Elevation (meters)

- 0–500
- 500–1,000
- 1,000–2,000
- 2,000–3,000
- 3,000–4,000

ROSS SEA

Cape Adare

George V Land Land

Cape Bickerton

SOUTHERN OCEAN

0   500 km

ANTARCTICA

OCEANIA

Acknowledgments

The authors are indebted to many members of the ABC-CLIO family for their fine work on this series. Special thanks are due to Vicky Speck, Martha Whitt, and Kevin Downing. We would also like to extend special thanks to our advisory board members, whose painstaking reviews played a significant role in shaping the final content of each volume, and to the contributors who lent their expertise and talent to this project.

Biographical Notes

Authors

KEVIN HILLSTROM and **LAURIE HILLSTROM** have authored and edited award-winning reference books on a wide range of subjects, including American history, international environmental issues, environmental activism, outdoor travel, and business and industry. Works produced by the Hillstroms include *Environmental Leaders 1* and *2* (1997 and 2000), the four-volume *American Civil War Reference Library* (2000), the four-volume *Vietnam War Reference Library* (2000), *Paddling Michigan* (2001), *Encyclopedia of Small Business, 2d ed.* (2001), and *The Vietnam Experience: A Concise Encyclopedia of American Literature, Films, and Songs* (1998).

Advisory Board

J. DAVID ALLAN received his B.Sc. (1966) from the University of British Columbia and his Ph.D. (1971) from the University of Michigan. He served on the Zoology faculty of the University of Maryland until 1990, when he moved to the University of Michigan, where he currently is Professor of Conservation Biology and Ecosystem Management in the School of Natural Resources and Environment. Dr. Allan specializes in the ecology and conservation of rivers. He is the author of *Stream Ecology* (1995) and coauthor (with C. E. Cushing) of *Streams: Their Ecology and Life* (2001). He has published extensively on topics in community ecology and the influence of land-use on the ecological integrity of rivers. He serves or has served on committees for the North American Benthological Society, Ecological Society of America, and the American Society of Limnology and Oceanography. He serves or has served on the editorial board of the scientific journals *Freshwater Biology and Journal of the North American Benthological Society*, and on scientific advisory committees for the American Rivers and Nature Conservancy organizations.

DAVID LEONARD DOWNIE is Director of Education Partnerships for the Earth Institute at Columbia University, where he has conducted research and taught courses on international environmental politics since 1994. Educated at Duke University and the University of North Carolina, Dr. Downie is author of numerous scholarly publications on the Stockholm Convention, the Montreal Protocol, the UN Environment Program, and other topics in global environmental politics. From 1994 to 1999, Dr. Downie served as Director of Environmental Policy Studies at the School of International and Public Affairs, Columbia University.

CHRIS MAGIN was educated at Cambridge University, England. He took an undergraduate degree in Natural Sciences and a Ph.D. in Zoology, conducting fieldwork on hyraxes in Serengeti National Park, Tanzania. Since then he has been a professional conservationist, employed by various international organizations, mainly in Africa and Asia. He currently works for Flora and Fauna International. His special areas of interest are desert ungulates, ornithology, and protected area management.

JEFFREY A. MCNEELY is Chief Scientist at IUCN-The World Conservation Union, where he has worked since 1980. Prior to going to IUCN, he spent three years in Indonesia, two years in Nepal, and seven years in Thailand working on various biodiversity-related topics. He has published more than thirty books, including *Mammals of Thailand* (1975); *Wildlife Management in Southeast Asia* (1978); *National Parks, Conservation and Development: The Role of Protected Areas in Sustaining Society* (1984); *Soul of the Tiger* (1985); *People and Protected Areas in the Hindu Kush-Himalaya* (1985); *Economics and Biological Diversity* (1988); *Parks for Life* (1993); *Expanding Partnerships for Conservation* (1995); *Biodiversity Conservation in the Asia and Pacific Region* (1995); *A Threat to Life: The Impact of Climate Change on Japan's Biodiversity* (2000); *The Great Reshuffling: The Human Dimensions of Invasive Alien Species* (2001); and *Ecoagriculture: Strategies to Feed the World and Save Wild Biodiversity* (2003). He is currently working on a book on war and biodiversity. He was Secretary General of the 1992 World Congress on Protected Areas (Caracas, Venezuela), and has been deeply involved in the development of the Convention on Biological Diversity. He is on the editorial board of seven international journals.

CARMEN REVENGA is a senior associate within the Information Program at the World Resources Institute. Her current work focuses on water resources, global fisheries, and species conservation. She specializes in environmental indicators that measure the condition of ecosystems at the global and regional level, and is also part of WRI's Global Forest Watch team, coordinating forest monitoring activities with Global Forest Watch partners in Chile. Ms. Revenga is lead author of the WRI report *Pilot Analysis of Global Ecosystems: Freshwater Systems* (2000) and a contributing author to the WRI's *Pilot Analysis of Global Ecosystems: Coastal Ecosystems* (2001). These two reports assess the condition of freshwater and coastal ecosystems as well as their capacity to continue to provide goods and services that humans depend on. Ms. Revenga is also the lead author of *Watersheds of the World: Ecological Value and Vulnerability* (1998), which is the first analysis of a wide range of global data at the watershed level. Before joining WRI in 1997, she worked as an environmental scientist with Science and Policy Associates, Inc., an environmental consulting firm in Washington, DC. Her work covered topics in sustainable forestry and climate change.

ROBIN WHITE is a senior associate with the World Resources Institute, an environmental think tank based in Washington, DC. Her focus at WRI has been on the development of environmental indicators and statistics for use in the *World Resources Report* and in global ecosystems analysis. She was the lead author of the WRI report *Pilot Analysis of Global Ecosystems: Grassland Ecosystems* (2000), which analyzes quantitative information on the condition of the world's grasslands. Her current work focuses on developing an ecosystem goods and services approach to the analysis of the world's drylands. A recent publication regarding this work is WRI's Information Policy Brief, *An Ecosystem Approach to Drylands: Building Support for New Development Policies.* Ms. White completed her Ph.D. in geography at the University of Wisconsin, Madison, with a minor in wildlife ecology. Before joining WRI in 1996, she was a policy analyst with the U.S. Congress, Office of Technology Assessment.

Contributors

ANGELA CASSER recently completed her Ph.D. in international environmental law at the University of Melbourne, where she has examined methods to improve the implementation of international freshwater agreements in both Australia and the People's Republic of China. Angela has written widely on the subject of freshwater, including groundwater and wetlands, and has also contributed written work to various international organizations including IUCN—the World Conservation Union—the World Wide Fund for Nature, and the Ramsar Convention Bureau. Casser is presently based at the Environmental Law Institute in Washington, DC, as a visiting scholar, and is cochair of the American Society of International Law's Environmental Interest Group for 2003.

A. M. MANNION is an Honorary Fellow (formerly Senior Lecturer) in the Department of Geography at the University of Reading, United Kingdom, where she lectured on biogeography/biodiversity, agriculture, environmental history, and environmental change from 1977 to 2001. She earned her Ph.D. in Geography (environmental history) at the University of Bristol, UK, in 1975. Her publications include seven books, more than thirty refereed articles in academic journals, and over thirty contributions to encyclopedias and other reference works.

KATHRYN MILES received her Ph.D. in literature from the University of Delaware and is currently an assistant professor of English and Environmental Studies at Unity College. She has worked as a freelance environmental writer for several newspapers and magazines, and has published on British modernism in academic journals. She is a member of ASLE (Association for the Study of Literature and the Environment), NAAGE (North American Alliance of Green Education), and the Virginia Woolf Society.

Population and Land Use

The South Pacific is a region of exceptional diversity, not only in terms of its flora and fauna but also in its human communities. The nations and territories of Oceania—defined here as Australia, New Zealand, Papua New Guinea, and twenty-one other states and territories dotting the surface of the world's largest and deepest ocean—contain a tremendous range of ethnicities and cultures, as evidenced by the fact that more than 2,000 distinct languages are spoken across the region. Lifestyles and community characteristics run the spectrum as well, ranging from the bustling cities of Australia and New Zealand, where standards of living are very high and technological innovations abound, to the remote jungle villages of Papua New Guinea, where natives continue to engage in subsistence forms of hunting and farming.

But while demographic and socioeconomic circumstances vary from island to island, the nations and territories in Oceania share many of the same fundamental concerns about their capacity to absorb continued population growth and steadily rising levels of resource consumption. Indeed, unsustainable land and resource use has emerged as a major concern across the South Pacific, from the island continent of Australia to Niue and Nauru and other small island nations.

Population and Land Use Trends in Australia

Population in Australia

Australia is an affluent and highly urbanized country that is seeing steady population growth. In mid-2002 its total population was estimated at 19.7 million (Population Reference Bureau, 2002), an increase of 11 percent from one decade earlier. Population growth forecasts have an inherent level

1

of uncertainty, but based on present trends, it is estimated that Australia's population at 2050 will reach 25 to 28 million, an increase of roughly 25 to 30 percent from present levels (Australia Bureau of Statistics, 2001; Population Reference Bureau, 2002).

Much of Australia's population growth in the last half-century is directly attributable to immigration from Europe, the former home of most of the 5.5 million migrants who have settled in the country since the conclusion of World War II. This steady stream of European migrants has boosted the percentage of Australians of European descent to approximately 94 percent of the total population. People of Asian and Middle Eastern descent account for nearly 5 percent of the population, while the indigenous Aborigines and Torres Strait Islanders account for about 1.5 percent of the population. These latter groups, reduced by the mid-twentieth century to a fraction of their former size by the repercussions of European colonialism—exposure to disease, cultural disruptions, theft of land, and general discriminatory treatment— have experienced rapid population growth in recent decades. Improved access to education, health care, and economic opportunities have all been cited as factors in this robust growth rate.

Most Australians live in urban settings. In fact, about 65 percent of Australia's population is concentrated in the nation's five major cities—Sydney, Melbourne, Brisbane, Perth, and Adelaide—and Sydney and Melbourne together accommodate more than 8 million people, more than 40 percent of the country's total. These and other population centers are located at various points on the country's coastline, especially along the southern and eastern coasts. In some of these cities, population and residential densities in the core of the metro area are on the increase, a trend sometimes called "reurbanization" (Krockenberger, 2002). But the prevailing growth trend is still suburbanization extending outward from the cities, a process that has been blamed for habitat loss and degradation; increased pressure on biodiversity; rising infrastructure expenses for new roads, water lines, and schools; and increased consumption of fossil fuels such as gasoline used in longer commutes (the total vehicle distance traveled by Sydney residents rose by 24 percent just between 1991 and 1998) (New South Wales Environmental Protection Authority, 2000; National Land and Water Resources Audit, *Landscape Health in Australia*, 2001). The famously rugged and arid interior of the country, meanwhile, remains only sparsely populated.

Few countries in the world can match Australia's wealth and standard of living on a per capita basis. Ranked among international leaders by such basic measuring sticks as literacy, educational level, life expectancy, and household income, Australia was one of only four countries to increase its share of the

Cities such as Sydney, Australia, have experienced enormous growth in recent decades.
FRANK KLETSCHKUS/IMAGESTATEPICTOR/PICTUREQUEST

global economy during the past twenty years, and during the 1990s its gross domestic product (GDP) grew at a higher rate than that of nearly any other industrialized country (Australian Bureau of Statistics, 2002). Much of this prosperity is the result of Australia's extensive investments in oil, mining, forestry, farming, and other natural resource industries, many of which have a strong export component.

Indeed, Australia's economy has been heavily reliant on the harvest, extraction, and management of its natural resources throughout its history, and recent years have been no exception. For example, in 2000 Australia's farming, forestry, and mining sectors accounted for 57 percent of the country's total export income (Australian Bureau of Agriculture and Resource Economics, 2001). Still, in Australia's most heavily populated states—New South Wales and Victoria—agriculture, mining, and forestry no longer enjoy unchallenged claims to land and resources. The primacy of these traditional powers is increasingly challenged by tourism and recreation, service industries, urban and suburban developments, and other constituencies.

The Past, Present, and Uncertain Future of Mining in Australia

Mining—the extraction of minerals, fossil fuels, and construction materials such as sand and gravel from the earth—has a long and colorful history in Australia. Coal was discovered in Newcastle within three years of European settlement, and exports of coal began before the turn of the nineteenth century. The discovery of gold in 1851 created a gold rush that doubled the European population of the continent within a decade. In fact, many regions of Australia were first opened to European settlement by prospectors or mining companies. Mining continues to make an important contribution to the nation's economy today. Australia is among the world's leaders in production of bauxite, lead, mineral sands, silver, uranium, zinc, coal, cobalt, copper, gold, iron ore, nickel, lithium, and industrial diamonds.

Although mining provides important economic benefits to the Australian people, it also carries a number of environmental costs. Particularly in its early days, mining caused considerable damage to the continent's land and water resources, as well as to its human and animal inhabitants. Some of the more common problems associated with mining and related processing operations include: disturbance and erosion of soil; disruption, overuse, or pollution of groundwater; contamination of surface water with sediments, chemicals, or heavy metals; and destruction of natural ecosystems through the creation of water-filled pits, heaps of

(continues)

Given Australia's comparatively low population density, it does not consume nearly as much of the world's natural resources as do the United States, China, India, and other countries with larger populations. Nonetheless, Australia's per capita consumption levels are among the highest in the world. At the beginning of the twenty-first century, Australia had the highest per capita emissions of greenhouse gases—the chemicals responsible for global climate change—on the planet. In addition, its per capita generation of municipal waste was second only to that of the United States, and per capita water use in Australia was the fifth highest in the world, even though the country occupies the driest inhabited continent on the planet. Its rate of degradation of arable land has also been cited as the highest in the world (Christoff, 2002).

Australia's high levels of personal income and overall material affluence are obvious factors in these elevated rates of consumption. Other factors frequently cited for Australia's high resource consumption levels include a popular belief that the continent's resources are virtually inexhaustible, and trust that ongoing technological innovations and scientific advances will be able to

mining refuse, and abandoned mining operations.

One of the most famous examples of the environmental devastation that can be wrought by mining can be found in Queenstown, Tasmania, which was the site of copper mining and smelting operations for many years. First the hills surrounding the city were clear-cut of timber to provide props for mine pits and fuel for smelters. Then sulfurous emissions from the smelting plant killed whatever vegetation was left on the hillsides downwind of town. The thin soil soon eroded away, filling the local river with gray sludge and leaving a barren, moonlike landscape that has become an unlikely tourist attraction.

Another example of the lasting environmental problems that can be caused by mining is the sediment-laden Ringarooma River in Tasmania. A

century of alluvial tin mining operations dumped an estimated 40 million cubic meters of sediment into the river. This material raised the riverbed near the mines by 4 to 6 meters (12 to 18 feet) between 1930 and 1970. Sediment was also carried 30 kilometers (18.6 miles) downstream and deposited in an estuary, where it accumulated to the point that a wharf that had once served oceangoing ships was rendered useless.

Yet another example of environmental damage from mining occurs at Captains Flat, located on the Molonglo River in New South Wales. Captains Flat was the site of zinc, copper, gold, and pyrite mining between 1874 and 1962. During this time, uncovered tailings dumps were spread over 15 hectares of land. When the dumps collapsed, they contaminated the river and

(continues)

downstream pastureland with heavy metals. The affected area was rehabilitated at great public expense beginning in 1979.

Proponents of Australia's mining industry note that it has become much more environmentally sensitive over the years. They point out that the rehabilitation of mining sites, which is considered routine (and often required by law) today, rarely occurred before the 1960s and 1970s. In 1996, the industry launched the Australian Minerals Industry's Code of Environmental Management. This code, which was agreed upon by forty-one companies representing 80 percent of Australia's mineral production, sets forth a series of environmental standards for mining operations. In addition, several individual companies have created their own environmental policies, which emphasize sustainable development.

Critics of the Australian mining industry claim, however, that companies changed their ways only after increased public scrutiny prompted new government regulation. They also point out that contemporary mining operations, while more environmentally sensitive than those of the past, still create environmental problems. For example, a tailings dam at the Jabiru uranium mine overflowed in 1995, contaminating nearby land and water with radioactive waste. Also in 1995, a gold mining operation near Parkes in New South Wales accidentally released cyanide used in gold processing. This toxic chemical was responsible for killing large numbers of birds and fish in the surrounding area. And environmentalists charge that routine mining operations also degrade local watersheds and other wildlife habitat.

Mindful of the public outrage that has accompanied heavily publicized

(continues)

adequately address the environmental problems that will crop up during the twenty-first century and beyond. The merits of these perspectives have been the subject of heated debate in Australia (and other parts of the world where resource consumption rates are high, such as North America and Europe) throughout the last decade, especially as consumption rates have spiraled upward in nearly every measurable sector. For example, end-use consumption of energy by the residential sector has increased by 60 percent since 1975, even though the general population registered only a 35 percent increase during that time (Australian State of the Environment Committee, 2001).

Together, Australia's rapidly expanding population and its appetite for energy, food, and material goods have had an appreciable impact on the health and integrity of the environment, both on the continent and around the world. In fact, studies issued in recent years make a strong case that the coun-

mining pollution incidents, the
governments of several Australian
states have become reluctant to
grant new mining permits without
making a full assessment of the
potential environmental impact of
the proposed operations. For
example, in 1996 the government of
New South Wales denied a permit for
a gold mine potentially worth $1.2
billion in order to preserve Lake
Cowal and its 170 species of
waterbirds.

The future of mining in Australia
appears likely to involve conflict
over opening new lands to mineral
exploration. Large sections of land
on the continent are currently off
limits to the mining industry. Some
of these lands have been set aside
for Aboriginal peoples, and others
have been protected as national
parks. Proponents of opening such
lands to mineral exploration argue
that it is necessary to maintain
Australia's economic health. They
claim that the industry can conduct
mining operations in an
environmentally sensitive manner
and rehabilitate disturbed areas
afterward. The industry faces stiff
opposition from environmentalists,
however, who feel that these lands
should be protected from the
potential damage associated with
mining activities.

Sources:

Aplin, Graeme. 1998. *Australians and
Their Environment*. Melbourne: Oxford
University Press.

Flood, Peter. 1992. "Wealth from Rocks."
In *The Unique Continent*. Edited by
Jeremy Smith. Queensland: University
of Queensland Press.

Young, Ann. 2000. *Environmental
Change in Australia since 1788*. 2d ed.
Melbourne: Oxford University Press.

try is presently traveling down environmentally unsustainable pathways in a host of areas, from farming and forestry to water use and energy policy (Australian Conservation Foundation, 2000; Christoff, 2002). "The historical increase in population—coupled with Australia's high standard of living and continuing growth in economic activity, rates of resource extraction and carbon emissions—has placed profound pressures on the Australian and global environment," summarized Peter Christoff, lead author of a major 2002 report on the state of Australia's environment. "Australia's severe environmental problems—including land degradation, water shortages, and declining biodiversity—will be exacerbated if an increasing population demands our present standard of living while still using existing technologies" (Christoff, 2002).

The commonwealth government and various state agencies have themselves acknowledged serious shortcomings in current land- and water-use practices (New South Wales Environmental Protection Authority, 2000; Australian State of the Environment Committee, 2001). As one national report flatly stated in 2001: "[T]he pressures on Australia's landscapes have intensified and the condition of Australia's lands continues to deteriorate" (Australian State of the Environment Committee, 2001).

Land Use

The Australian commonwealth's 2001 analysis of Australia's environmental standing cited six key land use issues confronting the country and its people: accelerated erosion, altered habitats, invasive species, secondary salinity and acidity, nutrient and carbon cycling, and soil and land pollution (ibid.). These and other manifestations of intensive land use, especially in Australia's more densely populated regions, have fundamentally transformed the natural character of vast tracts of land; in fact, more than half of the continent's total land area has been cleared, thinned, or otherwise significantly modified for human use (Organization for Economic Cooperation and Development, 1998). Indeed, one recent study states that 38 percent of all native forests, 25 to 30 percent of eucalypt woodlands, 30 percent of rain forest communities, 45 percent of heath communities, 90 percent of temperate woodlands, and a major share of native grasslands in coastal plains have been permanently cleared (Australian Bureau of Statistics, 2001; National Land and Water Resources Audit, *Australian Native Vegetation Assessment 2001*, 2001). "Today less than half of the continent has a level of naturalness equivalent to that of pre-European occupation. In Victoria, less than 5 percent of the land is in this category, and Tasmania, often considered a wilderness destination for trekkers, has only 35 percent of land classed as remote and highly natural" (Australian State of the Environment Committee, 2001).

This erosion of natural systems seems unlikely to slacken any time soon, given current practices. In the 1990s, more than 450,000 hectares were cleared of native vegetation on an annual basis for roads, homes, commercial developments, and extractive purposes, and there are indications that this rate of clearance is actually increasing (National Land and Water Resources Audit, *Australian Native Vegetation Assessment 2001*, 2001; Christoff, 2002). The Wilderness Society, for example, claims that from 1999 to 2001, more than 1 million hectares of native bushland were cleared across the state of Queensland—33 percent more than in the previous two-year period—despite the introduction of new measures to control illegal land clearing (Wilderness Society, 2003).

Historically, agriculture has been the single greatest driver of land alteration on the Australian continent. Cultivation and pastoralism (especially sheep herding) was the cornerstone of Australia's economy in the decades following European colonization, and today agriculture leaves its imprint on about 60 percent of the continent (approximately 450 million hectares). Agriculture remains the main cause of permanent land clearing and fragmentation of natural ecosystems, and it has been blamed for degrading water resources in ways that have endangered human health and diminished freshwater biodiversity. For example, more than one of four of Australia's river systems are now approaching or exceeding their limits for sustainable use, as irrigation-dependent farmers (and thirsty cities and towns) take greater and greater amounts of water out of the rivers (Christoff, 2002).

Agricultural practices have also been cited as a major element in the continent's soil quality woes. At the beginning of the twenty-first century, it was estimated that up to 5.7 million hectares of land are at serious risk or affected by dryland salinity caused by shallow groundwater tables, and that 17 million hectares could be affected by 2050. In fact, it has been estimated that Australia accounts for about 19 percent of the world's soil erosion, even though it has only 5 percent of its land mass. "There are—in human terms—no 'tolerable' rates of soil loss for many of Australia's soils. Salinity is now recognized as one of the greatest threats facing the country, with dire consequences for rural environment and social values. It could affect between 6 [and] 12 percent of the continent's total cropland and improved pasture within 30 to 50 years if effective action is not taken" (ibid.).

Of course, land alteration is not limited to rural farming areas. Coastal New South Wales, southern Queensland, and the coastal transport corridor extending from Sydney to Melbourne have all regularly posted growth rates of over 5 percent annually in recent years (State of the Environment Committee, 2001), as municipalities and developers labor feverishly to provide for the steady stream of rural Australians and immigrants settling in these areas.

Australia's commonwealth government, its six state and two territorial governments, and its multitude of local governments have taken some steps to address those land use patterns that threaten the country's ecological health and integrity. At the beginning of the twenty-first century, approximately 8 percent of Australia's land area was included in its national park system and was thus protected from many forms of development. In addition, vital coastal areas that provide habitat for both terrestrial and marine species have received particular attention. For example, 63 percent of Victoria's coastline is protected, and large expanses of coastline are safeguarded in New South Wales

(33 percent) and Queensland (25 percent) as well (Christoff, 2002). Australia's coastline is also dotted with two hundred marine protected areas (MPAs), ranging from small state- and territory-managed aquatic reserves to marine parks under the jurisdiction of the commonwealth.

But critics charge that sustainable land use ideals have not been adequately integrated into most policy areas at the state, territorial, or national (commonwealth) levels. Historically, states and territories have been regarded as the primary arbiters of resource management and land use policies within their borders, and their philosophies on environmental issues have ranged considerably from state to state (and from administration to administration within these states and territories).

Similarly, Australia's national government policies on land use and other environmental issues have shifted with the political winds over the past two decades. "Over the past 10 years, successive Australian governments have failed to integrate ecologically sustainable development into their policies and programs," charged one 2002 report by a consortium of Australia's leading environmental organizations. "Significant or potentially important institutional initiatives developed during the late 1980s and early 1990s were dismantled, undermined or collapsed through neglect during the past 10 years. The most important of these initiatives was the National Strategy for Ecologically Sustainable Development, which was abandoned in 1997. [At present] there is no national strategy to guide Australia towards ecological sustainability" (Christoff, 2002).

Supporters of Australia's national leadership during this period refute the charge that they are insensitive to environmental issues. They point out that Australia's first department dedicated solely to environmental affairs—Environment Australia—was created in 1996, and they claim that some of the land use policy changes pushed by environmentalists involve too much economic sacrifice. They also tout the 1997 creation of the Natural Heritage Trust, a self-described "environmental rescue plan" to restore and conserve natural resources by providing funding to community/grassroots groups for a host of environmental projects. Detractors, however, claim that these and other programs to implement sustainable land use practices and protect fragile ecosystems remain underfunded, and that they do not adequately address the root causes of unsustainable land use, such as policies that encourage—or at least do not discourage—wholesale land alteration. "Between 1996 and 2001, the Natural Heritage Trust funded the replanting of some 620,000 hectares of native vegetation," acknowledged Christoff. "At the same time, the national government refused to address the problem of native vegetation clearing, the major source of land degradation, salinity and loss of habitat and biodiversity. Consequently over 3 million hectares of bush were razed during the same time—leaving a deficit of over 2.4 million hectares in lost habitat and additional greenhouse emissions" (Christoff, 2002).

Population and Land Use Trends in New Zealand

Population

New Zealand's main North and South Islands and their myriad satellite islands provide about 27 million hectares of land for some 3.9 million people. According to current population trends, the country could hold more than 5 million people by the mid-twenty-first century (Population Reference Bureau, 2002). But even if these forecasts hold true, New Zealand would remain one of the least densely populated countries in the world. Isolated from other major world population centers and seemingly dedicated to preserving large swaths of its natural wealth from commercial exploitation, New Zealand simply has not received the same immigration and development pressures as most other developed nations. Moreover, the country does not appear to be anxious about this state of affairs, for it has maintained carefully calibrated immigration policies for the past quarter-century.

Today, approximately 85 percent of the population is concentrated in New Zealand's towns and cities, making the country one of the most urbanized in the world. Half the people live in the upper North Island, a quarter live in the lower North Island, and the remaining quarter live in the South Island. In some metropolitan centers—most notably Auckland and Christchurch—regional land and water resources are under increasing strain from robust population growth. In Auckland, environmental problems include freshwater shortages, diminished coastal water quality, and loss of wetlands and productive farmland on the city's fringe areas. In Christchurch, smog and other air quality problems traced to heavy emissions from automobiles and other sources is the highest-profile environmental issue.

On average, New Zealand's citizens enjoy a high standard of living and quality of life when compared with that of most of the rest of the world. The nation ranks among world leaders in numerous educational, health, and economic indicators (Statistics New Zealand, 2003), and its people have an international reputation as hardy lovers of the outdoors who revel in their country's wild mountains and forests. But considerable variation in health, education, and income exists among the different ethnic groups in New Zealand. People of European-only descent, who account for about 80 percent of the total population, post the highest scores in measurements of health, education, and income. Another 10 percent of New Zealand's population is composed of Asians, Indians, immigrants from other Pacific islands, and people of mixed ethnic backgrounds. The indigenous Maori people account for the remaining 10 percent of the population, and they are far behind the rest of the general population in virtually every socioeconomic category, including education, health, income, percentage of single parent families, home ownership rates, and rates of incarceration. But quantifiable improvements have been realized in recent years in some health and education categories, and the legal rights of the Maori have been greatly enhanced in recent years. In the meantime, the geographic distribution of Maori families has undergone a sea change in the past half-century. At the end of World War II, 75 percent of the Maori population lived in rural areas; by 1970 three out of four Maori lived in cities or towns, and today the percentage of Maori living in urban environments is roughly equivalent to that of the general population (New Zealand Ministry for the Environment, 1997; Loughran, 2000).

Land Use

Since permanent human settlements first became established in New Zealand 700 to 800 years ago, the landscapes of the North and South Islands have undergone extensive change. For example, indigenous forests once covered about 85 percent of the country's land area, but now they cover only about 25 to 30 percent, with the bulk of the remaining old-growth forests confined to mountainous areas and various low-lying pockets of the two islands (New Zealand Ministry for the Environment, 1997; UN Food and Agriculture Organization, 2001). Virtually all of the remaining indigenous forests are protected, and many other forests are now safeguarded from logging and other activities as well. But the government acknowledges that forests in low-lying coastal areas have been heavily fragmented by population pressures, and that they "will need considerable expansion if the biodiversity within them is to be sustained" (New Zealand Ministry for the Environment, 1997). Similarly, New Zealand's duneland ecosystems have been heavily modified by grazing, fires, coastal development, and introduced trees and grasses, and its grasslands have expanded dramatically as a result of earlier eras of deforestation and continued reliance on range-fed pastoralism (ibid.).

Today, nearly half of New Zealand's total land area is classified as pasture, a reflection of agriculture's continued importance to the overall economy. The livestock sector is particularly vital to the country's economic fortunes; all told, the country supports an estimated 57 million animals (primarily sheep and cattle) in free range agricultural systems (New Zealand Ministry of Agriculture and Fisheries, *Sectors/Animals*, 2002). But concerns have mounted

The Maori People of New Zealand

New Zealand Maori men perform a traditional war dance. ANDERS RYMAN/CORBIS

The Maori are a people of Polynesian origin who were the first human inhabitants of New Zealand. They arrived around 1200 A.D. from the Cook Islands, Society Islands, and Marquesas Islands in the Pacific Ocean. The first Maori settlers probably consisted of between 50 and 500 people who made a planned migration to New Zealand in a fleet of large canoes. As the Maori settled throughout New Zealand, they developed a distinctive culture. Their population grew rapidly as they exploited the islands' abundant supplies of fish, sea mammals, and birds. Later, when these food sources declined, they began to clear land for farming. Over time the Maori formed a stable relationship with the environment in their remote and rugged home. They developed customs to regulate resource use, conserve important food sources, and protect burial grounds and other significant lands.

The first European colonists arrived in New Zealand in the late eighteenth century. The Maori population was around 100,000 by the time British explorer James Cook established friendly relations with some tribes in 1769. By the early 1800s European ships visited New Zealand frequently, and the Maori traded commercial crops for weapons, tools, clothing, and books.

In 1840, British representatives and Maori chiefs signed the Treaty of Waitangi, which is sometimes regarded as New Zealand's founding document. The treaty established British rule over New Zealand, granted British citizenship to the Maori people, and recognized Maori land rights, though many treaty provisions remain in dispute today.

(continues)

New Zealand officially became a colony of Great Britain in 1841, at which time the number of European settlements grew rapidly. Conflicts over land claims led to violent clashes between these settlers and the Maori between 1843 and 1872—a period known as the New Zealand Wars. The Maori lost most of their traditional lands during this time. Some lands were confiscated by British authorities, while others were stolen through fraudulent or forced sales. As a result, less than one-sixth of New Zealand remained under Maori ownership by the 1890s, and most remaining Maori lands were poorly suited to farming.

The Maori population declined steadily during the 1800s as a result of the wars and the withering toll of European diseases, reaching a low point of 42,000 in 1896. But the population rebounded in the twentieth century with halting improvements in health care and improved access to basic sanitation systems. In fact, the number of Maori doubled between 1921 and 1951, then doubled again between 1951 and 1971, to reach 500,000 in 1996 (about 15 percent of New Zealand's total population).

The mid-1900s also saw a mass migration of Maori to New Zealand's cities. By the 1990s more than 80 percent of Maori lived in urban areas, compared with around 20 percent at the end of World War II. Unfortunately, greater distance from tribal authority and a loss of cultural support created problems for some Maori: they suffered higher rates of alcoholism, drug dependency, unemployment, and imprisonment than the general population. At the same time, however, the Maori benefited from improvements in health care and education.

During the second half of the twentieth century, the Maori underwent a sort of cultural and political renaissance. They gained some measure of political power and began calling for a revival of their traditional language and the return of their ancestral lands. In 1980, New Zealand formed a government investigative body called the Waitangi Tribunal to settle Maori legal claims and grievances based on the landmark 1840 treaty. Since that time, treaty obligations have been explicitly recognized in the nation's environmental laws and policies. For example, both national and local governments are required to consult with Maori communities before making decisions that affect them, including decisions about resource management and environmental issues.

This stipulation is a significant development, for over the course of their 800-year history in New Zealand, the Maori developed a set of environmental values and priorities that differ from those typically held by mainstream European environmentalists. The Maori tend to place less emphasis on protecting land or other resources based on their intrinsic or aesthetic value, for instance, and greater emphasis on protecting land with ancestral and mythological associations.

(continues)

Perhaps the most significant difference in Maori environmental views concerns water resources. In Maori belief systems, water is a living thing that is animated by a spiritual force. They have a unique perception of water quality and feel that water can suffer degradation from even small amounts of pollutants. As a result, the Maori tend to place a higher priority on sewage treatment and wastewater discharge issues than other people.

The Maori have waged several successful environmental campaigns against pollution of tribal waters over the years. In 1983 the Te Atiawa claim in the Waitangi Tribunal helped stop a proposed sewage pipeline that would have discharged chemicals from an industrial plant near traditional fishing grounds. Similarly, in 1984 the Kaituna claim helped divert a proposed pipeline that would have discharged sewage into the Kaituna River. Such victories ensured that the Maori voice would continue to be heard on environmental and other issues in New Zealand. In 1995, Queen Elizabeth II of Great Britain offered a formal apology and promised to provide compensation to the Maori people for the historical abuses they have suffered at the hands of European colonists.

Sources:

Alves, Dora. 1999. *The Maori and the Crown: An Indigenous People's Struggle for Self-Determination.* Westport, CT: Greenwood.

Cleave, Peter. 1998. *The Maori State.* Palmerston North, New Zealand: Campus Press.

New Zealand Ministry for the Environment. 1997. *The State of New Zealand's Environment.* Wellington: Ministry for the Environment.

Sinclair, Karen. 2003. *Maori Times, Maori Places: Prophetic Histories.* Lanham, MD: Roman and Littlefield.

in recent years over the impact of these herds on the environment due to episodes of severe overgrazing and degradation of waterways from animal waste and erosion of riverbanks.

New Zealand's primary laws controlling the environmental effects of land use are the Resource Management Act 1991, which formally mandates sustainable management as a guiding principle in a wide array of policy areas, and the Conservation Act 1987, which provides for formal protection of ecologically valuable forests, wetlands, and other natural areas. But several other notable laws have been passed in recent years as well, including legislation specifically designed to combat pests and invasive species; ensure sustainable logging of forestlands; and protect human communities and ecosystems alike from hazardous materials. New Zealand policy-makers have also moved to address long-term shortcomings in monitoring and research of land management issues.

Population and Land Use
Trends in Pacific Island States

Population

The Pacific Islands region occupies a 30-million-square-kilometer (11.5-million-square-mile) section of the Pacific Ocean, an area more than three times larger than the United States or China, amounting to nearly 6 percent of the earth's surface. The islands that dot this expanse of ocean feature a high degree of ecosystem and species diversity, considerable economic and cultural dependence on the natural environment, and an exceptional variety of cultures, religions, and languages. Indeed, the current demographic makeup of Oceania reflects the Pacific Islands' historic attraction as a migration destination. Today, Melanesians, Micronesians, and Polynesians whose ancestors hailed from Southeast Asia share citizenship with people whose families once lived in India, Europe, the United States, China, the Philippines, and other far-flung places.

Within Oceania, three generally recognized subregions exist—Micronesia (consisting of the Federated States of Micronesia, Palau, Guam, Northern Mariana Islands, Marshall Islands, Kiribati, Nauru); Polynesia (consisting of Tuvalu, Wallis and Futuna, Tonga, Tokelau, Samoa, American Samoa, Niue, Cook Islands, French Polynesia, Pitcairn Island); and Melanesia (consisting of Papua New Guinea, Solomon Islands, Vanuatu, New Caledonia, Fiji).

Nine of the entities listed above are independent nations (Fiji, Kiribati, Nauru, Papua New Guinea, Solomon Islands, Tonga, Tuvalu, Vanuatu, and Samoa). Within these countries, hereditary chieftains of the past have been replaced in most cases by popularly elected legislative governments. Oceania also features a half-dozen self-governing states that maintain some sort of link with the countries that once ran them (Cook Islands and Niue with New Zealand; the Federated States of Micronesia, Palau, and Northern Mariana Islands with the United States). The rest are territories that are still administered by other nations.

Population growth has been significant in the last half-century across most of Oceania. Approximately 7.5 million people lived in the South Pacific (not including Australia and New Zealand) at the close of the 1990s, with 4.8 million located in Papua New Guinea alone (Secretariat of the Pacific Community, 1998). At the close of the 1990s, children under fifteen years of age accounted for about 40 percent of the population in Pacific Island Countries (PICs), an indication that fertility rates have risen in recent years. If current trends continue, it has been forecast that Pacific Island population will reach

Table 1.1 Geographical Data on Pacific Island Countries (PICs)

Country	Last census	at last census	Mid-year population estimate 2002	Urban Population %
American Samoa	2000	57,291	60,000	48
Cook Islands	2001	18,027*	17,900	59
Fed. St. of Micronesia	2000	107,008	110,700	27
Fiji	1996	775,077	823,300	46
Guam	2000	154,805	159,900	38
Kiribati	2000	84,494	86,900	37
Marshall Islands	1999	50,840	53,200	65
Nauru	1992	9,919	11,900	100
Niue	1997	2,088	1,882	35
North Mariana Islands	2000	69,221	73,300	90
New Caledonia	1996	196,836	229,300	71
Palau	2000	19,129	19,900	71
Papua New Guinea	2000	5,190,786	5,471,200	15
Pitcairn	1999	47	47	88
French Polynesia	1996	219,521	239,800	53
Samoa	2001	174,140*	175,000	21
Solomon Islands	1999	409,042	439,400	13
Tokelau	2001	1,537*	1,538	0
Tonga	1996	97,784	101,100	36
Tuvalu	1991	9,043	10,100	42
Vanuatu	1999	186,678	199,600	21
Wallis and Futuna	1996	14,166	14,700	0

*Preliminary census results.
SOURCE: Secretariat of the Pacific Community, 2000

the 10 million mark between 2010 and 2015, with the fastest growth occurring in towns and cities. Some countries, including the Federated States of Micronesia, Vanuatu, the Solomon Islands, Papua New Guinea, and the Marshall Islands, could double or even triple their current populations by 2050 if current growth trends hold (Population Reference Bureau, 2002).

Many PICs are in the midst of major transitions from subsistence-oriented economies to economies predicated on industrialization, commercialization, and tourism. Agriculture remains the leading source of employment and income in most PICs, but manufacturing, mining, forestry, fishing, and other activities are accounting for a steadily rising slice of the economic pie in places such as Papua New Guinea, New Caledonia, and Fiji (UN Environment Programme, 1999), and tourism has experienced explosive growth in a number of states and territories.

Hotel in Moorea, French Polynesia. PHOTODISC, INC.

On many islands, however, prevailing forms of commercial development have aroused serious concerns about financial fairness and long-term environmental sustainability. For example, resorts and other forms of tourism development have become a major employer and source of income for some islands, but these sorts of capital-intensive enterprises are often beyond the reach of natives. Regional economies have thus become reliant on foreign companies that have been faulted for repatriating the bulk of their profits to their home countries and contributing little to overall community development. In addition, land clearing and pollution associated with resorts, factories, canneries, and other commercial developments have in many cases diminished the ecological integrity of coral reefs, rain forests, and other natural resources that remain vital to the welfare of families that rely on artisanal fishing and other subsistence activities for their livelihoods (Ueki, 2000).

Foreign aid is an important source of income in the Pacific Islands as well, but the donor profile has changed over the years. The United States and the United Kingdom significantly reduced their aid packages to the region in the 1990s, and Australian development assistance has not kept pace with inflation. However, countries such as China, Taiwan, and France have filled the breach. Eager to increase their influence in Oceania, these nations have boosted their overseas aid packages to targeted countries (Von Strokirch, 2002).

Urban population levels are presently low in Oceania as a whole, but there is considerable variation among states and territories. For example, only 13 percent of the population of the Solomon Islands live in cities, and countries such as Papua New Guinea (15 percent) and Vanuatu (21 percent) retain primarily rural populations. Other countries are heavily urbanized, however, in part because small land areas necessitate congregation of inhabitants in a few coastal areas. Nauru's population, for example, has been classified as 100 percent urban. Other countries with high urban populations include New Caledonia (71 percent) and Palau (71 percent) (Population Reference Bureau, 2002).

On the whole, movement toward increased urbanization is the rule rather than the exception across Oceania, as towns and cities are seen as places of economic opportunity and centers of cultural and social Westernization—both of which are attractive to many young people in PICs. However, the exodus from rural communities to towns and cities has also been cited as a contributing factor in troubling social trends in many PICs, including declines in employment, graduation rates, and household incomes, as well as increases in the incidence of substance abuse, crime, and HIV/AIDS infection (Secretariat of the Pacific Community, 1998). Population growth in towns and cities is also placing significant stress on local ecosystems and biodiversity. Environmental degradation and unsustainable consumption of limited natural resources is now a recognized problem in many PICs. "In general, urban growth across the Pacific is proceeding so fast that governments simply cannot keep pace with facilities and services. Urban areas of the Pacific are now manifesting lifestyles and conditions that were unheard of as recently as 20 years ago. Water is scarce and groundwater often polluted, toilets few. . . . In the larger towns, the search for environmentally safe and socially acceptable sites for solid waste disposal has become a perennial concern, which is, for several towns at least, seemingly insoluble. In smaller settlements and coastal peri-urban situations, mangrove areas or beaches have become the casual dumping grounds for much of the waste, ranging from derelict cars to household refuse" (UN Environment Programme, 1999).

According to many conventional economic and social indicators, a significant percentage of Pacific Island populations live in poverty. In some states these numbers can be misleading, as "many communities still enjoy a high degree of subsistence affluence obtained from traditional resource management systems. For many of the people, health and general social indicators, not purely economic ones, tell the real story" (ibid.). In others, such as Papua New Guinea, low scores do reflect grim conditions. Papua New Guinea's scores are the lowest in Oceania in numerous sectors, including life expectancy (fifty-seven, which is eight years below the average in the developing world) and infant mortality rates, and severe impoverishment is evident in many communities (Asian Development Bank, 2000; Bourke, 2001).

Other Oceanic states that perform very poorly on UN indexes of human development and poverty are Vanuatu and the Solomon Islands, the latter of which has been rocked so badly by political instability and violence in recent years that its major industries (palm oil, gold, fish canning, and tourism) have been thoroughly disrupted (Von Strokirch, 2002). Countries that fall in the middle ranks of developing nations include the Federated States of Micronesia, Kiribati, Nauru, and the Marshal Islands. The Cook Islands, Fiji, Samoa, Tonga, and Tuvalu perform the best on UN indexes of human and economic development among countries in Oceania, but recent political unrest in Fiji has undercut socioeconomic progress in that country (UN Development Programme, 1999; Von Strokirch, 2002).

All told, Pacific Island countries enjoy relatively high per capita incomes, high per capita aid, and productive subsistence sectors when compared with other developing countries around the world. But poverty levels may have inched upward in recent years, pushed by high business costs (such as the expense of transporting goods to market), aging infrastructure, rapid urban population growth, and the erosion of traditional support networks (Von Strokirch, 2002).

Land Use

Until relatively recently, respect for natural resources and knowledge of natural environmental processes were "intrinsic" to the "everyday life and cultural perspectives" of Oceania's communities (Ueki, 2000). In the last century or so, however, colonization, commercialization, and Westernization of Pacific Island communities have eroded traditional types of resource stewardship and increased pressure on extremely finite land and water resources. Indeed, most islands of the South Pacific have very limited supplies of freshwater, arable land, forest, and coastal areas, and as the UN Environment Programme has noted: "[L]imited land makes many terrestrial and near shore resources very vulnerable to overexploitation and to pollution from poorly planned waste disposal" (UN Environment Programme, 1999).

In the early twenty-first century, numerous inhabited islands in Oceania are under enormous development pressure, and many projects are proceeding with little or no consideration of the repercussions for wild habitat, biodiversity, or subsistence livelihoods. In the small island state of Palau, for example, tourism projects in various stages of development include massive resort communities carved into coastal areas and construction of an 85-kilometer (53-mile) asphalt loop around the mostly undeveloped island of Babeldoab. Conservationists contend that these projects are being undertaken without adequate regard for their impact on habitat, wildlife, and ecosystem functions. In some places, Palaun families have already detected signs of environmental degradation. "Women are noticing increased siltation in their taro patches as runoff increases. Fishers are reporting decreases in the volume of their catches, and in fish size. The ecosystem of Koror's port area has been altered by increased algae growth attributable to sewage outflows, virtually closing these traditional fishing grounds for gleaning" (Ueki, 2000).

In general terms, commercial and residential developments are applying the greatest pressure on coastal lands in Oceania, while principal causes of land degradation further inland include overgrazing, deforestation, and commercial cultivation (these contribute to coastal land conversion as well). These forces, which are being propelled in part by high population growth, are wholly displacing traditional land management systems on some islands and placing a particularly heavy environmental burden on atolls and other small islands with limited land and other natural resources (UN Environment Programme, 1999).

In some PICs, pressure to convert natural areas to more commercial purposes reflects an understandable appetite for greater material comfort and a more Westernized mode of living. But in some countries, development and exploitation pressures are rooted in grinding poverty. In poverty-riddled Papua New Guinea, for example, conservationists have long decried the state's approval of huge logging concessions to foreign-owned companies in areas of high biodiversity (Barry, 2002), and in 2002, Papua New Guinea announced its intention to pass a variety of tax incentives, such as reduction of the corporate tax rate for new petroleum projects by one-third, as part of a desperate effort to beckon international mining and oil companies to its shores. Long dependent on metal mining and oil for about 80 percent of its export revenues and increasingly strapped for cash to pay for the most basic health and education programs, Papua New Guinea sees increased natural resource extraction as its only economic option.

The island states and territories that compose Oceania are well aware that recent events—rapid commercial development, urbanization and population growth trends, and weakening of traditional conservation regimes—all are freighted to potentially significant ecological costs. But perspectives on appropriate responses to these threats vary considerably. For example, in Palau, where development pressure has surged in recent years, many citizens worry that commercial expansion of the tourism, agriculture, and fisheries sectors poses formidable threats to the environment, and they urge greater restraint on the part of community leaders. "Others hope that development will yield desirable economic benefits without destroying the balance of nature. Still others believe that the environment must be sacrificed to a certain extent in order to achieve economic growth and material prosperity" (Ueki, 2000).

By the close of the 1990s, very few Pacific Island Countries had developed or implemented land-use policies of any strength, despite widespread recognition that many of the region's fragile ecological resources are in growing jeopardy. International aid agencies, environmental groups, and research organizations alike assert that this is an indefensible abdication of responsibility that must be addressed swiftly and decisively if Oceania is to preserve a significant measure of its natural and biological wealth in the twenty-first century. "It is essential that efforts to develop and implement sustainable land management policies are given the priority that the issue deserves" (UN Environment Programme, 1999). Fortunately, Oceania remains a region in which the message of sustainable resource use still has resonance. Indeed, even though many PICs are moving away from subsistence livelihoods to economies founded on tourism and other commercial activity, they still retain cultures "steeped in respect and understanding of the natural environment" and communities that are supportive of policies protecting wild places and the creatures contained therein (Ueki, 2000).

Sources:

Aplin, Graeme. 1998. *Australians and Their Environment.* Melbourne: Oxford University Press.

Asian Development Bank. 2000. *A Pacific Strategy for the New Millennium.* Manila: ADB.

Australian Bureau of Agriculture and Resource Economics. 2001. *Australian Commodity Statistics 2001.* Canberra: Commonwealth of Australia.

Australian Bureau of Statistics. 2002. *Australian Social Trends 2002, Population.* Canberra: ABS.

———. 2001. *Australia's Environment: Issues and Trends 2001.* Canberra: ABS.

Australian Conservation Foundation. 2000. *Natural Advantage: A Blueprint for a Sustainable Australia.* Melbourne: ACF.

Australian State of the Environment Committee. 2001. *Australia State of the Environment Report 2001.* Canberra: Environment Australia/CSIRO.

Barry, G. 2002. *An Analysis of Papua New Guinea's Implementation of the Convention on Biological Diversity with a Focus on Forests.* Moreton-in-Marsh, UK: Fern.

Bourke, R. M., M. G. Allen, and J. G. Salisbury, eds. 2001. *Food Security for Papua New Guinea.* Canberra: ACIAR.

Christoff, Peter. 1998. "From Global Citizen to Renegade State: Australia at Kyoto." *Arena Journal* 10.

———. 2002. *A Continent in Reverse.* Victoria, Australia: Australian Conservation Foundation et al.

Easton, B. H. 1997. *The Commercialization of New Zealand.* Auckland: Auckland University Press.

Economic and Social Commission of Asia and the Pacific. 1995. *Review of the Environment and Development Trends in the South Pacific.* Port Vila, Vanuatu: ESCAP.

Flannery, Tim. 1995. *The Future Eaters: An Ecological History of the Australian Lands and People.* New York: Braziller.

Krockenberger, Michael. 2002. "The State of Our Environment." *Habitat Australia* 30 (June).

Loughran, Robert J., Paul J. Tranter, and Guy M. Robinson. 2000. *Australia and New Zealand: Economy, Society and Environment.* London: Arnold.

Mannion, A. M. 2002. *Dynamic World: Land-cover and Land-use Change.* London: Arnold.

National Land and Water Resources Audit. 2001. *Australian Native Vegetation Assessment 2001.* Canberra: CSIRO.

———. 2001. *Landscape Health in Australia.* Canberra: Commonwealth of Australia.

New South Wales Environmental Protection Authority. 2000. *NSW State of the Environment 2000.* Sydney: NSW EPA.

New Zealand Ministry of Agriculture and Fisheries. 2002. *Sectors/Animals.* Available at www.maf.govt.nz (accessed November 26, 2002).

———. 2002. *Sectors/Horticulture.* Available at www.maf.govt.nz (accessed November 26, 2002).

New Zealand Ministry of Agriculture and Forestry. 2001. *Forestry Sector Issues.* Wellington: MAF.

New Zealand Ministry for the Environment. 1997. *The State of New Zealand's Environment.* Wellington: Ministry for the Environment.

Organization for Economic Cooperation and Development. 1998. *Australia: Environmental Performance Review.* Paris: OECD.

Population Action International. 2000. *People in the Balance: Population and Natural Resources at the Turn of the Millennium.* Washington, DC: PAI.

Population Reference Bureau. 2002. "2002 World Population Data Sheet." Washington, DC: PRB.

Secretariat of the Pacific Community. 1998. *Pacific Island Populations.* Noumea: SPC.

Statistics New Zealand. Available at http://www.stats.govt.nz/ (accessed February 2003).

Toyne, P. 1994. *The Reluctant Nation: Environment, Law, and Politics in Australia.* Sydney: ABC.

Ueki, Minoru F. 2000. "Eco-Consciousness and Development in Palau." *Contemporary Pacific* 12 (fall).

UN Development Programme. 1996. *The State of Human Settlements and Urbanization in the Pacific Islands.* Suva, Fiji: UNDP.

———. 1999. *Pacific Human Development Report 1999: Creating Opportunities.* Suva, Fiji: UNDP.

UN Environment Programme. 1999. *Pacific Islands Environment Outlook.* Available at www.unep.org (accessed December 2002).

UN Food and Agriculture Organization. 2001. *Global Forest Resources Assessment 2000.* Rome: FAO.

Von Strokirch, Karin. 2002. "The Region in Review: International Issues and Events 2001." *Contemporary Pacific* 14 (fall).

Wilderness Society. 2003. "Queensland Clears over 1 Million Hectares of Bushland in 2 Years." January 24. Available at http://www.wilderness.org.au/projects/Woodlands/lc_crisis.html (accessed February 2003).

World Wide Fund for Nature Australia. 2001. *Greening the 2001 Agenda: Priority Environmental Initiatives for Commonwealth Government 2002–2005.* WWF-Australia, July.

Biodiversity

—A. M. MANNION

Oceania—defined here as the continent nation of Australia, New Zealand, and twenty-two other island countries and territories sprinkled over more than 40 million square kilometers (15.5 million square miles) of the South Pacific—is the most fragmented of all the continental regions; its unique combination of continental landmass, linked island groups, and isolated islands is the product of a varied geological history influenced by the splitting and clashing of geological plates, the ups and downs of global temperatures, the influence of marine processes, and of coral island and reef formation. These factors have exerted tremendous influence on Oceania's biodiversity—the number of species of flora, fauna, and insects occupying an ecosystem, country, continent, or other defined region. Temperate forests and grasslands, tropical vegetation communities such as savanna (a combination of grass-dominated ground cover with trees and shrubs at various densities), deserts, rain forests, and wetlands are all represented across Oceania, as are alpine environments in Australia and New Zealand. The current state of all of these ecosystems reflects the influence of climate over millions of years, notably annual temperature and precipitation regimes, as well as centuries of human activity.

Because of their relative isolation, Australia, New Zealand, and the thousands of other islands of the South Pacific have served as incubators for a rich tapestry of biodiversity featuring the planet's highest levels of endemism—species found nowhere else in the world—per unit of land area or number of human inhabitants (UN Environment Programme, 1999). Avian and marsupial species in Oceania, for example, are among the most abundant and unique on the entire planet, and in Southwest Australia, nearly 80 percent of the approximately 5,500 plant species found in the region exist nowhere else. Papua New Guinea's Lake Kutubu contains 11 endemic fishes within its boundaries, while 75 percent of New Caledonia's 3,250 vascular plant species (ferns, flowering plants, and trees) are endemic in nature (Jaensch, 1996). In

New Zealand, meanwhile, 88 percent of its 35 native freshwater fish species are endemic in nature (Conservation International, 2002). Similar examples of high endemism abound all across this region. Moreover, the full extent of the Pacific region's stunning array of terrestrial and marine biodiversity remains unknown; it has been estimated that only a fraction of the region's total species have thus far been identified (South Pacific Regional Environment Programme, 1992).

But many of the habitats upon which this biological wealth depend for sustenance are under considerable stress from unsustainable forms of development and exploitation. Indeed, the forests and coasts of Oceania have experienced widespread alteration, primarily for agriculture, logging, mineral extraction, and urbanization. It has been estimated, for example, that Oceania has lost almost 80 percent of its frontier forests, and that three-quarters of what remains is under moderate or high pressure from human activity (Bryant, 1997). As a result of these widespread habitat alterations, some species have been driven to extinction and many others are now vulnerable or endangered.

Monitoring and Protecting Biodiversity in Oceania

Across Oceania, there is considerable regional variation in the amount of biodiversity research that has been undertaken. Consequently, it is difficult to fully ascertain the number of extant, extinct, and threatened plant and animal species across Oceania's vast realm. Indeed, the full extent of species endangerment and loss can only be gauged in countries where systematic surveys have taken place. But investment in research efforts has increased in recent years, and the region's high level of biodiversity and concentration of endemic species has made it a focus of research and conservation activism among international nongovernmental organizations (NGOs).

For example, Micronesia and Polynesia—an area of more than 1,400 islands (including eleven nations, eight territories, and the U.S. state of Hawaii) scattered across a 21.6-million-square-kilometer (8.3-million-square-mile) expanse of the southern Pacific Ocean—is known to hold at least 6,557 plant species and 342 terrestrial vertebrate species (Conservation International, 2002). Australia, meanwhile, is home to an estimated 1,900 animal species, including 700 distinct reptile species (World Conservation Monitoring Centre, 1992). And New Zealand holds 2,300 plant species (81 percent of which are endemic) and entirely endemic populations of reptiles (61 species), amphibians (4 species), and mammals (3 species) (Conservation International, 2002).

Placing a Dollar Value on Biodiversity

Historically, activism in behalf of habitat and species conservation and protection goals has focused on the aesthetic, spiritual, and cultural benefits associated with biodiversity preservation. In New Zealand, for example, it has been observed that "we are shaped by . . . symbols of our natural environment and our relationship to it—whether by cabbage trees or kahikatea forest, weta or whitebait. We would be impoverished Kiwis indeed if our national icons went the way of the huia and the moa [extinct species formerly native to New Zealand]" (New Zealand Department of Conservation, 2000).

But increasingly, conservationists are touting the economic value of protecting biological wealth and preserving healthy ecosystems. For example, one study found that the total annual value provided by New Zealand's indigenous biodiversity could be more than double the value of the country's gross domestic product (Patterson and Cole, 1999). According to this analysis, the total annual value of indigenous biodiversity on New Zealand land amounted to $46 billion. This total included $9 billion in direct value (food and raw materials from agriculture and horticulture and timber from forests); $7 billion from "passive values" (value of future use options, value of biodiversity to future generations, and value of biodiversity preservation for its own sake); and $30 billion from indirect uses of ecosystem services provided—free of charge—by healthy flora and fauna, such as production of food, purification of water, regulation of regional and global climate, and provision of pollination and pest control. In addition, the value of the ecosystem services provided by New Zealand's marine ecosystems was placed at $184 billion annually. The estimated total annual value of indigenous biodiversity thus reached $230 billion in the mid-1990s; by comparison, total gross domestic product for the country during the same period was less than $90 billion annually.

Moreover, it is widely acknowledged that human communities currently make use of only a small portion of the biological resources that surround them. "New Zealand's biodiversity represents a pool of untapped opportunities," contended the country's Department of Conservation in its 2000 report, *New Zealand's Biodiversity Strategy*. "Like the endemic sponge, discovered off the Kaikoura coast, that produces a cancer-fighting substance, there are almost certainly other species with potentially useful and commercially valuable compounds. Scientists believe that most of these have not yet been discovered."

Sources:

New Zealand Department of Conservation. 2000. *The New Zealand Biodiversity Strategy*. Wellington: Department of Conservation.

Patterson, M., and A. Cole. 1999. *Assessing the Value of New Zealand's Biodiversity*. Occasional Paper Number 1, School of Resource and Environmental Planning, Massey University (February).

The fortunes of the multitudes of tree, shrub, mammal, bird, reptile, and fish species that currently exist in Oceania fall along a vast spectrum. Many are undoubtedly thriving, enjoying robust health in largely unspoiled habitat. But others are being pushed down the path toward extinction by pollution, habitat loss, or predation by invasive species. Australia, which has by far the largest terrestrial holdings in the region—and comparatively extensive environmental research programs—contains many of Oceania's known threatened species. It has 537 species formally recognized in the World Conservation Union-IUCN *Red Book of Threatened Species* as threatened within its borders, including mammals (63 species), plants (35), birds (37), reptiles (38), amphibians (35), and mollusks (175). Other nations within Oceania with large numbers of threatened species include Papua New Guinea (266 species, including 142 plant species and 58 mammal species); New Caledonia (244 species, including 214 plant species); New Zealand (125 species, including 63 bird species); French Polynesia (108 species, including 47 plant species and 23 bird species); and Fiji (92 species, including 65 plant species) (World Conservation Union, 2002). The UN Environment Programme, meanwhile, has described the biological diversity of the Pacific Islands as a whole as "among the most critically threatened in the world" (UN Environment Programme, 1999).

In recognition of the growing threat to their natural heritages, virtually all of Oceania's governments have issued formal conservation objectives. In addition, many nations in Oceania are signatories to international conventions focused on species or habitat conservation, including the Convention on International Trade in Endangered Species (CITES) of 1973, the Tropical Forestry Action Plan (TFAP) of 1985, and the Convention on Biological Diversity (CBD), which requires nations to develop a national biodiversity strategy. The nations of Oceania are signatories to the CBD, so each has a commitment to improve existing laws and enact new legislation to protect biodiversity and associated habitat.

Of course, these goals have to be reconciled with other priorities, such as the provision of food, employment, and housing for human communities. For large states of Oceania such as Australia and New Zealand, such conservation efforts are often fraught with difficulties stemming from political, social, and economic considerations, but the conservation challenges for small island nations are perhaps even more daunting, since the margin of error in protecting species is so slim. Moreover, setting aside protected areas that nourish vulnerable plants and animals is difficult because of limited land area and competing land use demands. Nonetheless, many Pacific Island states have set aside lands for conservation, including several protected areas that are internationally recognized for their importance in biodiversity preservation.

Regional Biodiversity Trends

The islands of Oceania have distinct floral and faunal communities with high rates of endemism—a reflection of geological history, isolation from other ecosystems, and adaptation to a range of microhabitats. But maintaining the ecological integrity of wilderness systems is a challenge for all states, and especially for the larger islands, which harbor the overwhelming majority of Oceania's endemic and endangered species.

Australia

In 2001, Australia's National Land and Water Resources Audit produced the *Australian Native Vegetation Assessment,* which gives a detailed account of the nation's vegetation communities. Some twenty-three major vegetation groups have been recognized based on the species present and the community structure (for example, open or closed canopy forests). The most widespread species are those of acacia and eucalyptus, which form open and closed forests, woodlands, shrublands, and some grasslands. These groups occupy approximately 36 percent of the land mass, while hummock grasslands, the second most important vegetation type, occupy 26 percent, predominantly in the country's arid interior. In terms of human impact, aboriginal peoples influenced Australia's natural vegetation cover through the extensive use of fire (wildfires have also been an important historical factor in shaping vegetation dynamics). More recently, European settlers who arrived in Australia in the late 1700s harnessed fire to clear land for farming.

The arrival of Europeans marked a major turning point in Australia's environmental and cultural history. Not only did Europeans begin to transform large tracts of forests and grasslands into arable fields and pastures, a process that accelerated after the 1830s, but they also introduced many plant and animal species that have competed with native species and in some cases driven them to extinction. Since European annexation the major impact has been the alteration of land cover for agriculture, especially in the southeast, the south, and the southwest, mainly for wool and cereal production (Young, 1996). Other impacts include mining and urbanization, but those forces are relatively minor in scope. All told, it is estimated that native vegetation has been cleared from approximately 13 percent of Australia's total land surface—a misleading percentage, since much of the country's interior is desert—and most areas of plant life that remain near populated areas have been highly modified and fragmented (National Land and Water Resources Audit, 2001). For example, 45 percent of Australia's heathlands that existed prior to European settlement have been cleared, primarily for farming and grazing, as have one-third of the country's tall open eucalyptus forests—the

The emu is one of many endemic bird species in Australia. COREL

latter lost to logging, grazing, and dam projects (National Land and Water Resources Audit, 2001). Indeed, the continent has lost more than 80 percent of its original frontier forest, including significant expanses of species-rich, unique forest types. Today, Australia's remaining frontier forests are confined almost exclusively to Tasmania, Cape York, and the northwestern region (Bryant, 1997).

Australia is justly proud of the rich array of fauna that still can be found roaming its reefs, deserts, and skies. It leads the world in terms of the range of snake and lizard species, and its many endemic bird species include the emu—the world's second largest flightless bird—and some 55 parrot species, 20 percent of the world total. The country supports no large carnivores, and the kangaroo is the largest herbivore.

But while some species continue to thrive or maintain stable populations, others have suffered dramatic declines. Since European settlement, several bird and mammal species exclusive to Australia have become extinct, including the lesser bilby and several species of hopping mice and hare wallabies. Many other animals are on the brink of extinction, from tree frogs to skinks. At the close of the twentieth century, Australia held 38 threatened plant species (5 critically endangered species, 7 endangered species, and 26 vulnerable species) and 499 threatened animal species (49 critically endangered, 119 endangered, and 331 vulnerable species) (World Conservation Union,

2002), in addition to 35 animal species believed to have gone extinct since 1500. "The conservation status of many components of terrestrial biodiversity [in Australia] remains disturbing," concluded the Australian Department of the Environment and Heritage. "Some 8 percent of Australia's higher plants, 14 percent of birds, 23 percent of marsupials, 8 percent of reptiles, 18 percent of amphibians and 9 percent of freshwater fish are extinct, endangered, or vulnerable at the national level. Australia's record of mammal species extinctions is the worst of any country. In the 1800s and 1900s, Australia has lost ten species of the original marsupial fauna of 144 species and eight of the 53 species of native rodents" (Australia State of the Environment Committee, 2001).

There are two major reasons for this loss of biodiversity: habitat loss and fragmentation from the clearance of native vegetation, and the introduction of alien plant and animal species that have wreaked havoc on delicately balanced ecosystems. The rate of land clearance has accelerated across Australia in recent decades, with as much land cleared during the past half-century as in the 150 years before 1945. In 1999 alone, it was estimated that Australian governments granted permits for the clearing of more than 1 million hectares of vegetation, much of it essential to regional ecosystems (ibid.). In addition to this large-scale land conversion, Australia has acquired an estimated 2,200 exotic plants that have become naturalized in the country's soil, including blackberry, gorse, lantana, mesquite, mimosa, and athel pine. Some of these plants were deliberately introduced, such as the radiata pine for the establishment of plantations in the southeast; others were introduced accidentally—for example, as unnoticed cargo on ships laden with crops from Europe. A number of these alien species have left a pronounced mark on the environment. The prickly acacia, for example, was introduced from Africa to provide shade and fodder in dry grasslands, but it is now crowding out native grasses (Williams and West, 2000). Introduced animals, meanwhile, include the rabbit, fox, camels, cane toad, deer, and water buffalo, and domesticated animals such as the cat. The impact of some of these species has been largely benign, but others have had significant ramifications for endemic species. Feral cats, for instance, have been widely blamed for declines in the populations of the endangered numbat and other small mammals in southwest Australia.

Southwest Australia is touted as both the richest and the most vulnerable region for biodiversity in the country. Designated by Conservation International as one of the world's twenty-five "Biodiversity Hotspots," the province has a Mediterranean climate that nurtures nearly 5,500 species of plants, almost 80 percent of which are exclusive to the region. In addition, 80 percent of the region's 30 amphibian species and 26 percent of its 191 reptile species are endemic in nature. In terms of endangered animals, the total

Table 2.1 Introduced Mammals That Have Established Persistent Wild
Populations in Australia

Common name	Reason for introduction	Status
Indian palm squirrel	zoo release	sparse, one isolated population
Black rat	commensal	abundant, widespread
Brown rat	commensal	common, major coastal cities
House mouse	commensal	abundant, widespread
Dingo	commensal	common, widespread except Tasmania and pastoral region
Feral dog	commensal	common, usually near centers of human population
Red fox	hunt	abundant, widespread except for northern Australia
Domestic cat	commensal	abundant, widespread
European rabbit	hunt	abundant, widespread except for northern Australia
European hare	hunt	common, southeast Australia
Feral horse	draught, transport	abundant, northern and central Australia
Feral donkey	draught	abundant, western and common central and western Australia
Arabian camel	draught, transport	sparse, central western Australia
Fallow deer	hunt	rare, isolated populations, eastern Australia, common Tasmania
Hog deer	hunt	sparse, isolated populations, southeast Australia
Axis deer (Chital)	hunt	common, limited to one isolated population, northeast Australia
Indian sambar	hunt	common, isolated populations, southeast and northern Australia
Rusa deer	hunt	rare, limited to a few local populations
Red deer	hunt	common, limited to scattered local populations
Feral goat	meat, milk	abundant, widespread except for northern and cental Australia
Water buffalo	draught, meat	common, limited to northern Australia
Banteng	draught	common, limited to northern Australia
Feral cattle	meat	common, northern and western Australia
Zebu	draught, meat	common, limited to northern Australia
Feral pig	meat	abundant, eastern Australia

SOURCE: ABS data used with permission from the Australian Bureau of Statistics. http://abs.gov.au. Australia's Environment: Issues and Facts (Cat. No. 4140.0, p. 37)

number is small compared with some other parts of the world. But conservationists contend that each species lost makes the world a little more barren. For example, only five reptile species found in southwest Australia are classified as threatened, but one of these is the western swamp turtle, which, with an estimated wild population of fewer than 100, is possibly the most endangered freshwater turtle on the planet (Conservation International, 2002). As with most other corners of Australia, chief threats to biodiversity and habitat in southwest Australia include agricultural development, mining and other extractive industries, and invasive species.

Australia has taken a number of steps to protect biodiversity in its southwest quadrant and elsewhere, including the designation of national parks and reserves as well as internationally recognized world heritage sites and biosphere reserves. But these protected areas shield relatively small percentages of the country's wild habitat. For instance, only 7.3 percent of Australia's tropical forests and 14 percent of its temperate forests enjoy formal protection (Mackay, 2002). Australia's 1999 Environment Protection and Biodiversity Act is supposed to ensure that stringent conditions apply to any proposed development that may affect the habitats of threatened or migratory species. Such legislation injects environmental considerations into a wide range of policy areas. Continued intercontinental trade, however, is expected to further expose Australia to the inadvertent introduction of plant and animal species.

New Zealand

New Zealand's diverse landscape supports a rich and wonderful variety of flora and fauna, from the world's only flightless parrot (kakapo) to a species of frog that lays eggs that hatch adult frogs (*Leiopelma* species). A vast island that was once a part of the ancient supercontinent Gondwanaland, New Zealand's long isolation from other land masses bestowed upon it a high degree of endemism in plants, birds, and reptiles. Its biological diversity was further shaped by evolutionary adjustments made by species so that they could exist in the various ecozones present across the island, from rugged ocean coastlines to subtropical forests to mountain meadows. As a result of these factors, "a collection of biological oddities has evolved. They include giant flightless weevils, flightless crickets, which include the world's most massive insects, giant carnivorous land snails, the world's most anatomically primitive frogs, the world's largest gecko, tiny flightless wrens, one of the largest eagles that ever lived, and an array of huge, plant-eating flightless birds—the moa" (Mansfield, 1996). Today, these creatures exist in highly distinctive ecosystems that range from the braided river systems of the eastern South Island to the kauri forests of the northern North Island (New Zealand Department of Conservation, 2000).

New Zealand's biodiversity also has been shaped by its long history of settlement, first by Polynesians and later by Europeans. Both of these groups altered the land to suit themselves in numerous ways, large and small. Today, the cumulative impact of these modifications is plain to see. Temperate rain forests once covered 85 percent of the archipelago, but these have been reduced to approximately 20 percent of their former extent. Indeed, only 59,400 square kilometers (about 22,900 square miles)—22 percent of New Zealand's total land area—remains in its original state (Conservation International, 2002). Much of the country's remaining wilderness is limited to remote areas such as the southwest of the South Island, a mountainous region with a fjord-studded coastline that has much more economic value as a tourist destination than as a site for agricultural or logging. Its biologically rich marsh and lowland areas, conversely, have been reduced to fragmented islands adrift in a sea of agricultural and industrial development and human settlements. "The history of people on these islands [of the New Zealand archipelago] has been brief but enormously destructive," summarized one analysis. "Destruction of the New Zealand bird fauna is so comprehensive, the ornithologist Professor Jared Diamond once declared that New Zealand no longer has a bird fauna—just the wreckage of one" (Mansfield, 1996).

New Zealand is also grappling with a serious exotic species problem. The annexation of New Zealand by Great Britain in 1840 triggered an influx of European immigration and the establishment of trade with Europe. This development, as well as the development of subsequent trade links with Australia and the Pacific Rim countries, introduced numerous exotic species to New Zealand's shores. Indeed, the governing bodies of both New Zealand and Australia encouraged so-called acclimatization societies, which fostered the introduction of familiar homeland species. Europeans opened the floodgates, bringing not only plants and animals for agriculture, horticulture, and forestry but also weeds and ornamentals.

It has been acknowledged that some introduced species have actually performed beneficial ecological services. For example, the banksia plant is a food source for native birds; the gorse scrub serves as a nursery for native plant seedlings; and blackbirds and some other introduced birds have become important dispersers of indigenous plant seeds. But examples of environmental loss directly attributable to invasive species are numerous, and in many places they threaten to overwhelm native ecosystems. "New Zealand now has the highest number of introduced mammals of any country in the world and the second highest number of introduced birds. In the case of vascular plants, we now have more introduced species in the wild than native ones"

(New Zealand Department of Conservation, 2000). Examples of plants now considered environmental weeds include hawkweed, a problem in South Island's tussock grasslands; heather, which was deliberately planted in tussock grasslands to provide a habitat for grouse; and lodgepole pine, introduced to afforest upland slopes for erosion control. Transplanted animal pests that have caused damage to native ecosystems include possums, goats, deer, rats, stoats, and feral cats. The Australian brush-tailed possum has been a particularly notorious invader; with no true predators (except humans) to check its population growth, it has developed into a voracious consumer of plants, bird eggs, land snails, and small invertebrates (World Wide Fund for Nature and World Conservation Union, 1995; Towns and Ballantine, 1993). "Introduced biodiversity is neither all 'good' nor all 'bad'; threats or benefits of individual introduced species most often depend on the situation in which they arise," admitted the New Zealand government. "[But] collectively, invasive pests pose the greatest single threat to our remaining natural ecosystems and habitats and threatened native species" (New Zealand Department of Conservation, 2000).

Together, the twin forces of habitat destruction and introduction of invasive species, in combination with other human actions, have led to the extinction of a stunning number of species over the past 800 years, including 32 percent of indigenous land and freshwater birds; 18 percent of sea birds; at least 12 invertebrates such as snails and insects; 1 species of fish; 1 species of bat; and 3 distinct species of frog. In addition, another 1,000 plant, animal, and fungi species across New Zealand have already vanished from places where they were once found, a pattern that typically precedes total species extinction. Finally, researchers believe that many presently unknown species (such as marine or invertebrate animals) may be extinguished before they are even discovered (New Zealand Ministry for the Environment, 1997). All of these factors led Conservation International to designate the New Zealand archipelago as one of the planet's twenty-five significant "biodiversity hotspots" (Conservation International, 2002).

Currently, New Zealand supports approximately 2,300 known vascular plants (including ferns, flowering plants, and trees). These represent a relatively low level of diversity, but 81 percent are endemic, including 35 genera of plants (a taxonomic grouping larger than a family but smaller than a species) found nowhere else in the world. Plants of particular note include the fern *Loxoma cunninghamii,* described as one of the earth's "living fossils" because it, along with three species from Central America, constitute a family of ferns closely related to those that existed some 60 million years ago (Conservation

The tuatara lizard is the sole survivor of a group of reptiles that flourished 150 million years ago in the Mesozoic era in the South Pacific islands of New Zealand. JAMES L. AMOS/CORBIS

International, 2002). Researchers in New Zealand estimate that more than 300 plant species are currently under threat, including 199 higher plant species and 85 lower plant species (with subspecies and varieties accounting for the remaining 18) (New Zealand Department of Conservation, 2002). The World Conservation Union-IUCN's 2002 *Red List of Threatened Species*, meanwhile, formally lists 21 plants in New Zealand as endangered.

Faunal biodiversity in New Zealand is also low in comparison with continental regions, but the country has high levels of endemism. "Both species of New Zealand bat are endemic, as are all four frogs, all 60 reptiles, more than 90 percent of insects and a similar percentage of marine molluscs . . . and a quarter of all bird species. In contrast, Great Britain, which separated from continental Europe only 10,000 years ago, has only two endemic species: one plant and one animal. Half a dozen islands in the Hauraki Gulf have a greater level of endemism than the whole of Britain" (New Zealand Department of Conservation, 2000). Many of these species are typified by stable or growing populations. But others have suffered from the impact of exotic species, habitat loss, pollution, and other factors. Indeed, the IUCN 2002 *Red List of Threatened Species* in New Zealand includes 8 mammals, 63 birds, 11 reptiles, 1 amphibian, 8 fishes, and 5 mollusks.

Despite its problems, however, New Zealand still remains a rich repository of biodiversity. Its biological wealth includes more than 100 species of endemic flightless crickets, the largest fauna of lizards on any temperate archipelago, breeding grounds for 75 percent of the world's penguin species, more than half of the world's albatrosses, and half of the world's petrels, prions, and shearwaters (Mansfield, 1996; Towns et al., 1990).

New Zealand has also exhibited a heightened awareness of biodiversity conservation issues in the last half-century. The country's first laws pertaining to conservation were passed in the 1860s, though they prohibited the hunting of birds and fish introduced from Europe. The first law to protect indigenous species was the Wild Birds Protection Act of 1864; various other laws to protect specific types of wildlife were enacted between 1875 and 1950, and all were brought together with the Wildlife Act of 1953. During this time many national parks and reserves were established. In the late 1990s New Zealand formally acknowledged the protection of indigenous habitats and biological diversity as one of its eleven most important environmental issues. Toward these goals, the government developed the New Zealand Biodiversity Strategy, which was unveiled in 2000. Important components of this strategy include the Department of Conservation, the main government agency responsible for biodiversity and its conservation, and the extensive network of terrestrial and marine protected areas it oversees.

Reversing Extinction through Cloning:
The Case of the Tasmanian Tiger

The thylacine was one of the most unusual animals to roam the Australian continent in modern history. The formal name of the species, *Thylacinus cynocephalus,* was taken from Greek words meaning "pouched dog." It was more widely known as the Tasmanian tiger or Tasmanian wolf, though human struggles to classify it also led to the nicknames zebra wolf and opossum hyena. The thylacine was a carnivorous marsupial weighing about 65 pounds, with a short brown coat and black stripes along its back. Although its closest living relatives were fellow marsupials like kangaroos and opossums, it evolved as a predator with behavior more like that of a wolf. Its range once included all of Australia, but in modern times it thrived mainly on the island of Tasmania, where it hunted wallabies and other grazing species.

The demise of the thylacine began with the arrival of European settlers in Tasmania in the early 1800s. Viewing the Tasmanian tiger as a threat to their introduced flocks of sheep, these settlers relentlessly trapped, shot, and poisoned every one they could find. The Tasmanian government sponsored an extermination program beginning in the 1840s that had paid more than 2,000 bounties by 1900 ("Revive the Extinct Tasmanian Tiger—through Cloning?" 2002). The thylacine population was further reduced by a loss of habitat as land was cleared for agriculture and grazing. As a result of these factors, the species was virtually wiped out within a century. The last known thylacine died in captivity in Hobart, Tasmania, in 1936, just two months after the Tasmanian government afforded legal protection to the species.

Although the thylacine has been extinct for many years, it remains a popular symbol in Australia; its likeness appears on items from license plates to beer labels and sports team logos. The thylacine attracted global interest in 1999, when the Australian Museum in Sydney announced its intention to resurrect the species through cloning. The museum's collection included a female baby thylacine that had been taken from its mother's pouch in 1866 and preserved in a jar of alcohol. A team of scientists was able to recover surprisingly good DNA samples from the specimen, to which it added DNA from two other preserved pups in 2001. They planned to sequence thylacine DNA (have the genetic code "read" in the proper order by a sophisticated computer) in hopes of someday creating a living clone and perhaps even a breeding population of the long-dead species.

Researchers admit that they face long odds in creating a living creature; one molecular biologist gave the project a 30 percent chance of success over the next 200 years (Weidensaul, 2002). They made an important breakthrough in May 2002, however,

(continues)

when they successfully replicated thylacine genes using a process called Polymerase Chain Reaction (PCR). But the biggest obstacles still lie ahead. Current methods of cloning, which have been used to produce clones of livestock, require a living cell to be inserted into a host egg from which all genetic material is removed. Of course, no living cells exist for extinct species like the thylacine. In this case, scientists must fill in the gaps in thylacine DNA with that of other marsupials to create artificial chromosomes. This cloning technique is beyond the ability of today's science and is expected to remain so for the foreseeable future.

The efforts of the Australian Museum to bring the thylacine back from extinction sparked a heated debate that involved scientists, ethicists, and conservationists. Opponents of the cloning experiment argued that its huge expense (sequencing the thylacine genome alone was expected to cost $15 million) drained money from more important government programs, including efforts to protect endangered species that are not yet extinct. They also claimed that cloning was impossible for the species because no living animal is a close enough relative for a successful surrogate birth. Some ethicists said that resurrecting a long-dead creature was an immoral exercise and berated researchers for "playing God." Some conservationists worried that if the program were ultimately successful, it would only create another endangered species in a world that is already full of them. They

also wondered whether successful cloning of the thylacine might serve to reduce public concern about endangered species, by convincing people that the species can always be brought back from extinction later.

Supporters of the cloning effort argued that mankind was morally obligated to restore the thylacine and other extinct species if it became scientifically feasible. Some scientists noted that sequencing the thylacine DNA was an important exercise in itself, because it would allow valuable comparisons to be made with the genetic codes of living marsupials, like the Tasmanian devil and numbat. Conservationists also have claimed that reintroduction of the thylacine would provide a needed capstone predator in Tasmanian ecosystems. Finally, museum representatives said that the cloning effort would help improve Australia's scientific reputation. "To actually reverse extinction would be the biological equivalent of the first walk on the moon," said Australian Museum director Michael Archer ("Revive the Extinct Tasmanian Tiger—through Cloning?" 2002).

As the cloning program proceeds for the legendary Tasmanian tiger, projects to clone extinct and endangered species are also underway in other parts of the world. Targeted imperiled and extinct species include the gaur, a wild ox once found in India and Southeast Asia; the Asiatic cheetah, which is found in small numbers in Iran; and the giant pandas of China. In addition, Oxford University scientists have sequenced the genome of two

(continues)

extinct species of moa—flightless birds once found in New Zealand—in hopes of someday resurrecting them.

Sources:

2002. *The End of Extinction: Cloning the Tasmanian Tiger* (documentary film). The Discovery Channel, July 7.

Paddle, Robert. 2000. *The Last Tasmanian Tiger: The History and Extinction of the Thylacine.* Cambridge and New York: Cambridge University Press.

2002. "Revive the Extinct Tasmanian Tiger—through Cloning?" *Christian Science Monitor,* July 11.

2002. "Tasmanian Tiger Cloning Breakthrough." *Australian Museum Online,* May 28. Available at http://www.austmus.gov.au/thylacine/news release.htm.

Weidensaul, Scott. 2002. "Raising the Dead." *Audubon* (May–June).

Papua New Guinea

One of the largest nations in the Pacific, the total landmass of Papua New Guinea is 85 percent mainland, with its 600 satellite islands composing the remaining 15 percent. Once a part of the ancient continent of Gondwanaland, Papua New Guinea is now the most biologically diverse country in Melanesia. Its vegetation communities include tropical moist (rain) forests and wetlands. The former are varied in structure and composition because of marked altitudinal contrasts that give rise to variations in soil, rainfall, and annual temperature regimes.

Papua New Guinea houses 5 to 7 percent of the world's biodiversity, with a high proportion of endemics, on less than 1 percent of its total land area (Papua New Guinea Department of Environment and Conservation, 1995). Indeed, it is ranked fifteenth in terms of absolute diversity and eleventh when country size is considered (World Conservation Monitoring Centre, 2002). Approximately 40 percent of Papua New Guinea's original forest cover remains, despite a long history of shifting cultivation and a high incidence of natural fire (Bryant, 1997). This is the largest intact tropical forest in the Asia-Pacific region and the third-largest in the world after the Amazon and Congo basins. It is also the cornerstone of much of the country's biological wealth, from its 75 species of bat and 71 species of marsupials to 56 endemic butterfly species, including the Queen Alexandra birdwing, the world's largest butterfly. But mining operations, agricultural clearing, and clear-cut logging threaten much of the remaining forests. Logging operations have emerged as a particularly dire threat, as clear-cuts dismantle species-rich tropical forests and increase sediment loads carried by rivers to the sea, where they degrade the quality of coastal and coral reef ecosystems (Bryant, 1997).

Like its neighbors, Papua New Guinea has its share of deliberately and accidentally introduced alien species. Plant invaders include the aquatic weeds salvinia and water hyacinth, both of which are widespread in Papua New Guinea wetlands and rivers. In addition, 21 species of freshwater fish have been introduced, including several species of trout, though only half have become established; other introduced species include mollusks—for example, the giant African snail—insects such as parasitic wasps, and introduced mammals including the domestic dog and cat, pig, cattle, buffalo, goat, rat, various species of deer, and horse.

The impact of invasive species, coupled with habitat loss and alteration caused by development pressures and pollution, has been considerable. Indeed, all sectors of Papua New Guinea's biological wealth have experienced severe attrition. According to the IUCN 2002 *Red List of Threatened Species,* Papua New Guinea is home to 266 threatened species (58 mammal species, 32 bird species, 9 reptile species, 13 fish species, 2 mollusk species, 10 other invertebrate species, and 142 plant species).

Papua New Guinea is a signatory to the Convention on Biological Diversity, but it does not yet have a formal biodiversity strategy in place, or well defined plans for forest exploitation. The forests constitute a major resource, and their exploitation is the chief real and potential cause of biodiversity loss. Timber harvesting in Papua New Guinea began in the early twentieth century—mainly in lowland forests—but it was not until the 1980s that concerns about environmental damage and corruption at government level in relation to logging concessions were articulated. This led to a review of logging policies (the Barnett Commission) and the formulation of a New National Forest Policy by 1990. But despite sound intentions there remains considerable cause for concern. Conservationists contend that Papua New Guinea forests are still under the control of large, foreign-owned companies that are annually logging at least 125,000 hectares in unsustainable fashion. In addition, logging concessions continue to be approved in areas of high biodiversity and in areas where the rights of indigenous people will be compromised (Barry, 2002). These trends engender concerns that Papua New Guinea's forests will be ravaged in the same manner as those of Indonesia and parts of Malaysia.

Invasive Weed Species Threatens Kakadu National Park

Australia's geographic isolation helped protect it against invasion by exotic species of plants for centuries. When Europeans arrived on the continent, however, they brought with them a variety of plants, both intentionally and unintentionally. In fact, many of the most troublesome weeds now found in Australia were brought over intentionally for use in gardens and then escaped into the surrounding bush. Lacking natural enemies to keep them in check, some of these nonnative species spread out of control. Over time, such invasive species displace native plants and animals, thus altering entire ecosystems and threatening biodiversity.

One of the most problematic weeds in Australia is *Mimosa pigra,* commonly known as the "giant sensitive plant" because its leaves close up quickly when touched. This woody plant, which prefers a tropical climate with well-defined wet and dry seasons, is native to Central America but is now causing problems in Africa and Southeast Asia as well as in Australia. *Mimosa pigra* grows in dense thickets up to six meters (20 feet) tall that effectively prevent light from reaching the ground below. The species thus crowds out native vegetation and communities of animals.

Mimosa pigra is believed to have been brought to Australia intentionally prior to the 1890s. It apparently started out as a display plant in the Darwin Botanic Gardens in the Northern Territory, where it remained for many years. Even after it escaped to the wild, the species did not become a nuisance until a combination of factors assisted its spread in the 1970s. A series of floods carried the plant's seeds—which remain viable in water and can float—onto land that had been severely degraded through overgrazing and trampling of the native vegetation by herds of feral water buffalo (Beckmann, 1992).

Mimosa pigra soon proved itself to be an ideal plant for these conditions. It is fast-growing (achieving a growth rate of up to 1 centimeter per day in favorable conditions), produces abundant seeds that mature quickly, can survive drought and flood, and is inedible to water buffalo and other common animals of the region. The species spread quickly across the coastal floodplains of the Northern Territory, eventually stretching over 450 kilometers (280 miles) from Western Australia into Queensland. The worst infestation occurred along the Adelaide River. *Mimosa pigra* transformed the species-rich tropical wetlands, sedgelands, and grasslands of this region into monospecific stands and reduced the diversity of plant and animal species found there. The weed had a particularly harmful effect on ducks, egrets, geese, magpies, lizards, and other fauna that depended on diverse woody plants, abundant grass cover, or open sedgelands.

(continues)

As *Mimosa pigra* spread across the northern reaches of Australia, scientists grew concerned that the weed would threaten the biodiversity of Kakadu National Park, a World Heritage Site. Thanks to its diverse geography and habitat, Kakadu contains the richest flora in the region. Some 1,700 species of plants have been recorded there, including 97 species that are considered rare. In addition, Kakadu is among the most weed-free parks in the world; as of 1995, only 5.7 percent of the plants found there were nonnative (Environment Australia, 2002).

Mimosa pigra poses a significant threat to Kakadu's plant and animal life. Experts estimate that the weed could eventually become the dominant species in 29 percent of the park's 13,000 square kilometers (5,020 square miles), and could become a significant feature in an additional 54 percent. In fact, only 17 percent of the protected area is believed to contain habitat unsuitable for *Mimosa pigra*. Furthermore, the most severe damage would likely occur in Kakadu's wetlands, which are home to numerous species of birds that attract many of the park's visitors (Beckmann, 1992).

Park officials have developed a management plan for *Mimosa pigra* and other weeds, which are defined as "any naturalized (established and reproducing in the wild) plant that is not native to Kakadu." As part of this plan, the park has employed four people full-time since the 1980s to monitor and eradicate invasive plant species. They have managed to prevent *Mimosa pigra* from gaining a permanent foothold within the park's boundaries through the use of herbicides and biological controls.

As part of the efforts to control the spread of *Mimosa pigra* in the Northern Territory, scientists have studied the plant and its natural predators in Mexico. They discovered that more than 200 species of insects and several species of fungi prey upon the plant in its home range. As a result, *Mimosa pigra* is not an aggressive invader in Central America, but rather an interesting addition to the local flora.

By the late 1990s, Australian officials had introduced 11 new species (9 insects and 2 fungi) in hopes of finding an effective biological control for *Mimosa pigra* (Marko, 1999). The first introductions, which took place in 1989, were of two species of stem-boring moths from Mexico that kill mature plants by tunneling into the stems. One of these species, *Neurostrota guinniella,* has become established and spread throughout the range of *Mimosa pigra* in Australia. The moths have apparently had some success in slowing the spread of the weed, and experts hope that the other introduced predators will provide additional help in the near future.

Sources:

Australian National Botanic Gardens. "Environmental Weeds in Australia." Available at http://www.anbg.gov.au/ weeds/weeds.html (accessed November 2002).

(continues)

Beckmann, Roger. 1992. "*Mimosa pigra* Threatens Kakadu." In *The Unique Continent*. Edited by Jeremy Smith. Queensland, Australia: University of Queensland Press.

Environment Australia. "Kakadu National Park: Plants, Animals, Landforms." Available at http://www.ea.gov.au/parks/kakadu/plantsanimalsland/plants.html (accessed December 2002).

Lonsdale, W. M. 1993. "Rates of Spread of an Invading Species: *Mimosa pigra* in Northern Australia." *Journal of Ecology* 81.

Marko, Michelle. 1999. "Controlling Invasion of the Exotic Shrub *Mimosa pigra* in Tropical Australian Wetlands." *Restoration and Reclamation Review*. Available at http://www.hort.agri.umn.edu/h5015/99papers/marko.htm.

New Caledonia

Originally part of Gondwanaland, the thirty-six islands of the French territory of New Caledonia became isolated 80 million years ago. Today, its main island of Grand Terre and the smaller Loyalty Islands contain a wealth of species diversity, including numerous species found nowhere else in the world. Indeed, high levels of endemism are present in New Caledonia's plant diversity (77 percent of its 3,332 known plant species), reptile diversity (86 percent of its 65 species), and mammal diversity (67 percent of its 9 species). But the terrestrial, marine, and freshwater habitats that support this abundance of life are under pressure on a host of fronts, making it one of the world's most vulnerable centers of biodiversity (Conservation International, 2002).

Four major terrestrial vegetation types are present in New Caledonia, as well as coastal mangroves. But only 5,200 square kilometers (2008 square miles) of vegetation—28 percent of the original total—remain in generally unspoiled condition. Evergreen rain forests were once the most extensive, covering about 70 percent of the territory's land mass, but removal to facilitate open cast nickel mining—which generates approximately 90 percent of the territory's total foreign exchange—has relegated these forests to scattered patches in the mountainous interior. Indeed, unsustainable mining, hunting, and logging have been the chief causes of biodiversity loss in an island group that has historically made little provision for environmental protection and conservation. For example, there are twenty-five reserves that cover only 527 square kilometers (203 square miles) out of a land area of 18,000 square kilometers (6,900 square miles). In addition, 83 percent of the territory's threatened plant species are not found in any of these protected areas (ibid.). Other factors in the erosion of New Caledonia's biological wealth include the intentional and accidental introduction of alien species and illicit trade in endangered bird and marine species.

Vanuatu

This independent state comprises eighty-two islands, with Espiritu Santo and Malekule accounting for about half of the total land area of 1.219 million hectares. These islands, which formed in the last 10 million years, feature mountainous interiors girded by coastal strips. There has been little clearance when compared with most other Pacific Islands states, and about 75 percent of the land remains covered in natural vegetation. Nonetheless, overall biological richness and endemism are modest when compared with the holdings of other Pacific Island states (World Wide Fund for Nature, "Vanuatu Rain Forests," 2002).

Agriculture and forestry are Vanuatu's primary sources of employment and wealth generation. Agriculture is mainly subsistence in nature, comprising yam and taro production, while commercial forestry is important in the more accessible lowland areas. According to the UN Food and Agriculture Organization, the quality of the natural forests for commercial purposes is low, and much of the forest is inaccessible on account of steep terrain; both characteristics are advantageous for habitat preservation. Local traditions have also served to conserve Vanuatu's natural heritage. Moreover, the government has compiled a National Forest Plan (NFP) that emphasizes sustainable resource use, and it is in the midst of formulating a Biodiversity Strategy and Action Plan. Yet despite these positive factors, 23 species of flora and fauna in Vanuatu have been classified in the IUCN 2002 *Red List of Threatened Species,* and that number will rise considerably if rising water levels associated with global warming submerge coastal habitats.

The Solomon Islands

The Solomon Islands comprise six large volcanic islands in two parallel chains and numerous small islands and atolls. There is much variation in biodiversity and human activity among the islands, most of which bristle with lowland rain forests that support a variety of endemic flora and fauna. Of 47 mammal species found in the Solomon Islands, for instance, more than half (26) are endemic or near endemic. These include nine rodents and 17 bats, of which three of each are endangered. Of 199 bird species, 91 are of restricted range and 69 are endemic. Three bird species are classified as critically endangered and 4 others as endangered (World Wild Fund for Nature, 2002).

The Solomon Islands' high degree of endemism means that many species are susceptible to extinction as a result of competition from invasive species. An even greater threat, however, is habitat loss and degradation from unsustainable logging and shifting cultivation, both of which have been fueled by high rates of population growth. Both local and international concerns have been raised about the high rate of logging, and a new Forest Act was passed in 1999 to encourage sustainable practices. But monitoring and enforcement of new regulations have been limited, and the Solomon Islands have yet to offer formal protection to any of its land holdings.

Polynesia and Micronesia

Conservation International has designated the islands of Micronesia and Polynesia (including Fiji) as one of the globe's twenty-five biodiversity hotspots. These 1,400-plus islands dot 21.6 million square kilometers (8.3 million square miles) of the southern Pacific—an area approximately 2.6 times the size of the continental United States—but their total land area amounts to only 46,000 square kilometers (17,760 square miles). In terms of geologic character, these tiny islands range from mangrove-ringed coastal wetlands to open woodlands and cloud forests. This diverse array of ecosystems—the hotspot contains twelve distinct vegetation biomes or ecosystem regions—has combined with the isolation of the islands to produce a startling number of endemic species. But both endemic and more widely distributed species within this region are at risk from human-induced disturbance. Indeed, less than 21 percent of the region's original vegetation remains in a natural state, and invasive species introduced by way of human activity have disrupted numerous habitats (Conservation International, 2002).

More than 6,550 species of vascular plants are known to exist across Polynesia and Micronesia, of which 51 percent are endemic in nature. In addition, 9 of the region's 16 known mammal species are endemic, as are 174 of the area's 254 bird species. Indeed, BirdLife International ranks Polynesia and Micronesia as the sixth-richest area of bird endemism in the world (Stattersfield, 1998). Endemic species also account for nearly 54 percent of the 69 reptile species found in Polynesia and Micronesia, and all three amphibian species in this sector of the South Pacific are endemic. Finally, these waters support a high level of marine diversity. The waters off the tiny island nation of Palau, for example, contain 300 distinct species of coral and 7 species of giant clam. Endemism is also significant, especially in remote tropical waters (Conservation International, 2002).

As in other areas of Oceania, biodiversity on the islands of Micronesia and Polynesia has been adversely affected by human activities. According to Conservation International, Polynesia and Micronesia contain 88 threatened species of flora and fauna, with 24 species critically endangered. In addition, it reports that nearly 40 species have become extinct in the region since 1500, with bird species suffering disproportionate damage. In fact, BirdLife International reports that 22 of the region's endemic avian species disappeared after the arrival of Europeans (ibid.; Stattersfield, 1998).

Leading threats include unsustainable logging, clearing of land for agricultural purposes, and development for housing and transportation. "Small islands, because of their limited area, are heavily impacted by conversion of natural vegetation to anthropogenic landscapes. In many Pacific islands, there is no natural lowland vegetation left, because the land is under such demand from human populations" (Conservation International, 2002). But many observers believe that alien species constitute an even greater menace to native communities of animals and plants. On the island of Guam, for example, the brown tree snake was introduced a half-century ago. Since that time, it has been directly linked to the extinction of nine native bird species and all endemic lizard species on the island. In Tahiti, meanwhile, a South American tree species, *Miconia calvescens,* has overwhelmed native vegetation and now covers 65 percent of the island (ibid.). Finally, the threat of sea level rise from global warming constitutes a growing threat to biodiversity (and human populations) in this region, as many low-lying islands may ultimately disappear entirely beneath the waves.

Fiji

On Fiji, all of the factors threatening biodiversity across the rest of Polynesia and Micronesia can be seen in microcosm. The Republic of Fiji consists of 300 islands, but two of them—Viti Levu and Vanua Levu—account for 87 percent of the total land area. The tropical forests of Fiji support rich fauna and flora relative to other oceanic island groups in the Pacific. Moreover, many species are exclusive to Fiji, including half of its plant species. Indeed, some species are endemic to specific islands, such as the orange, golden, and whistling fruit doves, each of which is confined to a specific island group.

But these and other remarkable species face potential threats from a host of human activities. Agriculture is a mainstay of the Fiji economy and employs half the adult population; it has also transformed forested areas into arable land producing sugar cane, coconut, ginger, and tropical fruits. Indeed, agriculture and associated forest exploitation is the leading cause of habitat and biodiversity loss on Fiji's two main islands.

Evidence from archaeological sites indicates that prior to human colonization the Fijian islands had a richer fauna (and probably flora) than they have now. Many extinctions have already occurred, including that of a land crocodile and a giant land iguana; the monkey bat, one of Fiji's few mammal species, is considered to be critically endangered. Altogether, Fiji contains 92 species known to be threatened, including 65 species of plants, 5 species of mammals, 12 species of birds, and 6 species of reptiles (World Conservation Union-IUCN, 2002). Fiji's recent efforts to counteract declining species populations have included creation of a protected area network and implementation of a formal biodiversity strategy and action plan. But analysts believe that any effective conservation strategy will have to squarely address the unsustainable agricultural practices that currently prevail across Fiji.

Sources:

Australia State of the Environment Committee. 2001. *State of the Environment Australia 2001.* Canberra: Environment Australia/CSIRO.

Barry, G. 2002. *An Analysis of Papua New Guinea's Implementation of the Convention on Biological Diversity with a Focus on Forests.* Moreton-in-Marsh, UK: Fern.

Bryant, Dirk, D. Nielson, and L. Tangley. 1997. *The Last Frontier Forests: Ecosystems and Economies on the Edge.* Washington, DC: World Resources Institute.

Conservation International. 2002. "Biodiversity Hotspots." Available at www.biodiversityhotspots.org (accessed October 24, 2002).

Crisp, M. D., S. Laffan, H. P. Linder, and A. Monro. 2001. "Endemism in the Australian Flora." *Journal of Biogeography* 28.

Cronin L. 1989. *The Concise Australian Flora.* Frenchs Forest, NSW, Australia: New Holland.

Davis, S. D., et al., eds. 1997. *Centres of Plant Diversity: A Guide and Strategy for Their Conservation.* Cambridge, UK: WWF-World Wide Fund for Nature and World Conservation Union-IUCN.

Environment Australia. 2002. *Threatened Species and Ecological Communities.* Available at www.ea.gov.au (accessed November 1, 2002).

Jaensch, Roger. 1996. "An Overview of the Wetlands of Oceania." In *Wetlands, Biodiversity and the Ramsar Convention.* Edited by A. J. Hails. Gland, Switzerland: Ramsar.

Mackay, Richard. 2002. *The Atlas of Endangered Species.* London: Earthscan.

Mansfield, Bill. 1996. "Ecosystem Restoration on Mainland New Zealand." Paper delivered at IUCN World Conservation Congress, Montreal, October 18.

Mittermeier, Russell A., Norman Myers, and Cristina Goettsch Mittermeier. 1999. *Hotspots: Earth's Biologically Richest and Most Endangered Terrestrial Ecoregions.* Washington, DC: CEMEX, Conservation International.

National Land and Water Resources Audit. 2001. *Australia's Native Vegetation.* Canberra: National Land and Water Resources Audit.

New Zealand Department of Conservation. 2000. *The New Zealand Biodiversity Strategy: Our Chance to Turn the Tide.* Wellington: Department of Conservation.

———. 2002. *National Parks.* Available at www.doc.govt.nz (accessed November 3, 2002).

New Zealand Ministry for the Environment. 1991. *New Zealand's National Report to the United Nations Conference on Environment and Development.* Wellington: Ministry for the Environment.

———. 1997. *The State of New Zealand's Environment.* Wellington: Ministry for the Environment.

Papua New Guinea Department of Environment and Conservation, Conservation Resource Centre, and the Africa Centre for Resources and Environment. 1995. *Papua New Guinea Country Study on Biological Diversity.* Waigani: Department of Environment and Conservation.

Samoa Department of Land Survey. 1998. *National Report to the Convention on Biological Diversity.* Samoa: Government of Samoa.

South Pacific Regional Environment Programme. 1992. *The Pacific Way: Pacific Island Developing Countries' Report to the United Nations Conference on Environment and Development.* Manila, Philippines: Asian Development Bank and UN Development Programme.

Stattersfield, A. J., and D. R. Capper, eds. 2000. *Threatened Birds of the World.* London: BirdLife International.

Stattersfield, A. J., et al. 1988. *Endemic Bird Areas of the World: Priorities for Biodiversity Conservation.* Cambridge, UK: BirdLife International.

Towns, D. R., and W. J. Ballantine. 1993. "Conservation and Restoration of New Zealand Island Ecosystems." *Trends in Ecology and Evolution,* no. 8.

Towns, D. R., C. H. Daugherty, and I. A. E. Atkinson, eds. 1990. *Ecological Restoration of New Zealand Islands.* Wellington: New Zealand Department of Conservation.

UN Development Programme. 2002. *The Federated States of Micronesia: National Biodiversity Strategy and Action Plan.* UNDP.

UN Environment Programme. 1999. *Pacific Islands Environmental Outlook.* Available at http://www.unep.org (accessed December 2002).

Williams, J. A., and C. J. West. 2000. "Environmental Weeds in Australia and New Zealand: Issues and Approaches to Management." *Austral Ecology* 25.

World Conservation Monitoring Centre (WCMC). 1992. *Global Biodiversity: Status of the Earth's Living Resources.* London: Chapman and Hall.

————. *Papua New Guinea Country Characteristics.* Available at www.wmcm.org (accessed November 7, 2002).

————. *Papua New Guinea Rainforests.* Available at www.wcmc.org (accessed November 10, 2002).

World Conservation Union—IUCN. 2002. *Red List of Threatened Species.* Available at www.redlist.org (accessed November 25, 2002).

World Wide Fund for Nature. 2002. "Solomon Islands Rain Forests." Available at www.worldwildlife.org/wildworld/profiles/terrestrial (accessed March 2003).

————. 2002. "Vanuatu Rain Forests." Available at www.worldwildlife.org/wildworld/profiles/terrestrial (accessed March 2003).

World Wide Fund for Nature and World Conservation Union-IUCN. 1995. *Centres of Plant Diversity: A Guide and Strategy for Their Conservation.* Cambridge: WWF.

Young, Ann. 1996. *Environmental Change in Australia since 1788.* Melbourne: Oxford University Press.

3

Parks,
Preserves, and
Protected Areas

O ceania is a region of vast size and attendant habitat and species diversity. It includes the continent nation of Australia as well as New Zealand, Papua New Guinea, and another 10,000 islands divided among twenty-one countries and territories distributed over more than 40 million square kilometers (15.5 million square miles) of the South Pacific. As one moves across this corner of the globe, an incredible array of unique wilderness areas and habitats nourishing high concentrations of endemic and threatened species can be found. Areas contributing to Oceania's high levels of biodiversity include rugged mountain ranges and gorges, towering old-growth forests, colorful tropical reefs, white sand beaches, mangrove swamps, untamed rivers, and remote desert landscapes.

During the past century, many nations in Oceania have erected protected area networks to preserve these areas. A multitude of these parks and sanctuaries were created out of a spirit of ecological stewardship; others were established to preserve aesthetically pleasing lands or accommodate the recreational pursuits of citizenry and tourists. Whatever the motivation, the end result has been the creation of parklands and reserves of extensive size and notable ecological value. This is especially true in Australia and New Zealand, economically advanced nations that account for an overwhelming percentage (almost 94 percent) of Oceania's total land area. Notable protected areas in these countries range from Australia's Great Barrier Reef Marine Park, the largest marine protected area on the planet, to New Zealand's Te Urewera National Park, home of the largest forested wilderness remaining on the country's North Island, and Whanganui National Park, which shields the wild Whanganui

River as it flows from its mountain origins into the Tasman Sea. But noteworthy parks and reserves exist elsewhere in Oceania as well. Indeed, numerous small but ecologically important protected areas dot the far-flung island nations of the South Pacific.

Unfortunately, many protected area networks in Oceania are suffering degradation from a host of internal and external forces. Even parks in Australia and New Zealand, which have shown a strong commitment to wilderness conservation principles, have been affected. These threats range from levels of tourism that compromise the integrity of park habitat to destructive land use practices inside or adjacent to the boundaries of protected areas. These activities include unsustainable forms of logging, mining, farming, commercial development, and expansion of towns and cities. In addition, inadequate investment in protected area networks—including monitoring and maintenance of existing parks—is a problem in Papua New Guinea and other Pacific Island states, and expansion of systems to provide greater protection of valuable and vulnerable habitat and species is an emerging priority throughout the region.

Classification of Protected Areas

Protected areas around the world are managed for a wide range of purposes, including scientific research, wilderness protection, preservation of species and ecosystems, maintenance of environmental services, protection of specific natural and cultural features, tourism and recreation, education, sustainable exploitation of natural resources, and maintenance of cultural and traditional attributes. The specific design, objectives, implementation, and management of protected areas all vary in accordance with the home country's cultural, political, economic, and ecological orientations. Indeed, classification systems used by individual countries vary in accordance with objectives and levels of protection, and title designations are different from country to country as well. Therefore, comparing protected areas in different regions of the world, or in different countries within one region, can be a challenging task.

To help countries decide what type of area to establish, select preservation objectives, and set management guidelines to achieve those objectives, the World Conservation Union (also known as IUCN from its former name—the International Union for the Conservation of Nature) maintains a classification system for protected areas that is recognized around the world. Classifying individual protected areas into this system based on their stated management objectives, regardless of their local designations, also makes information comparable across national and regional boundaries, permitting an assessment of the effectiveness of different protected area categories. Data on all but the smallest of the world's parks and reserves are collected by the WCPA and used to create the *United Nations List of Protected Areas,* the definitive listing of protected areas around the globe.

The World Conservation Union classifies each formally designated protected area in one of six management categories. Category I parks and reserves are protected areas managed primarily for science or wilderness protection. Strict nature reserves (Category Ia) includes ecological reserves, biological reserves, ecological stations, and other areas that are managed purely for biodiversity protection and scientific research and do not tolerate human visitation other than by scientists. Wilderness areas (Category Ib) are protected areas managed primarily for wilderness ecosystem protection; they allow human visitation only at a primitive level—that is, without assistance from human-established infrastructure such as roads and housing.

Category II protected areas are national parks managed for both ecosystem protection and human recreation. This is the most common category of protected area everywhere, because it is both the oldest of the categories and the one that is best suited to achieve the two objectives of greatest interest to the general public—conservation and recreation.

Other management classifications are available for natural monuments and landmarks that are managed primarily for conservation of specific natural features such as mountains, lakes, or canyons (Category III), species and habitat protection areas that are managed primarily for conservation, though subject to tree felling and other active forms of management (Category IV), protected landscapes and seascapes with dual conservation and recreation management mandates (Category V), and "managed resource protection areas" (Category VI), which seek to balance biodiversity protection with extractive activities like logging conducted in a sustainable manner.

Protected Areas in Australia
Australia contains a far greater number of parks, marine reserves, conservation areas, and other types of protected areas than any other nation in the South Pacific. In addition, the total area of land and sea protected under the Australian flag is more than thirteen times the size of the combined protected area systems of New Zealand, Papua New Guinea, and the other Pacific Island states.

According to a late 1990s report sponsored by the World Commission on Protected Areas, Australia contains 5,647 recognized protected areas covering 1.046 million square kilometers (0.4 million square miles), approximately 13.6 percent of its total land area (this percentage includes both actual protected land area—about 8 percent—and marine protected areas). The mean size of Australia's parks and reserves is a little over 185 square kilometers (71 square miles); by comparison, the mean size of protected areas in Europe is only 65 square kilometers (25 square miles), while the mean size of protected areas in South America is 1,280 square kilometers (494 square miles) (Green and Paine, 1997).

Most of Australia's protected areas are in the following three IUCN categories: (1) 2,191 strict nature reserves and wilderness areas (Type Ia and Ib), covering nearly 273,000 square kilometers (105,000 square miles)—3.55 percent of Australia's total land area; (2) 672 national parks (Type II), covering more than 237,000 square kilometers (105,000 square miles)—3.1 percent of the continent's total land area; and (3) 309 multiple-use reserves (Type VI), covering more than 476,000 square kilometers (184,000 square miles)—6.2 percent of the country's total land area (ibid.).

Australia's own Collaborative Australian Protected Areas Database (CAPAD), meanwhile, paints a similar portrait of the country's protected area network, though numbers are slightly different because of the creation of new parks and evolving management philosophies for existing parks. According to this source, at the end of the 1990s, Australia contained 5,251 terrestrial (land) protected areas divided into forty-one distinct types of parks, reserves, and sanctuaries, from Aboriginal national parks and botanical gardens to state parks and wilderness protection areas. These protected areas encompass more than 61 million hectares and protect 7.84 percent of mainland Australia (including Tasmania). According to CAPAD statistics, the most numerous protected areas are Type IV species and protection habitat areas—1,397 protected areas covering more than 325,000 hectares. But the most significant categories by area are nature reserves and wilderness areas (Type Ia and Ib), which afforded protection to more than 19 million hectares in 1,981 units; national parks (Type II), which covered another 25.2 million hectares within 603 units; and managed resource protection areas (Type VI), which accounted for more than 11.7 million hectares distributed among 376 units (Environment Australia, 2000).

In addition to its land-based parks and reserves, Australia has designated about 200 marine protected areas (MPAs), ranging from small state- and territory-managed aquatic reserves to marine parks under the jurisdiction of the Commonwealth. These MPAs, which operate in accordance with IUCN guidelines and categories, covered nearly 61 million hectares in 2000. Australia's commonwealth government was responsible for only thirteen of them, but these federal parks and reserves account for the lion's share of protected marine habitat, at more than 53 million hectares. Queensland accounts for another 5.4 million hectares of marine protected area within its eighty-two MPAs, the most of any single state or territory in Australia. Other states and

Table 3.1 Australia's Terrestrial Protected Areas by Type

Designation – Protected Area Type	Number	Area (hectares)	Jurisdiction
Aboriginal National Parks	4	531,485	NT
Botanic Garden	1	90	COMM
Conservation Areas	119	486,390	TAS
Conservation Parks	394	5,933,630	QLD, SA, WA
Conservation Reserves	63	317,233	SA, NT
Feature Protection Areas	26	1,703	QLD
Flora Reserves	103	29,036	NSW
Forest Reserves	191	176,122	TAS
Game Reserves	21	36,847	TAS, SA
Historic Sites	26	15,960	TAS
Historical Reserves	15	9,801	NT
Hunting Reserve	1	1,605	NT
Indigenous Protected Areas	6	507,087	SA, VIC, TAS
Karst Conservation Reserves	4	4,409	NSW
Management Agreement Areas	1	19,930	NT
Marine Parks (Terrestrial Component)	4	704	WA
Miscellaneous Reserves	9	2,425	WA
National Parks	511	28,172,191	ALL
National Parks, Scientific	7	52,181	QLD
Native Forest Reserves	6	1,473	SA, NT
Natural Features Reserves	1,522	160,336	VIC
Nature Conservation Reserves	328	180,758	VIC
Nature Parks	14	26,896	NT
Nature Reserves	1,441	11,547,443	NSW, ACT, TAS, WA
Other Conservation Area	41	409,972	TAS, NT
Other Parks	9	52,463	VIC
Protected Areas	4	13,380	TAS, NT
Recreation Parks	12	2,994	SA
Reference Areas (outside PA)	36	21,074	VIC
Regional Reserves	10	10,656,316	TAS, SA
Reserves	11	22,814	NSW
Resources Reserves	21	257,703	QLD
Scientific Areas	40	11,545	QLD
Section 5(g) Reserves	28	147,340	WA
Sites of Special Scientific Interest	4	11,550	COMM
Specially Protected Areas	4	1,142,060	COMM
State Parks	31	183,452	VIC
State Recreation Areas	2	230	TAS
State Reserves	50	17,869	TAS
Wilderness Parks	3	202,050	VIC
Wilderness Protection Areas	5	70,074	SA
Totals	5,128	61,438,611	

(continues)

Table 3.1 *(continued)*

Protected Area Types within other PAs	Number	Area (hectares)	Jurisdiction
Reference Areas (within PA)	104	90,306	
Wilderness Zones (within PA)	19	640,000	
Totals	123	730,306	
Combined Totals	5,251	62,168,917	double counting
Total of all PAs in Australia		61,438,611	
Total of PAs in External Territories		1,165,581	
Total of PAs in mainland Australia (incl. Tas.)		60,273,030	

PAs as % of total land area (ha) of the Australian mainland (incl. Tas.)

Total land area of mainland Australia	768,432,663
Total land area of PAs in mainland Australia	60,273,030
% PAs in Australia	7.84

% land protected on the Australian Mainland (incl. Tas.)	7.84

SOURCE: Collaborative Australian Protected Areas Database 2000. Copyright Commonwealth of Australia reproduced by permission.

territories with significant systems include New South Wales (fifty MPAs, 128,000 hectares), South Australia (seventeen MPAs, 252,000 hectares), Western Australia (eight MPAs, 1.4 million hectares), and Northern Territory (seven MPAs, 230,000 hectares) (Australian State of the Environment Committee, 2001). Australia's most famous marine protected area is Great Barrier Reef Marine Park, which is managed for multiple uses ranging from tourism to fishing, but nonetheless provides protection to 344,800 square kilometers (133,100 square miles) of ocean rich in flora and fauna. This park is managed by a separate commonwealth agency, the Great Barrier Reef Marine Park Authority.

Management and oversight of Australia's vast array of parks, wilderness areas, and marine reserves is divided among nine jurisdictions—the com-

Table 3.2 Australia's Marine Protected Areas (MPAs), November 2000

Jurisdiction	Number of MPAs	Area in MPAs (ha)	Management Plans produced
Commonwealth (incl. Great Barrier Reef Marine Park	13	53,329,431	5
New South Wales	50	127,707	4
Victoria	12	50,312	7
Tasmania	5	77,110	0
South Australia	17	252,371	1
Western Australia	8	1,393,387	4
Northern Territory	7	230,426	0
Queensland	82	5,421,117	6
Total	*194*	*60,881,861*	*27*

SOURCE: Australian State of the Environment Committee. 2001. *Australia State of the Environment 2001.* Independent Report to the Commonwealth Minister for the Environment and Heritage. CSIRO Publishing on behalf of the Department of the Environment and Heritage. Copyright Commonwealth of Australia reproduced by permission.

monwealth (federal) government, six states (New South Wales, Queensland, South Australia, Tasmania, Victoria, and Western Australia), and two self-governing territories (Australian Capital Territory and Northern Territory). Among Australia's states and territories, New South Wales has long been a recognized leader in conservation, and it has a particularly noteworthy history of protecting wilderness areas. Indeed, New South Wales's 1967 National Parks and Wildlife Act, which provided for the declaration of wilderness areas within national parks, marked the first time that the wilderness concept appeared in Australian legislation, and it proved to be a model for the commonwealth and other states. Since that landmark legislation, New South Wales has declared seventeen wilderness areas (IUCN Type Ia or Ib) within its boundaries, and it has remained a leading proponent of the wilderness ideal (Environment Australia, 2000).

Threats to Australia's Protected Area Network

Large, unspoiled wilderness areas can still be found in many areas of Australia. Their continued existence is the result of several factors, including climatic and topographic conditions that make some regions inhospitable for settlement or economic activity; the existence of a protected area system that shields forests, rivers, reefs, and other biologically rich ecosystems from development and degradation; and the country's relatively small population in relation to its land area. Indeed, the latter factor is perhaps the leading contributor to the continued existence of large wilderness areas in Australia. For example, Australia averages 7 people per square mile across its land area. By comparison, the United States contains 77 people per square mile, China contains 347 people per square mile, and Germany contains 598 people per square mile (Population Reference Bureau, 2002).

Nonetheless, even some parks and reserves enjoying Australia's highest levels of conservation protection have suffered erosion in the realms of ecological integrity and species health. This erosion is attributable to both internal factors, such as heavy and inappropriate tourist activity, and external factors, such as nearby logging and mining activities that fragment habitat and deposit pollutants into waterways running through the parks.

In Australia—like most other countries in the world—large areas of habitat have already been sacrificed for development, leaving behind "islands" of remnant habitat surrounded by "oceans" of agriculture, logged forests, highways, cities and towns, and other kinds of development. This is especially true of Australia's coastal areas in the south and west, where the beautiful tropical forests and coastal areas that nourish many species of flora and fauna have also attracted heavy concentrations of Australian families and businesses. In Queensland, for example, populations of the southern cassowary—a six-foot-tall, flightless bird that once roamed throughout the coastal rain forest—have been decimated by residential development that has destroyed much of the wide-ranging creature's habitat. In 1999 the cassowary was officially designated as an endangered species.

To a large degree, these historical patterns of development have dictated the shape and management priorities of today's protected areas. "In many cases these 'islands' are all that is left to conserve and there is no choice about the design of reserves" (Beattie, 1995). In some cases—as with the southern cassowary—the protected areas that have been cobbled together have not been of sufficient size or strength to safeguard fragile species from the pressures of the outside world (Pressey, 1995).

Australia is also grappling with the struggle to "accommodate tourism and recreation—which are essential in maintaining public support for protected area networks and other environmental protection measures—while also maintaining ecological integrity" (Beattie, 1995). Indeed, ecotourism is a steadily growing force in the overall fortunes of Australia's travel industry, and businesses and communities near tourist destinations such as the Great

Tourists travel by boat through the wetlands of Kakadu National Park in Australia's Northern Territory.
MICHAEL S. YAMASHITA/CORBIS

Barrier Reef are heavily dependent on these protected areas for their continued existence. But in some parks, such as Kakadu National Park, where the
number of visitors increased from 45,800 in 1982 to 240,000 in 1994–1995
(Aplin,1998), existing infrastructure (parking lots, visitor centers, restrooms,
campgrounds, and so on) can become woefully inadequate. Consequently,
pressure to accommodate growing numbers of visitors through increased investment in infrastructure is strong. But detractors contend that in some cases
these "improvements" compromise the ecosystems and endanger the species
that the park/reserve/sanctuary is charged with protecting. "The desires of
tourists may clash with the objectives held for protected lands, so it is hardly
surprising that it is difficult to achieve minimal impact in highly valued landscapes" (Young, 2000). In some protected areas, however, park managers have
addressed rising levels of visitation in ways that suggest a recognition of the
primacy of the protected area's conservation mandate. Measures to counter
visitor pressure include pricing policies, restrictions on daily visitation levels,
and internal zoning of reserves to provide varying levels of public access.

Protecting Wilderness and Biodiversity in the Twenty-first Century

At the beginning of the twenty-first century, Australia has set aside approximately 8 percent of its total land area for conservation. But it has signaled, both
in word and deed, its interest in further expanding its protected area network.

One priority among Australian conservationists is to extend a greater level of protection to habitats that sustain threatened species. At the close of the twentieth century, less than one-quarter of Australia's endangered and vulnerable plant species were found in national parks or proclaimed reserves. The remainder were located in areas receiving no special protections from development. Many of these habitats are almost certainly safe from exploitation, for they are in remote regions or are of little interest to mining, timber, agricultural, or real estate interests. But others are more vulnerable, for they contain exploitable natural resources in large enough quantities to be of potential commercial interest, or they lie in the path of expanding residential and commercial developments.

A related shortcoming of Australia's existing protected area network is the under-representation of open woodlands and grasslands. This state of affairs is directly linked to (1) Australian settlement patterns, which targeted open areas for grazing and crop cultivation; (2) the frequency with which states and territories added to protected area systems by incorporating land available at little or no cost—a practice that has been termed "conservation on the cheap" (Adam, 1992); and (3) the understandable desire to provide protection for mountain forests, rocky coastlines, high desert plateaus, and other aesthetically attractive regions that seem symbolic of the wilderness ideal. Conservationists laud the protections that have been afforded to the latter types of regions, but they believe that the rush to preserve these areas (an effort made considerably easier by their perceived low economic value) pushed protection of species-rich grasslands and open woodlands that had been spared by the first waves of Australian settlement far down the conservation priority list.

Today, the remnants of these ecosystem types still provide important habitat for a wide array of flora and fauna, but they are also vulnerable to exploitation in many parts of the country (Aplin, 1998; Pressey, 1995). For Australia's reserve systems to cover the full natural diversity of a region, then, greater attention will need to be paid to grasslands, open woodlands, and other under-represented but ecologically valued habitat types. "The resources for nature conservation are limited, competition with extractive uses is often fierce, and many species and habitats have limited life expectancies unless formally protected," observed one study. "Poor decisions about protected areas are therefore difficult to correct and can have a high price, if not for people then for other species. Unfortunately, poor decisions are all too frequent. Formal protection is commonly biased towards areas with least potential for economic or subsistence use and least in need of conservation action" (Pressey, n.d.).

Protected area design issues are also being explored at the commonwealth, state, and territorial levels. In response to rising numbers of threatened and endangered species, some analysts have called for increased linkage of individual protected areas through the creation of wildlife corridors in order to create larger blocks of contiguous protected area. Indeed, conservationists and wildlife biologists around the world have touted linked networks of protected areas as a way of preserving habitat and wildlife by providing otherwise isolated populations of animals with the means to migrate and breed with distant populations, thus strengthening the entire ecosystem's biodiversity. In Australia, the scaffolding of such an arrangement would include a combination of undeveloped public land and conservation easements on private land, with management responsibilities divided among commonwealth, state, and territory agencies. On the other hand, some conservationists have called for increased emphasis on the creation of numerous smaller reserves that might buffer species against chance extinction—from disease, for example—more effectively than would a single large protected area.

Other conservation priorities frequently cited in examinations of Australia's existing protected area system include greater protection of "keystone species"—those species that sustain numerous species by providing shelter or food or habitat maintenance—and greater regulation of mining, logging, development, as well as other activities in areas adjacent to parks and reserves so that practices that degrade land, water, and air within protected areas are minimized.

Much of the groundwork for further expansion of Australia's system of protected areas has already been completed, as commonwealth, state, and territorial governments have passed a number of pieces of conservation legislation within the last fifteen years. For example, the creation and implementation of Regional Forest Agreements (RFAs)—joint agreements between the commonwealth and state governments that provide a twenty-year "blueprint" for management and use of forests in a particular region—is, according to government agencies, helping Australia meet its professed goal of establishing a "world-class" forest reserve system across Australia (Commonwealth of Australia, 2000). These agreements have already been credited with significantly expanding the area of Australian forests contained in conservation reserves and other protected areas (UN Food and Agriculture Organization, *Global Forest Resource Assessment 2000*, 2001). However, Australian environmental organizations such as the Australian Conservation Foundation (ACF) claim that the RFAs mark an abrogation by the commonwealth government of its responsibility to protect natural areas with high conservation value, instead leaving this important duty to states and territories that may not have the funds or inclination to do so. The ACF has also charged that conservation goals stipulated in the RFAs have been subverted and that the agreements are "supporting unsustainable logging levels, massive job loss, destruction of old growth and high conservation value forests, all heavily subsidized by the taxpayer" (Australian Conservation Foundation, 2002).

Several other initiatives launched in the mid-1990s have helped to increase the representativeness of the nation's system of conservation reserves. These initiatives include the National Reserve System Program and related state and territory programs, the Indigenous Protected Area program, new multitenure management schemes, and a surge in contributions from nongovernment entities such as the Trust for Nature and Bush Heritage Fund (Environment Australia, "Parks and Reserves," 2003). In addition, the 1999 passage of the Environment Protection and Biodiversity Conservation Act (EPBC Act) gives the Commonwealth a valuable new tool for establishing and managing protected areas; within two years of the law's passage, twenty-one reserves had been declared under the EPBC Act, comprising six national parks, five national nature reserves, five marine parks, three marine reserves, and two botanical gardens (ibid.).

Australia has also shown increased recognition of the ecological, economic, and cultural importance of the continent's oceans and coastal areas. In the early 1990s the country's state, territory, and commonwealth governments agreed to establish a National Representative System of Marine Protected Areas (NRSMPA) that will contribute to the long-term ecological viability of marine and estuarine systems and protect Australia's biodiversity. Since that time, a variety of marine parks, marine national parks, marine and intertidal habitat areas, coastal reserves, marine management areas, fish habitat protection areas, aquatic reserves, seaward extensions of national parks, marine nature reserves, and marine reserves have sprouted across the continent. The naming conventions and management priorities of these protected areas vary by jurisdiction, but "they share a common intent to protect the marine and estuarine environment, particularly habitats such as reefs, seagrass beds, tidal lagoons, mangroves, rock platforms, coastal, deep ocean and underwater seabed areas and any marine cultural heritage" (Australian State of the Environment Committee, 2001). Conservation groups, however, have urged the extension of formal safeguards to much larger areas of coastline, both in heavily populated and rural areas of the country.

Australia also remains an active participant in various international conservation agreements. A member of the RAMSAR Convention since the 1980s, the country contains sixty-three recognized Wetlands of International Importance (RAMSAR Convention, 2002). It also contains fourteen World Heritage properties. Most of these natural areas of "universal importance" were nominated and inscribed with little controversy. Others, such as the Tasmanian World Heritage Area and the Wet Tropics of Queensland, aroused fierce opposition from state governments and commercial interests at the outset but have since garnered acceptance from state authorities and local communities (McNeely, 1994).

Finally, Australia has shown a willingness to take bold steps in expanding its protected areas system. In 2002 it announced its intention to create the world's largest highly protected marine reserve, one that would—unlike the Great Barrier Reef—be free of fishing, energy development, and other forms of exploitation. This massive new reserve, totaling 6.5 million hectares, will be created around the remote Heard Island and McDonald Islands group, located 4,500 kilometers (2,790 miles) southwest of the Australian mainland. According to scientists, this sub-Antarctic island group remains free of foreign species introduced directly by human activity. It also contains valuable habitat and food supplies for the southern elephant seal, the sub-Antarctic fur seal, several penguin species, and two albatross species.

That same year, Australia formally established the country's largest protected area deep in the outback desert. The protected area, called Ngaanyatjarra, will be managed by Aboriginal peoples that have long sought to protect the region's culture and environment from outside disturbances. But the Australian government will still assist in some aspects of the park's operation, including combating alien species, protecting water sources and other natural features, and establishing ecologically sensitive ecotourism ventures. The targeted area covers more than 98,000 square kilometers (38,000 square miles) and incorporates portions of the Gibson, Great Sandy, and Great Victoria deserts. It is the fifteenth indigenous protected area proclaimed in Australia, and the largest ever.

Australia's Indigenous Protected Areas

Indigenous Protected Areas (IPAs) are tracts of land controlled and managed by traditional Aboriginal peoples for the purposes of promoting biodiversity and cultural resource conservation. This program was created in the wake of the 1993 Native Title Act, which granted extensive new land rights to Aboriginal communities that had historically been victimized by the machinations of white governments and industries.

At the close of the twentieth century, indigenous people owned or managed about 15 percent of the Australian continent, including large swaths of semi-arid and arid rangelands that nurture many endemic species of flora and fauna. This has not escaped the notice of the country's conservation scientists, who have been keen to identify and fill gaps in the country's existing system of protected areas. "[This scientific approach] has shown [that] many types of landscapes and ecosystems . . . are poorly represented in the existing National

Sandstone monolith known as Ayers Rock, or Ululu (its Aboriginal name). COREL

Reserve System and that some such areas occur only on Indigenous owned lands" (Environment Australia, "Indigenous Protected Areas," 2003).

The IPA was thus created, both to help ensure that Aboriginal land rights were respected and to address gaps in Australia's protected area network. Nantawarrina was the first Indigenous Protected Area declared, in August 1998. It covers 58,000 hectares and is adjacent to the southern boundary of Gammon Ranges National Park in South Australia. Title to the land is held by the South Australian Aboriginal Lands Trust on behalf of the Adnyamathanha people from Nepabunna, and by all accounts this community has done a laudable job of balancing biodiversity conservation and cultural values. In June 2000 the Nepabunna community even won a UN Environment Day award in recognition of its work in Nantawarrina. Other notable IPA reserves include Watarru Indigenous Protected Area, a globally significant haven for reptile species that covers 1.28 million hectares, including parts of the rugged Birksgate Ranges; the 100,000-hectare Dhimurru IPA in the Northern Territory, which contains sacred sites of the Yolngu people and vital habitat for threatened species of marine turtles and sea birds; and Warul Kawa (Deliverance Island), an island IPA located in the Torres Strait that is an important nesting site for three species of sea turtle and a significant cultural and spiritual site for the Torres Strait Island people. By February 2001, the IPA program included thirteen distinct properties encompassing 3.1 million hectares.

Since that time, two additional protected areas, including the aforementioned Ngaanyatjarra, have been incorporated into the program, and other additions are expected in the future (ibid.).

Protected Areas in New Zealand

Composed of two large islands—North and South Islands—and numerous smaller islands, New Zealand contains vast areas of rugged beauty that are renowned throughout the world. Public appreciation of these natural riches is widespread throughout the country, which features a high standard of living and low population densities (37 people per square mile) (Population Reference Bureau, 2002). This combination of factors has created a fertile environment for the creation of a large and impressive system of protected areas. Indeed, few nations around the world can match the conservation program that has been erected by New Zealand over the past half-century.

As the twentieth century drew to a close, New Zealand had 235 protected areas recognized by the World Conservation Union-IUCN. These areas covered 63,338 square kilometers (24,455 square miles), nearly 24 percent of New Zealand's total land area. Within this system, the most significant protected area type was national parks (Type II protected areas according to IUCN classifications), with thirteen parks covering 28,629 square kilometers (11,054 square miles)—10.8 percent of New Zealand's total land area. Other protected area categories providing protection to extensive land area included fifty-four wilderness areas and nature reserves (Type Ia and Ib parks) covering 15,760 square kilometers (6,085 square miles)—5.94 percent of the total land area—and seventeen protected landscapes/seascapes managed for both recreation and conservation (Type V parks), covering 13,699 square kilometers (5289 square miles)—5.17 percent of the total land area (Green and Paine, 1997). Since this survey, New Zealand has continued to add to its network of protected areas, approving numerous smaller reserves and sanctuaries and opening a fourteenth national park—the 157,000-hectare Rakiura National Park on Stewart Island—in 2002. Today, New Zealand reports that fully one-third of the country's total land area is protected in some type of park or reserve.

New Zealand's Department of Conservation (DOC) manages six types of protected areas in "conservation units," standard groupings of parcels of land used in the DOC's National Land Register. As of early 2002, these holdings included reserves (2,977 conservation units encompassing 1.234 million hectares), national parks (14 parks divided into 27 conservation units, with a total land area of 3.4 million hectares), conservation areas (3,799 conservation units totaling 4.314 million hectares), wildlife areas (4 conservation units covering 88 hectares), marine mammal sanctuaries (2 conservation units—

Auckland Islands and Banks Peninsula—totaling 2.328 million hectares), and protected private lands, consisting in large measure of conservation covenant arrangements (441 conservation units totaling 81,250 hectares). New Zealand also boasts three World Heritage Sites of cultural and natural heritage of "outstanding universal value": Tongariro National Park; Te Wahipounamu—South West New Zealand (consisting of Westland/Tai Poutini National Park, Mount Aspiring National Park, Aoraki/Mount Cook National Park, and Fiordland National Park); and Sub-Arctic Islands of New Zealand (including Auckland, Campbell, Antipodes, and Bounty Groups and the Snares islands).

Some of the lands in New Zealand that receive protection from development would probably be spared from heavy human use anyway by virtue of their location and topographical features. For example, the centerpieces of many of the country's national parks are mountain ranges that are unsuited for settlement and farming or minimally adorned with accessible resources (such as timber) that would interest commercial resource extraction operations. But New Zealand has also set aside extensive areas of species-rich natural forest for preservation. In fact, fully 77 percent of natural forests in New Zealand are government-owned and managed as protected areas by the country's Department of Conservation. All of these forests—nearly 5 million hectares in total—are subject to conservation management plans. In addition, New Zealand has arranged for the protection of 70,000 hectares of privately owned natural forests through a variety of conservation covenant agreements (UN Food and Agriculture Organization, *Global Forest Resource Assessment 2000*, 2001). This level of forest protection—unmatched anywhere else in the world—is the cornerstone of the country's protected area network, and the single greatest key to New Zealand's hopes of preserving its natural ecosystems and its many species of flora and fauna for future generations.

Still, New Zealand's heavy emphasis on conservation has not gone unchallenged or been entirely devoid of controversy. Regarding the natural forests of New Zealand, "there remains a distinct tension between preservationist and multiple-use management philosophies," acknowledged one global forest study. "In recent years, there has been a marked shift towards further reducing the already modest industrial forestry activities in natural forests. At the same time, this has removed a significant component of the natural forests' ability to generate funds for improved management. Natural forests managers have consequently become increasingly reliant on direct government funding for effective management, and in some areas this has fallen short in providing adequate protection from degradation by introduced pests, most notably by red deer and the Australian brush-tailed opossum" (ibid.).

Finally, New Zealand's efforts to protect marine biodiversity and ecosystems through the establishment of protected areas has traditionally lagged behind its land-based conservation programs. Whereas about one-third of New Zealand's land is under some form of protection, marine reserves cover just 0.1 percent of the coastal sea around the North and South Islands. However, the country appears to be moving decisively to rectify this gap in coverage. One objective of its recently minted New Zealand Biodiversity Strategy (NZBS) is to expand the network of marine protected areas (using marine reserves and other forms of legal protection) so that it fully represents the range of New Zealand's coastal and marine ecosystems and habitats. By 2010, it hopes to have approved protection for 10 percent of the seas surrounding the island's two major islands. Toward this end, the Department of Conservation is laboring to create up to fifteen new marine reserves by 2005, and tangible progress toward this goal has already been made. In 2002, for instance, the Minister of Conservation approved three new marine reserve applications—at Te Matuku Bay on Waiheke Island (700 hectares), at Taputeranga on the south coast of Wellington (969 hectares), and at Paterson Inlet on Stewart Island (1,140 hectares). (These applications also require the consent of the ministers of Fisheries and Transport before they can be approved as marine reserves.)

In addition, New Zealand has sought to update its Marine Reserves Act 1971, the basis for its current marine reserve system. A proposed successor to the 1971 legislation—the Marine Reserves Bill—was introduced to Parliament for consideration in October 2002. This bill seeks to address several perceived deficiencies in the existing system. For example, it includes new provisions for meeting obligations of the Treaty of Waitangi, the 1840 treaty in which the United Kingdom proclaimed sovereignty over New Zealand in return for promises to respect the land-ownership rights of indigenous Maori peoples. It also seeks to join marine protection efforts with other environmental legislation passed in recent years, and it legalizes the creation of marine reserves within New Zealand's exclusive economic zone (EEZ)—the area of ocean extending from the outside edge of New Zealand's territorial sea (which extends 12 nautical miles out from the coastline) to 200 miles from inhabitable land.

Protected Area Systems in Other Oceanic States

Progress in establishing and maintaining protected area networks in other Oceanic states has been fitful since the 1970s, when Pacific Island states including Tonga, Western Samoa, Papua New Guinea, Kiribati, the Cook Islands, and Vanuatu devoted considerable resources toward establishment of protected areas, with a special focus on economically and ecologically valuable marine and coastal areas. This spate of activity declined dramatically in the 1980s, despite proliferating regional initiatives and meetings specifically designed to encourage protected area designation and biodiversity protection. In the 1990s, meanwhile, campaigns to safeguard ecologically significant natural areas from development produced meaningful success in only a handful of countries.

In the late 1990s Oceanic states excluding Australia and New Zealand had a total of 152 protected areas recognized by the World Conservation Union-IUCN. These parks and reserves covered a total of 13,113 square kilometers (5,063 square miles) and had a mean size of 86 square kilometers (33 square miles). Approximately one-third (50) of parks and reserves in the IUCN's Pacific category were Type IV protected areas—habitat/species management areas subject to active forms of management, including forest clearing and other activities seen as helpful to meeting management goals. The next most common type of protected area was managed resource protection areas (Type VI); Oceania contained 34 of these multiple-use zones, which seek to balance environmental conservation with recreational activities (hiking, camping) and extractive activities (logging, mining, hunting). Only 27 of the 152 designated protected areas in the Pacific states were Type Ia or Ib reserves, receiving the highest levels of conservation protection (Green and Paine, 1997).

Among these Pacific Island states, Papua New Guinea has the most extensive protected area network. It ranks second in Oceania (again excluding Australia and New Zealand) in terms of both the number of protected areas and the total land area protected. But these figures are misleading, for Papua New Guinea's total land mass dwarfs that of the other Oceanic nations. Indeed, Papua New Guinea's 464,000 square kilometers (179,000 square miles) of land area make it considerably larger than New Zealand, let alone tiny states such as Tonga (751 square kilometers [290 square miles of land]), the Marshall Islands (179 square kilometers [69 square miles]), Tuvalu (26 square kilometers [10 square miles]), and Nauru (23 square kilometers [9 square miles]) (Population Reference Bureau, 2002).

A closer look at Papua New Guinea's protected area system reveals a network rotting from inattention and mismanagement. The country's twenty-six formally recognized parks and reserves protect 10,341 square kilometers (3,993 square miles), only 2.23 percent of its total land area. Many of the protected areas that do exist are managed by tribal communities rather than the government, which devotes little funding or energy to scientific research, wildlife monitoring, or visitor services. "The present system [in Papua New Guinea] has evolved largely since 1975 and is woefully inadequate for a country of the size and conservation importance of Papua New Guinea," concluded one IUCN survey (McNeely, 1994).

Elsewhere in Oceania, France's New Caledonia has forty-six protected areas, but these cover only 1,154 square kilometers (446 square miles)—6 percent of its total land area—and consist primarily of category IV reserves (habitat and species areas under active management regimes). No other

Pacific Island state has more than 300 square kilometers (116 square miles) set aside for conservation protection or more than fifteen formally designated protected areas. Most countries have less than 6 percent of their admittedly modest land area under some form of protection, and mangrove forests, which provide a host of important ecological functions, remain severely underrepresented in protected area systems across much of the South Pacific. In addition, membership in the RAMSAR Convention among Pacific Island countries is practically nonexistent. This is significant, for while wetland resources are limited in extent in many of these small island states, the region is characterized by coral reefs, a vital wetland type recognized by the RAMSAR Convention, and it contains globally significant reefs in terms of both endemism rates and biodiversity.

One of the chief obstacles to development of protected area networks has been the region's entrenched system of land and resource ownership. Government control and ownership of land in most Pacific Island countries is the exception rather than the rule. In fact, in many parts of Oceania, private groups "can lay claim to the ownership of the resources of the land and coastal marine areas including reefs and fishing grounds. Pacific Island people have unusually strong cultural, spiritual and economic links with their land and coastal marine environment resulting from their dependence on terrestrial and marine resources for subsistence. In such circumstances the compulsory acquisition of land for protected areas and the denial of resource user rights is out of the question and governments have not seen protected areas establishment as a high enough priority to warrant expenditure on compensation or the possible political impact of difficult or failed negotiations" (ibid.).

Other impediments to the establishment of parks, reserves, sanctuaries, and other types of protected areas include high population growth rates, which have triggered displacement of traditional land management systems by new agricultural systems and further depletion of marginal forest lands and other habitats; rapacious mining and logging practices, which have destroyed entire ecosystems in places like Nauru; and an almost complete absence of comprehensive land-use policies. "It is essential that efforts to develop and implement sustainable land management policies are given the priority that the issue deserves" (UN Environment Programme, 1999).

This neglect has extended to existing parks and reserves as well. In Fiji's J. H. Garrick Memorial Reserve, for example, illegal logging operations carved up protected forest with impunity during the 1990s. Elsewhere, Queen Elizabeth II National Park in the Solomon Islands has been wracked by illegal land clearing and fuelwood theft ever since its establishment in 1954. Marine protected areas have also seen degradation as a result of inappropriate human activities (such as discharge of pesticides and heavy metals into coastal waters), infiltration by invasive species, and inadequate funding of agencies charged with fulfilling management and conservation mandates (McNeely, 1994; UN Food and Agriculture Organization, *Global Forest Resource Assessment 2000*, 2001; UN Environment Programme, 1999).

Despite these obstacles, some Pacific Island states have made noteworthy strides in the realm of habitat conservation. For example, forestry reserves built on notions of sustainability and environmental stewardship are slowly coalescing in some countries. This is an encouraging sign, given the pivotal place that forest systems occupy in many island ecosystems. And despite the formidable hurdles posed by traditional land tenure systems, many countries are slowly cobbling together protected area networks for themselves. Countries such as American Samoa, Fiji, French Polynesia, Niue, Samoa, and Vanuatu have all declared new parks or reserves in recent years, and New Caledonia has done an "exceptional" job of creating parks and reserves, according to the UN Food and Agriculture Organization (*Global Forest Resources Assessment 2000*, 2001). In addition, five Pacific Island states have formally declared their marine Exclusive Economic Zones (EEZs) to be whale sanctuaries, the first building blocks in an ambitious initiative to create a whale sanctuary across the entire South Pacific (South Pacific Regional Environment Program, 2002).

But most countries in Oceania have a long way to go before they will have protected area networks fully capable of safeguarding their natural and biological riches. In fact, observers believe that instituting such networks will require considerable assistance from international conservation and development assistance agencies—both governmental and nongovernmental—for the foreseeable future. Even with such aid, however, there is widespread concern that "unless government conservation agencies [in the Pacific Island states] are dramatically strengthened through the increased allocation of financial and manpower resources, little progress can be expected with the establishment of new protected areas in the region let alone with the effective management of existing areas" (McNeely, 1994).

Sources:

Adam, P. 1992. "The End of Conservation on the Cheap." *National Parks Journal* 36, no. 3.

Aplin, Graeme. 1998. *Australians and Their Environment: An Introduction to Environmental Studies*. Melbourne: Oxford University Press.

Australia Bureau of Rural Sciences. 1998. *Australia's State of the Forests Report 1998*. Canberra: BRS.

Australian Conservation Foundation. 2002. "Regional Forest Agreement Act Bad for Environment and Jobs." March 14. Available at http://www.acfonline.org. au/asp/pages/document.asp?IdDoc=667 (accessed March 2003).

Australian State of the Environment Committee. 2001. *Australia State of the Environment Report 2001.* Canberra: Commonwealth of Australia.

Beattie, Andrew J., ed. 1995. *Biodiversity: Australia's Living Wealth.* Sydney: Reed.

Bonyhady, T. 1993. *Places Worth Keeping: Conservationists, Politics and Law.* Sydney: Allen and Unwin.

Brennan, F. 1995. *One Land, One Nation: Mabo—Towards 2001.* Brisbane: University of Queensland Press.

Brunckhorst, David J., ed. 1994. *Marine Protected Areas and Biosphere Reserves: Toward a New Paradigm.* Canberra: Australian National Conservation Agency, UN Scientific and Cultural Organization.

Cole, D. N., and P. B. Landres. 1996. "Threats to Wilderness Ecosystems: Impacts and Research Needs." *Ecological Applications* no. 6.

Commonwealth of Australia. 2002. *Regional Forest Agreements, 2002.* Available at www.rfa.gov.au.

Dick, R. 1997. *NPWS State Reserve System Program: Past, Present and Future.* Sydney: New South Wales National Parks and Wildlife Service.

Environment Australia. 1997. *National Reserve System—Terrestrial and Marine Protected Areas in Australia.* Canberra: Department of Environment and Heritage.

———. "Collaborative Australian Protected Areas Database (CAPAD) 2000." 2000. Available at www.ea.gov.au/parks/nrs/capad/2000 (accessed January 2003).

———. "Indigenous Communities and the Environment." Available at www.ea.gov. au/indigenous (accessed January 2003).

———. "Indigenous Protected Areas." Available at www.ea.gov.au/indigenous/ ipa/index.html (accessed January 2003).

———. "Parks and Reserves." Available at www.ea.gov.au/parks (accessed January 2003).

Frazier, Scott. 1996. *An Overview of the World's Ramsar Sites.* Berkshire, UK: Wetlands International.

Great Barrier Reef Marine Park Authority. "Protecting the Great Barrier Reef World Heritage Area." Available at www.gbrmpa.gov/corp_site/info_services/ publications/brochures/protecting_biodiversity (accessed January 2003).

Green, M. J. B., and J. Paine. 1997. "State of the World's Protected Areas at the End of the Twentieth Century." Paper presented at IUCN World Commission on Protected Areas Symposium, Albany, Australia, November.

Hall, C. M. 1992. *Wasteland to World Heritage: Preserving Australia's Wilderness.* Melbourne: Melbourne University Press.

McNeely, J. A., J. Harrison, and P. Dingwall, eds. 1994. *Protecting Nature: Regional Reviews of Protected Areas.* Gland, Switzerland: IUCN.

New Zealand Department of Conservation. 2000. *The New Zealand Biodiversity Strategy: Our Chance to Turn the Tide.* Wellington: DOC.

————. "Marine Reserves." Available at www.doc.govt.nz/conservation (accessed January 2003).

Population Reference Bureau. 2002. *2002 World Population Data Sheet of the PRB: Demographic Data and Estimates for the Countries and Regions of the World.* Washington, DC: PRB.

Pressey, R. L. 1995. "Conservation Reserves in New South Wales: Crown Jewels or Leftovers?" *Search,* no. 26.

Pressey, R. L., et al. n.d. "Effectiveness of Protected Areas in North-Eastern New South Wales." Armidale: New South Wales National Parks and Wildlife Service.

Preston, G. 1997. *Review of Management Regimes for Coastal and Oceanic Resources in Pacific Island Countries.* Apia: South Pacific Regional Environmental Programme.

Ramsar Convention on Wetlands. 2002. "The RAMSAR List." Available at www.ramsar.org (accessed November 2002).

South Pacific Regional Environment Program. 2002. *Action Strategy for Nature Conservation in the Pacific Islands Region, 2003–2007.* Apia, Samoa: SPREP.

Stevens, Stan. 1997. *Conservation through Cultural Survival: Indigenous Peoples and Protected Areas.* Washington, DC: Island.

UN Environment Programme. 1999. *Pacific Islands Environmental Outlook.* www.unep.org (accessed December 4, 2002).

UN Food and Agriculture Organization. 2001. *Global Forest Resources Assessment 2000.* Rome: FAO.

————. 2001. *State of the World's Forests 2001.* Rome: FAO.

World Conservation Monitoring Center. 2001. "WCMC Protected Areas Database." Available at http://unep-wcmc.org/protected_areas/data/nat_warning.htm (last revision, October 29).

World Conservation Union-IUCN. 1998. *1997 United Nations List of Protected Areas.* Gland, Switzerland: IUCN.

Young, Ann. 2000. *Environmental Change in Australia since 1788.* 2d ed. Melbourne: Oxford University Press.

Zbicz, D. C., and M. J. B. Green. 1997. "Status of the World's Transfrontier Protected Areas." Paper presented at the International Conference on Transboundary Protected Areas as a Vehicle for International Co-operation, September 16–18, 1997, Somerset West, South Africa.

4

Forests

Australia, New Zealand, and the other twenty-two island states and territories of the South Pacific region known as Oceania contain approximately 200 million hectares of forest, about 5 percent of the global total (UN Food and Agriculture Organization, *Global Forest Resources Assessment 2000*, 2001). But the forests that grace Oceania's 10,000 islands—many of them virtual specks scattered across on the surface of more than 40 million square kilometers (15.5 million square miles) of sea—have a biological significance far out of proportion to their size. Indeed, these forests, which are overwhelmingly tropical or subtropical in nature, contain some of the world's richest storehouses of rare and endemic species. In addition, healthy forests are important components in overall watershed health, for they mitigate erosion, store freshwater, and filter pollutants. And in many Pacific Island states, timber and non-timber products harvested from the forest are cultural and economic cornerstones of urban and rural communities alike. Unfortunately, the quality of stewardship of this resource is uneven across the region. In Australia and New Zealand, where most of Oceania's forests are located, attention to sustainable use of forest resources is high. In many other Pacific Island states, however, unsustainable rates of logging, massive land-clearing campaigns for agriculture, and other human activities have destroyed large swaths of species-rich forests and left many others imperiled.

Oceania's Forest Resources

Almost all of the states and territories within Oceania contain forests that are tropical in character. Tropical rain forest species drape all three subregions of Oceania—Polynesia, Micronesia, and Melanesia—with the largest intact tracts found in Papua New Guinea (PNG). These species even thrive in Australia's northeastern Queensland state, recipient of the country's highest levels of annual precipitation. Elsewhere in arid Australia, tropical dry forests

Table 4.1 Oceania: Forest Resources by Subregion

Subregion	Land area	Forest area 2000						Area change 1990–2000 (total forest)		Volume and above-ground biomass (total forest)	
		Natural forest	Forest plantation	Total forest							
	000 ha	000 ha	000 ha	000 ha	%	ha/ capita	000 ha/ year	%	m³/ha	t/ha
Australia and New Zealand	795,029	159,547	2,938	162,485	20.4	7.2	−243	−0.1	58	65
Other Oceania	54,067	34,875	263	35,138	65.0	4.7	−122	−0.3	34	58
Total Oceania:	849,096	194,775	2,848	197,623	23.3	6.6	−365	−0.2	55	64
Total World:	13,063,900	3,682,722	186,733	3,869,455	29.6	0.6	−9,391	−0.2	100	109

SOURCE: UN Food and Agriculture Organization Global Forest Resource Assessment, 2000

and shrublands and subtropical forests (both dry and humid) persist, albeit primarily in coastal regions. In the lower latitudes of the South Pacific, regions such as New Zealand's South Island, Australia's southeastern coast, and the island of Tasmania feature temperate oceanic forest, while mountain forest systems are limited to the high altitude regions of Australia (such as the Tasmanian Highlands and the Australian Alps) and New Zealand (such as the Southern Alps of South Island).

Mangrove forests are among Oceania's most ecologically and commercially vital forest resources, for they provide a host of major benefits to human and animal communities alike. These benefits include protection of coastal villages and cities from storm surges and other severe weather events, stabilization of coastal shorelines against erosion, and provision of habitat for a wide assortment of creatures. Indeed, mangrove stands have been described as hybrid terrestrial/marine ecosystems, for they are capable of supporting terrestrial species in their canopies while at the same time nourishing fish, shellfish, and other marine species at their base (Nybakken, 1993).

The Indo-Pacific realm (the western part of the Pacific and the Indian Ocean in its entirety) is one of two globally recognized centers of mangrove diversity; the other is centered around the Caribbean, northeastern South America, and western Africa. A significant portion of the Indo-Pacific's mangrove forests can be found garnishing the perimeter of Australia, which ranks behind only Indonesia and Brazil in total mangrove area (Spalding, 1997). Other major mangrove forests still exist in Papua New Guinea (such as the

Figure 4.1 Forest Area per Capita, by Region

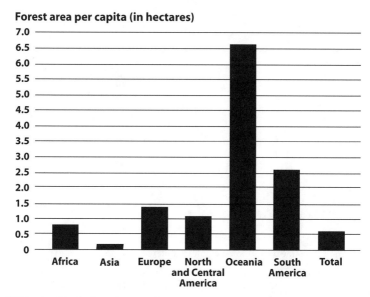

Forest area per capita (in hectares)

SOURCE: UN Food and Agriculture Organization Forest Resources Assessment, 2000

200,000-hectare forest along the Gulf of Papua), Fiji, and the Solomon Islands. But in these and other Pacific Island states, human population pressure on the coastal zones where mangrove forests exist has increased dramatically in recent years, and concerns about their future are mounting (Jaensch, 1996).

Regional Trends

The people of Oceania enjoy more forest area per capita (6.6 hectares) than any other region in the world. But this figure is skewed by conditions in New Zealand and Australia, which feature low populations and about 94 percent of Oceania's total forest resources by land area. Collectively, New Zealand and Australia boast 7.2 hectares of forest area per capita; by contrast, per capita forest area for the remainder of Oceania is 4.7 hectares (UN Food and Agriculture Organization, *Global Forest Resources Assessment 2000*, 2001).

Most ancient or "old-growth" forests in Oceania have been cut, including those of Australia and New Zealand. All told, about 80 percent of these forests have been lost, according to one study (Bryant, 1997), and 75 percent of the remaining forest is under moderate or high threat. But in Australia and New Zealand, where the majority of these forests were located, some cut-over areas once again support mature forests, and remaining old-growth forests are

Table 4.2 Harvest from New Zealand's Planted Forests (Actual to 2000 and Forecast to 2040)

Year	Actual Volume (million m^3)	Year	Forecast Volume (million m^3)
1950	0.9	2000	18.0
1955	1.8	2005	28.8
1960	3.0	2010	31.3
1965	4.4	2015	32.0
1970	6.8	2020	34.6
1975	7.4	2025	41.9
1980	9.4	2030	43.3
1985	9.0	2035	51.4
1990	11.1	2040	52.5
1995	16.0		
1999	15.7		

SOURCE : NEFD Wood Supply Forecasts 2000.

NOTE:

1. This table illustrates the forecast wood supply in context with historical harvest levels.

2. The forecast starts in 2005.

3. The forecast assumes a target clearfell age of 28 years for radiata pine and a new planting level of 40,000 hectares each year.

being conserved. Commercial forest plantations, which represent 1.4 percent of the total forest area in Australia and New Zealand, also account for a growing percentage of overall timber production. Still, logging of natural forests remains a polarizing issue in both of these countries—and especially Australia—as various constituencies labor to reach consensus on the industry's economic and environmental impact.

Elsewhere in Oceania, deforestation did not emerge as a serious issue until nineteenth-century European colonization. In the wake of European settlement, however, ambitious land-clearing efforts dramatically reduced forest area on numerous islands. Coastal and lowland forests were converted to plantations that produced coconut, cocoa, and banana crops on a commercial scale, or cut down to provide space and materials for the development of seaside communities and other agricultural operations. The emergence of commercial logging, with its arsenal of chainsaws and other efficient tree removal tools, has also contributed to forest loss in recent decades. But forest status varies widely by country and forest type; the French-controlled territory of New Caledonia, for instance, has implemented an array of conservation measures that have preserved large areas of natural forestland, while other states and territories, such as the Solomon Islands, are struggling to halt widespread forest degradation and loss.

Woodchipping Depletes Tasmania's Old-Growth Forests

A former forest of red gum trees (Eucalyptu comaldulensi), now reduced to lumber awaits woodchipping for the paper industry. Some environmentalists regard the production of paper pulp from woodchipping as a waste of resources. WAYNE LAWLER; ECOSCENE/CORBIS

The Australian state of Tasmania contains some of the world's great temperate forests, including such areas as the Styx Valley, Tarkine, Picton, Weld, Eastern Tiers, Great Western Tiers, and the Tasman Peninsula. But approximately 20,000 hectares of native forests are clear-cut each year in Tasmania, including 16,000 hectares on public land. About 75 percent of the forests cut on public land are old growth, containing trees more than 110 years of age (Wilderness Society, n.d.). As of 2000, only 18 percent of the island state's old-growth forest remained. Nearly half of those old-growth areas were immediately threatened by logging, and only 10 percent were permanently protected from logging (Forestry Tasmania, 2002). These statistics appeared to run counter to public sentiments. A 2001

survey conducted by the University of Tasmania found that 70 percent of Tasmanian citizens supported an end to logging in the state's remaining old-growth forests (Wilderness Society, n.d.).

Forestry Tasmania (FT) is the agency charged with managing state-owned forests on behalf of the public. FT controls 1.5 million hectares of land, or 22 percent of Tasmania. About 1.25 million hectares of this land is classified as "multiple-use native forest," which is open to logging. The agency has come under increasingly harsh criticism for its forest-management practices in recent years. For example, FT constructs logging roads that open up pristine areas of old growth for clear-cutting by private companies. Clear-cutting is usually followed by burning, which produces large quantities of smoke that

(continues)

is harmful to the atmosphere and discourages tourism. In addition, several of FT's controlled burns escape each year and consume thousands of hectares of forest.

FT has also faced criticism for replacing native forests with monospecific plantations. Such plantations, which replace clear-cuts 68 percent of the time in Tasmania, do not provide suitable habitat for native wildlife. In addition, FT engages in the controversial practice of using 1080 poison to kill the wallabies and possums that browse on plantation seedlings. Studies have shown that the poison often kills unintended bird and animal species, including some that are threatened or endangered.

Most logging of old-growth forests in Tasmania is undertaken to produce woodchips, another aspect of timber operations that has drawn the ire of conservationists. Most very old trees are transformed into woodchips—rather than sawn logs or veneer timber— because their age makes them more prone to rot. But woodchipping creates fewer jobs and economic benefits to local people than logging for other end uses. In fact, most of the woodchips are exported to Asia, where they are processed into paper products and packaging materials.

According to the Australian Bureau of Statistics, the export of woodchips from Tasmania reached a record level of 5.58 million tons in 2000, nearly double the level exported in 1995. Tasmania thus exported more woodchips than the rest of Australia combined. "Woodchips are now exported in such volumes that

it is uneconomic to rely only on sawmill waste and rejected timber from logging, such as branches and broken, diseased, or undersized trunks," observed one researcher. "Almost any tree species seems suitable [for conversion to woodchips], too. There is thus nothing selective about logging for woodchips, something the companies refer to quite proudly as 'efficient use with minimum wastage.' However, taking such logging waste out of the forests is not ecologically desirable if regrowth is an objective, and such a total removal increases the likelihood of erosion and siltation" (Aplin, 1998).

The increase in woodchipping can be attributed in part to the Tasmanian Regional Forest Agreement (RFA), which proponents claimed would achieve an appropriate balance between conservation and resource extraction, maximizing employment opportunities and economic benefits for Tasmanian citizens while simultaneously safeguarding the long-term health of area forests. But critics note that the practical result of the RFA was to abolish quotas and provide for unlimited woodchip export volumes, while the promised jobs and prosperity failed to materialize. In fact, the logging royalties paid to FT by private companies fall short of covering the costs of forest management, regrowth, and infrastructure. Critics point to FT's operating deficit and argue that Tasmanian forests are being sold off at a loss to the state, while the forest-products industry employs less than 2 percent of the Tasmanian workforce (Wilderness Society, n.d.).

(continues)

Environmental groups have launched a campaign to preserve some of the remaining Tasmanian old-growth forests. One focus of conservation efforts has been the Styx Valley, which is home to *Eucalyptus regnans*—the tallest hardwood tree and tallest flowering species in the world. Many trees in the valley are more than 400 years old and more than 90 meters (295 feet) tall. About 1,000 hectares of the Styx Valley is protected, while 22,000 hectares consist of state-owned forest and is being logged. Although a rule prohibits cutting of *Eucalyptus regnans* over 85 meters (278 feet) tall, environmentalists point out that this leaves many 300- and 400-year-old specimens available for logging. "I don't really see the value of saving something just because it's old," said one FT official (Clausen, 2001). In addition, lone trees that are spared the axe often fall within a few years because of increased vulnerability to wind.

Some environmentalists dream of creating Valley of the Giants National Park to preserve the entire Styx Valley area. Eager to publicize the idea, they have created walkways for viewing the giant trees and organized public tours that have proven popular. Some people believe that the giant trees of the Styx Valley could be as important a tourist attraction as California's redwoods and giant sequoias. "The Tasmanian forests are much more than just trees," one scientist stated. "They go back virtually unchanged for at least 60 million years. If you found a community of animals on earth that dated back, virtually unchanged, for 60 million years you would see most of that island state set aside as a sanctuary to preserve these

unbelievably wonderful animals. But because they are plants it's a different story. And yet these plants are the climate controllers and they are enormously important to our future. In allowing ancient ecosystems to be cleared and destroyed we are acting like a third-world country. Shredding the forests of antiquity for short-term corporate profit is simply stupid" (Saunders and Gee, 2002).

Sources:

Aplin, Graeme. 1998. *Australians and Their Environment.* Melbourne: Oxford University Press.

Clausen, Lisa. 2001. "Kings of the Forest: In Tasmania, Timber-Getters and Conservationists Tussle over the Fate of Australia's Tallest Hardwoods." *Time International,* December 17.

Forestry Tasmania. 1999. *Forestry Tasmania Annual Report 1999/2000.* Hobart, Tasmania: FT.

———. 2002. *Forestry Tasmania Annual Report 2002.* Hobart, Tasmania: FT.

Kirkpatrick, J. 1998. "Nature Conservation and the Regional Forest Agreement Process." *Australian Journal of Environmental Management* 5, no. 1.

Saunders, Kirsten, and Helen Gee. 2002. "Chips on Our Shoulders: Tasmanians Have Made Their Feelings Clear; Their Ancient Forests Are Worth More than Woodchips." *Habitat Australia* (February).

Wilderness Society. "Forestry Tasmania's Atrocious Environmental, Economic, and Social Record." Available at http://www.wilderness.org.au/ member/tws/projects/Forests /atrocious.html (accessed December 26, 2002).

Eucalyptus species in Cooloangubra State Forest, New South Wales, Australia. WAYNE LAWLER; ECOSCENE/CORBIS

Australia

The sixth-largest country in the world, Australia is an economically developed nation with low population and land use pressure, and its forest holdings are by far the most extensive in Oceania. Despite the presence of large tracts of arid land unable to support forests, Australia's 154.5 million hectares of forest—including more than 42 million hectares of commercial forest—cover more than 20 percent of its total land area. These forests are concentrated in a broad crescent around coastal Australia, with mangroves, acacia, and other coastal species giving way to open eucalyptus forests as one moves into the continent's interior. Eucalypt hardwood forests, including the tall mountain ash stands in Victoria and the alpine ash forests of New South Wales and Victoria, constitute around 80 percent of Australia's overall forest cover (UN Food and Agriculture Organization, *Global Forest Resources Assessment 2000*, 2001). Australia's natural forest resources are further supplemented by plantation estates covering another 1.4 million hectares. The bulk of these plantations cultivate exotic species of pine and other softwoods.

The current character of Australia's forests reflects millennia of alteration by humans. Australia's Aborigine peoples utilized burning as a land-clearing tool, and it is believed that their reliance on fire may have contributed to an overall diminishment of the rain forest and an attendant increase in the presence of more fire-tolerant vegetation (Flannery, 1995; Young, 2000). But the Europeans left a much more indelible imprint on Australian land, for they cleared large swaths of forest to make way for crop fields and sheep pastures, and to build their homes. Indeed, mid-nineteenth century land-selection laws in Australia required settlers to "improve" their land by clearing it of woods. However, demand for timber for housing, fuel, fences, and other purposes became so great that by the 1870s, the authorities felt compelled to hand down restrictions on certain types of clearing. For example, in New South Wales, regulations forbidding the removal of trees along rivers were issued, although they were rarely enforced, and several timber reserves were formally set aside around the continent. In 1873 South Australia authorities even began handing out financial rewards to landowners willing to plant trees on previously cleared land, and two years later the state established the continent's first forest service (Carron, 1985).

During the first half of the twentieth century, Australian timber reserves grew in number and size, but pressure on forests also escalated, especially in heavily forested coastal zones where communities and agricultural and ranching activities congregated. Ecological damage associated with these harvests was exacerbated by the absence of a regulatory framework for the logging industry. In the 1960s and 1970s, however, the country experienced a surge in opposition to commercial logging operations, which were feeding escalating domestic and foreign demand for timber products. Opposition coalesced around forest losses in several specific locales including Tasmania, where old-growth forests were being sacrificed to deliver pulpwood to Asian destinations, and New South Wales, where clear-cutting (or clear-felling, as the practice is known in Australia) of forests to provide Japan with wood-chips triggered storms of protest (ibid.; Young, 2000).

Since that time new forest conservation policies have been implemented, and existing regulations have been strengthened. In 1992, Australia showed a genuine commitment to sustainable forest management with passage of its National Forest Policy Statement, a formal declaration of its intention to sustainably manage all its forests for future generations, including conservation reserves, public and private commercial forests, and plantations. This statement put heightened emphasis on devising management models that met conservation goals while simultaneously addressing employment and other economic concerns. Other important initiatives included the development of an Australian Forestry Standard as a means of certifying forest management practices in Australia.

In recent years, Australia's rate of deforestation has been modest when compared with that of many other nations. From 1990 to 2000, Australia reported an annual deforestation rate of 282,000 hectares, a figure that is in part a reflection of improved forest assessment resources and methods. As a result of this relatively modest output—and increased mechanization in the timber industry—less than 1 percent of Australia's workforce is employed directly in forestry, milling, and wood processing.

Despite the more restrained extractive activity of recent years, however, decades of largely unregulated cutting have left their mark. By the late 1990s, Australia had lost an estimated 80 percent of its original indigenous (old-growth) forest, including extensive tracts of rare forest types that supported a wide array of flora and fauna. Today, Australia's remnant indigenous forests are confined almost entirely to Tasmania, Cape York, and remote locales in the northwest. Many of these still-existing old-growth forests have been added to the country's protected area system in recent years, but stands not shielded by law remain vulnerable in Tasmania—where only a fraction of the original old-growth forest cover remains—and elsewhere. In addition, conservationists remain harshly critical of ongoing logging activities in some non–old-growth rain forests, especially in southeastern Australia and Tasmania (Bryant, 1997; Clayton, 1996). For example, clear-cutting remains a dominant practice in many areas. This methodology has been criticized for destroying vital migration corridors and sanctuary areas in wilderness ecosystems, causing serious erosion and soil compaction, and compromising water quality in area rivers and streams. "Clear-felling is the equivalent of an army's scorched earth policy," charged one analysis, "cutting all timber and often clearing or otherwise effectively killing all undergrowth" (Aplin, 1998). Critics of this approach contend that selective harvesting of commercially valuable species would meet timber needs while simultaneously preserving the integrity of forest ecosystems. Defenders, however, cite clear-cutting as the most efficient means of gathering timber, and they point out that some clear-cut areas regenerate over time into young woodlands that better suit some species of flora and fauna.

At the close of the twentieth century, less than 30 percent of Australia's forests were privately owned, a notable contrast with Japan, Germany, the United States, and other developed countries with far higher rates of private ownership. However, private ownership of forests by timber companies and others is higher in places like Tasmania, which has experienced heavy rates of cut in recent years. All told, natural forests on private lands account for about 30 percent of Australia's total timber production, while plantations account for about 45 percent of total national output—a percentage that may well increase given continued investment in plantation estates.

The majority of Australian forests are owned and managed by public agencies at the local, state, and federal level. State forests are multiple-use public forests in which timber production is an important management priority. Crown lands are other public forests in which logging may or may not occur. In these state and crown forests, about 60 percent of land is tenured for logging. Conservation reserves are public forestlands that are set aside by the commonwealth government primarily for conservation or recreation. Distribution of Australian forests between these three categories is relatively even at 13 to 17 million hectares each, but the percentage of protected forest has increased steadily in recent years. Recent regional forest management agreements between states and the commonwealth have placed 42 percent of affected forests in formally recognized conservation reserves. Moreover, a variety of covenant arrangements have lent protected status to some privately owned forests. In addition, pastoral leasehold lands held by the government and subject to strict land-clearing regulations account for another 66 million hectares (UN Food and Agriculture Organization, *Global Forest Resources Assessment 2000,* 2001; Young, 2000).

Today, many Australian forests are managed through a system of Regional Forest Agreements. These joint agreements between the commonwealth and state governments provide a twenty-year "blueprint" for management and use of forests in a particular region. The overarching goal of these individual plans, according to authorities, is to establish a world-class forest reserve system across Australia; engage and educate industries, local communities, and other entities with vested interests in local forests; and "ensure internationally competitive and ecologically sustainable management of the national forest estate" (Commonwealth of Australia, 2000).

Australia's forest management schemes are informed by monitoring and inventory systems that match those of the world's leading forestry countries, and continuing investment in forestry research appears to be a national priority. Indeed, the UN Food and Agriculture Organization has commented that the nation's blend of financial wherewithal and political will has placed it in a position to "achieve very high standards of forest management," though it also acknowledges that various constituencies within Australia—environmental groups, timber companies, rural communities, and others—remain locked in a protracted and contentious effort to influence state and commonwealth forest management programs: "There remains considerable disparity in broader stakeholder perceptions of the appropriate emphasis that should be placed on nature conservation objectives compared with economic development objectives. A separate dimension relates to social aspects of forestry and, in particular, how the rights and aspirations of Aboriginal peoples and Torres Strait Islanders in respect to their forest interests can be reconciled within national and regional frameworks for sustainable forest management" (UN Food and Agriculture Organization, *Global Forest Resources Assessment 2000,* 2001).

These issues are in particular evidence in the northern and western reaches of Australia, where increased attention to indigenous land rights complicates both conservation and development objectives, and where notions of forest and biodiversity conservation are colliding violently with beliefs that the "Outback" constitutes the last untapped frontier of development opportunity on the continent (Australian State of the Environment Committee, 2001).

Indeed, debate over the management of Australia's forest resources has become so polarized that the quest to find common ground seems a more elusive, ephemeral goal with each passing year. "Private interests accuse government departments and agencies of poor management because they have not been commercial enough, while conservationists accuse private forest companies of being solely interested in profits," summarized one analyst. "The main argument of the companies is that public ownership by such large bodies as a state Forestry Commission, which in some states has a large number of geographically widespread areas to manage, means that management is too far removed from responsibility and accountability for a particular area of forest. . . . The counter-argument is that if those economic factors are over-emphasized, other forest values are neglected" (Aplin, 1998).

This clash—which is also being played out in the United States, Canada, Russia, Brazil, and many other countries with significant forest areas—is unlikely to conclude to anyone's complete satisfaction, given the high environmental, social, and economic stakes involved, and the unique aesthetic and spiritual appeal that forests have for many people. Conservationists have strived to take full advantage of this dynamic, putting particular emphasis on preservation of charismatic old-growth forests, which are recognized as last bastions of habitat for many threatened species on the continent, and on the establishment of large, contiguous refuge areas that encompass wildlife corridors and a multitude of habitat types. "But it is not only in old-growth forests that concerns about species extinction have been raised," noted one analysis. "It is necessary to conserve wildlife not only in reserves, but also in forest that is logged. Clear-felling, rather than selective logging, has become far more widespread over the last 20 years. Animals that forage over large areas, rely on hollows in old trees for shelter, or are 'central place foragers' [larger and more social creatures that search for food in all directions from a central nest or home] suffer under this practice" (Young, 2000).

Loggers, timber companies, and other proindustry advocates, however, contend that ecological damage from extraction activities has been overstated, and they claim that logging restrictions and bans in dry forest regimes have increased Australia's vulnerability to wildfires, a long-time nemesis. These fires burn large areas of forest and woodlands each year, and in 2002 bushfires singed an estimated 10 percent of the continent as widespread drought conditions created ample fuel and dried up creeks that might otherwise have served as natural firebreaks (Christie, 2003). Logging proponents argue that these conflagrations will worsen in the coming years without active efforts to reduce fuelwood loads.

Logging, sawmilling, and woodchipping operations also are an important source of revenue and jobs in rural communities that have traditionally relied on extraction-based activities for revenue. As a result, families that have long subsisted on timber-related jobs have watched the proliferation of forest preserves with mounting alarm. "The main concern in the forests of the New South Wales North Coast region, in Tasmania, and in North Queensland has been the possibility of a complete cessation of logging as areas are added to national parks and other reserves for conservation-related reasons. Conservationists point to possible new jobs in tourism and park management, but how realistic this is remains an open question, especially for the older men who have spent all their long working lives in logging or saw-milling" (Aplin, 1998).

New Zealand

New Zealand's natural forests receive less development/extraction pressure than those of any other country in Oceania. Like Australia, New Zealand has a high ratio of land area to population and is economically prosperous. In addition, it boasts a conservation-friendly social and political orientation, abundant forest resources (although few stands of original frontier forest remain), high standards of forest management and monitoring, and extensive, thriving forest plantations that meet virtually all of its current domestic and export needs.

Forest cover in New Zealand amounts to approximately 8.2 million hectares, approximately 30 percent of its total land area. More than 6.4 million hectares of this total consist of natural or indigenous forests, while plantation forests account for another 1.8 million hectares (New Zealand Ministry of Agriculture and Forestry, 2001). Natural forests in the country include cool temperate rain forests strung along the west side of South Island and throughout the mountainous North Island. These forests, composed primarily of beech, kauri, rimu, and tawa, are characterized by high forest canopies and dense understories. They have extremely high levels of biomass and are home to a great variety of animals and plants, including many endemic species—those found nowhere else in the world.

But although many of New Zealand's natural forests look mature and undisturbed, the country has actually lost a higher percentage of its original forest cover—90 percent according to one study—than any other state in Oceania. New Zealand's islands were the last of the world's large land areas to be settled by humans, but since colonization—first by the Maori, 700 to 800 years ago, then by Europeans—clearing for agriculture and other purposes has removed large swaths of frontier forest. Today nearly all old-growth forests still standing in New Zealand are under the protective shield of the country's extensive protected area network. The chief threats now facing these forest ecosystems are exotic or invasive species, such as the red deer and the Australian brush-tailed possum, which have decimated populations of some endemic flora (Bryant, 1997; World Wide Fund for Nature and World Conservation Union, 1995).

All told, the New Zealand Crown (federal government) manages about 77 percent of the country's natural forest resources through its Department of Conservation. These areas are managed as protected areas, with an emphasis on habitat and ecosystem conservation and provision of recreational opportunities. The remaining 23 percent of New Zealand's natural forest holdings are privately owned, but conservation is the guiding principle here, too. Landowners are legally bound by a 1993 amendment to the Forests Act of 1949 to manage their natural forest areas in ways that maintain their capacity to provide products and amenities in perpetuity while also retaining their ecological and scenic value. This emphasis on sustainable models of environmental stewardship extends to commercial harvesting of privately owned forests, which can only be undertaken with government-sanctioned sustainable management plans and permits (New Zealand Ministry for the Environment, 1997; New Zealand Ministry of Agriculture and Forestry, 2001).

In addition, New Zealand's commitment to preservation of wilderness forests and sustainable use of commercial forests is enshrined in a number of voluntary measures, including the New Zealand Forest Code of Practice and the New Zealand Forest Accord 1991. Moreover, several New Zealand forests have obtained Forest Stewardship Council certification, and a process to develop a national certification process consistent with international standards is being developed (UN Food and Agriculture Organization, *Global Forest Resources Assessment 2000*, 2001).

New Zealand's ability to protect and sustainably manage virtually all of its natural forests, whether on Crown or privately held land, is directly attributable to its formidable forest plantation industry. This network of plantation estates accounts for an incredible 99.7 percent of the country's total timber harvest. Plantation forests have been established throughout the country, with the largest concentration (about one-third of the total area) planted on the volcanic plateau of central North Island. Other major forest growing areas include Northland, East Coast and Hawkes Bay, Nelson and Marlborough, and Otago and Southland. These plantations, which covered about 1.8 million hectares in early 2001, are mainly composed of pine species capable of exceptional growth rates (New Zealand Ministry of Agriculture and Forestry, 2001).

Steady growth in plantation operations has also driven net gains in forest area for New Zealand in recent years. From 1990 to 2000, New Zealand reported an average net gain in forest area of 39,000 hectares per year, and the average annual area of new planting from 1995 to 1999 was 62,000 hectares. Virtually all of the country's plantation forests are under private ownership, with 91 percent either owned by private landholders or registered public companies. Only 3 percent of the total plantation area is held by the Crown government, with another 6 percent controlled by local or state bodies (ibid.).

At the close of the 1990s, about 60 percent of the wood produced by these operations was exported in some form, and this percentage is projected to rise markedly in the coming decade. Large plantation holdings will reach maturity

Clear cut area of a rain forest, Papua New Guinea. JAY DICKMAN/CORBIS

during that time, boosting annual harvests from the current 18 million cubic meters to 30 million cubic meters or more by 2010 (ibid.).

The robust growth of plantation estates in New Zealand and elsewhere troubles some conservationists, who have expressed concern that their monocultural character precludes the development of complex ecosystems seen in natural forests. But defenders say that their presence makes it easier for New Zealand to take conservation steps, such as its May 2002 decision to end logging of native rain forest on the west coast of the South Island of New Zealand. According to this new plan, 130,000 wooded hectares scattered across twenty-nine forests previously under the control of a state-owned timber operation will be transferred to the Department of Conservation, where they will be added to existing national parks or ecological areas. In some cases, these forests constitute the final links in the formation of contiguous protected area units of considerable size and ecological importance.

Oceania
Virtually all of the forests contained in the remainder of Oceania are tropical in nature, but species richness is greatest in the southwest Pacific (a geographic region known as Melanesia) and declines gradually as one moves east into the ocean's central (Polynesia) and northwest (Micronesia) sectors. In addition to geographic proximity to mainland areas, other factors influencing

Figure 4.2 Forest Cover (Percent of Total Land Area) in Some PICs

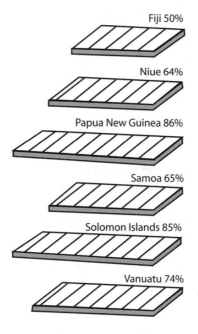

Fiji 50%

Niue 64%

Papua New Guinea 86%

Samoa 65%

Solomon Islands 85%

Vanuatu 74%

SOURCE: United Nations Environment Programme, 1999. *Pacific Island Environment Outlook.* Pg. 7. http://www-cger.nies.go.jp/geo2000/region/pieo.pdf

forest types on these islands include temperature, precipitation, and elevation. Among the most notable forest types are mangrove forests, which are concentrated in protected tidal zones; cloud forests, found at the highest points of Papua New Guinea and other countries with significant elevation gain; and dense lowland rain forests, many of which have been removed or degraded by human activity. The many coral atolls that are a feature in all three of these subregions support little in the way of trees or other vegetation (Mueller-Dombois and Fosenberg, 1998).

In terms of volume and land area, Papua New Guinea contains the overwhelming majority of forest in Oceania (excluding Australia and New Zealand). It accounts for 87 percent of forest area in the region, and despite troubling rates of deforestation, it continues to have a relatively high proportion of forest cover. Other countries with a high proportion of land in forest cover include the Solomon Islands, Fiji, New Caledonia, and Vanuatu, although all of these nations are much smaller than Papua New Guinea. Forest cover in the remaining Pacific Island states and territories is very small (UN Food and Agriculture Organization, *Global Forest Resources Assessment 2000,* 2001).

Many nations in this region are experiencing difficulty in managing their forest resources in a manner that will sustain both ecological and economic priorities over the long term. One basic problem in many countries is incomplete, dated, or otherwise questionable data on the extent and character of forest estates. This paucity of information makes it difficult for governments to make informed decisions about the management and care of their forests.

In addition, few Pacific Island states have passed meaningful legislation or programs to preserve existing forests—including endangered tree species— or reforest cleared areas. This shortcoming, claims the UN Environment Programme, "is threatening the local and regional biodiversity which constitutes the economic and cultural backbone of many Pacific peoples" (UN Environment Programme, 1999). After all, forest removal deprives people of a resource that provides protection from storms, nurseries for fish and other dietary staples, habitat for terrestrial species, aid in watershed protection, and a source of fuelwood and other forest products.

Moreover, poor stewardship of forests is adversely affecting the lives of Pacific Islanders in a host of undramatic but significant ways. For example, when forests are cleared or degraded, subsistence gardens that are a staple of many families' diets must be moved farther from villages, and fuelwood must be carried longer distances. These trends can have a negative impact on family nutrition, with a resulting increase in health care responsibilities for women. This development, in turn, can harm women's health and their ability to meet family and community responsibilities (ibid.).

Forest loss in the Pacific Islands is attributable to a combination of factors, including population growth, increased reliance on land-devouring shifting cultivation practices, erosion of traditional conservation controls in the community, pasture development, and increased commercial mining and logging activities. The latter factor has attracted particular notice in recent years, especially in Papua New Guinea, where the bulk of the region's forests are situated. But environmentally destructive logging practices—driven to a large extent by offshore demand—are also a pressing concern in the Solomon Islands, Vanuatu, Fiji, Niue, Samoa, and Tonga. Countries grappling with rampant conversion of forests to agricultural land, meanwhile, are typically those with heavy population densities, such as the Cook Islands, the Federated States of Micronesia, Kiribati, the Marshall Islands, Niue, Tokelau, Tonga, Tuvalu, and Samoa. In many of these countries, the traditional reliance on fire to clear land for agriculture has emerged as a particularly vexing problem. In recent years, for example, the Federated States of Micronesia have loss more forest area to human-caused wildfires than to timber extraction or other forms of land clearance (ibid.).

In Papua New Guinea, stewardship of forests is at a pivotal point. Prior to 1991, logging companies and private landowners were logging at a feverish pace that virtually exhausted all commercial forest resources in the New Ireland and West New Britain Provinces and, in addition, compromised species-rich coral reefs and coastal fisheries by increasing sedimentation loads in waterways that emptied into the sea (Papua New Guinea Forest Authority, n.d.). One study sponsored by the Asia Pacific Action Group during this period characterized the situation in one PNG province thusly: "It would be fair to say, of some of the companies, that they are now roaming the countryside with the reassurance of robber barons, bribing politicians and leaders, creating social disharmony and ignoring laws in order to gain access to, rip out, and export the last remnants of the province's valuable timber" (Marshall, 1990).

In 1991 the rapacious timber practices finally convinced Papua New Guinea's central government to make desperately needed proconservation changes to its forestry regulations, and today Papua New Guinea still possesses great swaths of tropical forest—about 40 percent of its original forest cover according to recent estimates. But the conservation measures implemented by PNG have only slowed—not stopped—the liquidation of the country's forest resources. Fully 85 percent of PNG's remaining stands of old-growth forest were under moderate or high threat from logging, mining, and agricultural operations in the late 1990s (Bryant, 1997). In fact, more than one-third of Papua New Guinea's total forest area—nearly 11 million hectares—had been included under logging concessions, with another 3 million hectares scheduled for allocation. Annual log harvest from these concessions in 1999 was 2.097 million cubic meters—a total that excludes the volume that was harvested using small-scale portable sawmills and removals as a result of land clearing for agriculture or other land uses. The primary markets for this timber include China (including Taiwan), Japan, the Republic of Korea, and the Philippines (UN Food and Agriculture Organization, *Global Forest Resources Assessment 2000*, 2001).

Solomon Islands is another Pacific Island country that is struggling to institute a more sustainable forest stewardship philosophy after years of short-sighted exploitation. At first glance, the situation does not appear dire. Approximately 88 percent of its tropical rain forests remain intact. But the country's rate of logging of accessible forest areas has steadily risen in the past four decades, with most timber exported to Asia. By the close of the 1990s, about half of the accessible rain forest had been logged over, and analysts warn that current rates of harvest will finish off these forests within a decade. Yet independent assessments indicate that the government continues to approve logging licenses that far exceed sustainable annual yields, and environmental impact assessments of logging proposals remain absent. These trends have prompted forecasts of dramatic declines in national timber output—and income—in the coming years. These observers note that reforestation or regeneration of carefully logged forests will take thirty to forty years, and that reforestation or regeneration of damaged areas—which are far more commonplace—will require forty-five to two hundred years (UN Food and Agriculture Organization, 1997; UN Environment Programme, 1999).

Fiji, meanwhile, has experienced significant declines in its natural forest cover, especially in lowland areas where agricultural activities and population centers are concentrated. But about 30 percent of Fiji's remaining forests receive varying levels of protection in parks and reserves, and in recent years it has kept its annual logging rate at sustainable levels. Moreover, the country has painstakingly developed significant mahogany and pine plantations that are expected to help relieve logging pressure on wild forests. Indeed, logs harvested from maturing mahogany plantations are expected to supplant national forests as the major source of Fiji timber (UN Food and Agriculture Organization, *State of the World's Forests 2001*, 2001).

Of all the Pacific Island countries, New Caledonia has received the most plaudits for its conservation-oriented forest management philosophy. "New Caledonia has done an exceptional job of creating parks and reserves," declared the UN Food and Agriculture Organization. "New Caledonia's forest situation appears to be stable, with reasonable harvest levels, progressive forest management, and a modest plantation program" (UN Food and Agriculture Organization, *Global Forest Resources Assessment 2000*, 2001).

The challenges facing other Pacific Island nations wishing to follow the forest conservation example laid out by New Caledonia are significant. For example, land tenure systems found in most of Oceania are a blend of individual and communal rights in which land itself cannot be sold, but the resources contained therein—including forests—can be sold. This situation has made the creation of parks and protected areas a difficult, though not insurmountable, challenge, and has often encouraged exploitive practices that turn these resources into cash or other land uses with little thought to the future (UN Food and Agriculture Organization, *State of the World's Forests 2001*, 2001).

But some countries have shown increased interest in addressing destructive logging and other land-use activities by promoting responsible and sustainable logging and farming practices. Efforts to strike an appropriate balance between natural reforestation and plantation establishment are also on the upswing. In addition, nonwood forest products (NWFPs) such as forest tree nuts, traditional medicinal plants, bee-keeping, and butterfly farming are increasingly recognized as a viable income-generating alternative to logging in some states. Many countries within Oceania are also signatories to international conventions and treaties focused on biodiversity conservation and other environmental issues. "Much remains to be done [in Oceania in the realm of forest conservation]," concluded the UN Food and Agriculture Organization, "but on balance significant progress is being made" (UN Food and Agriculture Organization, *Global Forest Resources Assessment 2000*, 2001).

If the countries of Oceania wish to build on their progress to date, however, observers believe that further emphasis will have to be placed on reducing the rate of logging or tree cover removal to sustainable levels; effective implementation of codes of logging practice (such as those recently created in Fiji, Vanuatu, and Papua New Guinea) and increased reliance on selected harvesting techniques to reduce the adverse impacts of logging on social, environmental, and biodiversity elements; and increased use of natural reforestation to provide the next forest crop. In addition, Pacific Island states need to give greater weight to the multitude of services that natural forests provide, including habitat for wildlife, reduction of soil erosion, and regulation of water flow and quality. "Given the critical importance of forests and trees to the region—socially, economically, and ecologically—it is imperative that the effective implementation of appropriate policies and practices for the sustainable use, management and development of forest and tree resources be a high priority policy issue for Pacific Island countries" (UN Environment Programme, 1999).

Sources:

Aplin, Graeme. 1998. *Australians and Their Environment.* Melbourne: Oxford University Press.

Australia Bureau of Rural Sciences. 1998. *Australia's State of the Forests Report 1998.* Canberra: BRS.

Australia National Land and Water Resources Audit. 2001. *Australian Agriculture Assessment 2001.* Canberra: National Land and Water Resources Audit.

———. 2001. *Australia's Native Vegetation.* Canberra: National Land and Water Resources Audit.

Australian State of the Environment Committee. 2001. *Australia State of the Environment Report 2001.* Canberra: Commonwealth of Australia.

Bryant, Dirk, D. Nielson, and L. Tangley. 1997. *The Last Frontier Forests: Ecosystems and Economies on the Edge.* Washington, DC: World Resources Institute.

Carron, L. T. 1985. *A History of Forestry in Australia.* Canberra: Australian National University Press.

Christie, Michael. 2003. "Bushfires Leave Country-Sized Scars on Australia," *PlanetArk,* February 13. Available at http://www.planetark.org.avantgo/dailynewsstory. cfm?newsid=19798 (accessed February 2003).

Clayton, Mark. 1996. "Chipping Away at Australia's Old-Growth Forests." *Christian Science Monitor,* April 24.

Commonwealth of Australia. 2002. *Regional Forest Agreements, 2002.* Available at www.rfa.gov.au (accessed February 2003).

Flannery, Tim F. 1995. *The Future Eaters: An Ecological History of the Australian Lands and People.* New York: Braziller.

Florence, R. G. 1996. *Ecology and Silviculture of Eucalypt Forests.* Collingwood, Victoria: Commonwealth Scientific and Industrial Research Organization.

Jaensch, Roger. 1996. "An Overview of the Wetlands in Oceania." In *Wetlands, Biodiversity and the Ramsar Convention.* Edited by A. J. Hails. Cambridge, UK: Ramsar.

Lieth, H., and M. J. A. Werger, eds. 1989. *Ecosystems of the World.* Amsterdam: Elsevier.

Marshall, G. 1990. *The Barnett Report: A Summary of the Report of the Commission of Inquiry into Aspects of the Timber Industry in Papua New Guinea.* Hobart, Australia: Asia Pacific Action Group.

McNeely, J. A., J. Harrison, and P. Dingwall, eds. 1994. *Protecting Nature: Regional Reviews of Protected Areas.* Gland, Switzerland: IUCN.

Mueller-Dombois, D., and F. R. Fosenberg. 1998. *Vegetation of the Tropical Pacific Islands.* New York: Springer-Verlag.

New Zealand Ministry for the Environment. 1997. *The State of New Zealand's Environment 1997.* Wellington: Ministry for the Environment.

New Zealand Ministry of Agriculture and Forestry. 2000. *National Exotic Forest Description: National and Regional Wood Supply Forecasts 2000.* Wellington: MAF.

———. 2001. *Forestry Sector Issues.* Wellington: MAF.

Nybakken, J. 1993. *Marine Biology: An Ecological Approach.* New York: HarperCollins.

Papua New Guinea Forest Authority. n.d. *Country Report—Papua New Guinea.* Rome: FAO.

Soulé, M. E., and John Terborgh. 1999. *Continental Conservation: Scientific Foundations of Regional Reserve Networks.* Washington, DC: Island Press.

Spalding, M. D., F. Blasco, and C. D. Field, eds. 1997. *World Mangrove Atlas.* Okinawa, Japan: International Society for Mangrove Ecosystems.

Thaman, R. R., and W. A. Whistler. 1995. *Samoa, Tonga, Kiribati and Tuvalu: A Review of Uses and Status of Trees and Forests in Land Use Systems with Recommendations for Future Actions.* Rome: FAO.

UN Environment Programme. 1999. *Pacific Islands Environmental Outlook.* Available at http://www.unep.org (accessed December 2002).

UN Food and Agriculture Organization. 1997. *Asia Pacific Forestry Sector Outlook Study.* Rome: FAO.

————. 1999. *State of the World's Forests 1999.* Rome: FAO.

————. 2001. *Global Forest Resources Assessment 2000.* Rome: FAO.

————. 2001. *State of the World's Forests 2001.* Rome: FAO.

World Wide Fund for Nature and World Conservation Union-IUCN. 1995. *Centres of Plant Diversity: A Guide and Strategy for Their Conservation.* Cambridge, UK: WWF.

Young, Ann. 2000. *Environmental Change in Australia since 1788.* 2d ed. Melbourne: Oxford University Press.

Agriculture
—A. M. Mannion

Agriculture is widespread throughout Oceania and is a primary economic activity. In Papua New Guinea and many other Pacific Island states, the production of sufficient food to support indigenous populations is an all-important activity, as is the need for agriculture to generate income through export. Indeed, farming is an essential component of the social and economic fabric of numerous Oceanic communities, large and small. However, historically unsustainable models of farming have also been cited as a leading factor in the loss of wilderness, natural habitat, and biodiversity across Australia, New Zealand, and the numerous island states of the South Pacific. Specific problems laid at the feet of the farming and ranching sectors include land degradation, including soil erosion and desertification (the spread of arid conditions and associated reduction in plant growth); the pollution of marine and freshwater environments by agrochemicals and animal waste; loss of floral and faunal biodiversity; and habitat alteration and fragmentation. Agricultural activities have also contributed to the deliberate and accidental introduction of alien plants and animals, some of which now threaten indigenous species with extinction through competition and habitat alteration. In addition, industrial farming's heavy consumption of fossil fuels has been implicated as a contributor to global climate change (Mannion, 1997; Mannion, 2002).

Agricultural Resources in Australia and Oceania
At the dawn of the twenty-first century, nearly 60 percent of the land area in "developed" Oceania (Australia and New Zealand) is used for agriculture. Land set aside for permanent pasture accounts for most of this total—approximately 52 percent of the total land area in these two nations is devoted to pastoral use—with less than 7 percent of the land area given over to arable cropping. In the developing nations of Oceania, comprising Papua New

Guinea (PNG) and other Pacific Island states, only about 4 percent of the total land area is used for agriculture, with land area divided almost equally between arable land and permanent pasture.

These percentages reflect the chasm between subsistence and industrialized agricultural systems that exists in this part of the world. In the subsistence-oriented agricultural systems that are dominant in many parts of Oceania, only sufficient food and materials to support an individual family are produced, and the energy input is human or animal labor. In the industrialized, commercial agricultural systems that typify the landscapes of Australia and New Zealand, commodities are produced for trade and export. The emphasis is on high productivity, often through generous doses of fertilization, irrigation, and mechanization.

Within the vast realm of Oceania, which includes tropical, subtropical, and temperate environments, there exists considerable variation between nations in terms of crops. Indeed, crops produced in the South Pacific range from the tropical fruits such as mango and coconut that are cultivated primarily on the smaller islands to vast quantities of wheat, maize, cotton, and assorted meat products generated in Australia and New Zealand.

Environmental Effects of Agriculture in Oceania

Oceania's natural landscapes have been influenced by agriculture for millennia. Aboriginal populations in Australia and Papua New Guinea dating back at least 50,000 years are known to have used fire to assist in the exploitation of plant and animal resources. Environmental alteration of the Pacific Islands region accelerated with colonization by Polynesian cultures. Another threshold was reached in the mid-eighteenth century with the advent of Europeans. Indeed, European colonialism prompted a new and extensive wave of environmental alteration, especially in Australia and New Zealand. European farming systems were introduced and an export trade developed to supply the expanding European markets whose populations were increasing in the wake of the Industrial Revolution.

During the twentieth century, Australia and New Zealand imposed dramatic alterations on their lands in order to enhance agricultural production. These changes ranged from damming of rivers for irrigation to massive land clearance for fields to overgrazing of natural pasturelands. Other Pacific Island nations also undertook extensive changes to natural areas for cultivation, ranching, and other purposes. Much of this alteration was localized around communities, leaving more remote islands and other land areas undisturbed. But in some cases, land degradation was more widespread.

Clearing of land via fire for agriculture, for example, compromised soil quality so much on Fiji's Viti Levu and Wallis and Futuna that only hardy ferns can now grow there (Nunn, 1994).

Although data on land degradation across the Oceania region are incomplete, it has been estimated that the Pacific region of the world—including Australia and New Zealand—contains more than 100 million hectares of degraded soil (UN Environment Programme, 1999). Overwhelmingly, the chief culprits in this degradation hail from the agriculture sector. Indeed, overgrazing, which renders soils vulnerable to wind and water erosion, has been cited as the leading cause of degradation, accounting for 80 percent of the total. Another 8 percent has been attributed to crop agriculture, while deforestation—some of which is undertaken for the specific purpose of making land available for plowing and grazing—accounts for the remaining 12 percent (Economic and Social Commission of Asia and the Pacific, 1995). This breakdown of causes is skewed, however, by large livestock operations in New Zealand and Australia; other Pacific Island countries equipped with less grazing land are much less dependent on sheep, cattle, and other livestock for their livelihoods.

Nonetheless, smaller Pacific Island nations with growing populations are increasingly faced with unsustainable demands on their limited land resources. "High population growth rates and the displacement of traditional land management systems by introduced agricultural systems, mining and forest utilization have placed serious stress on land resources and the communities that depend on them," reported the UN Environment Programme. Moreover, increased emphasis on cash crop schemes (which rely on large plantations) over traditional subsistence agriculture has encouraged incursions into valuable habitat areas, even when they are not well suited for farming. In Fiji and Samoa, for example, commercial agricultural systems have pushed subsistence gardens onto marginal soils and steep slopes vulnerable to erosion. In the Solomon Islands, meanwhile, pressure to squeeze every ounce of productivity out of existing fields has resulted in severe environmental degradation (UN Environment Programme, 1999).

Efforts to address these troubling trends are proliferating, especially in places like Australia and New Zealand, where recognition of environmental problems is high and where significant institutional and financial resources can be brought to bear. Australia's National Land Management Program—or LandCare, as it is more commonly known—is an indicator that land-use issues have assumed heightened priority in the region. But establishing environmentally desirable practices will be difficult without adjustments in other policy areas. "[There] is a widespread belief that the most important task to

Table 5.1 The Extent of Agriculture in Oceania for the Year 2000

	Total area of Oceania 1000 ha	Area of arable Land 1000 ha	% of total land area	Area of permanent pasture 1000 ha	% of total land area	Total agricultural area 1000 ha	% of total land area
Developed	801,175	51,859	6.47	418,200	52.20	477,080	58.92
Developing	55,265	600	1.09	701	1.27	2357	4.26
Total	856,440	52,459	6.12	418,901	48.91	474,437	55.40

SOURCE: UN Food and Agriculture Organization, 2002.

achieve a more sustainable agriculture is the raising of community awareness and changing of farmers' attitudes to their land. [In reality], what is required are profitable and practical conservation farming techniques and management strategies. Where these are not available the best assistance is research directed at producing . . . solutions, rather than a reliance on evangelical calls to better farming and changing attitudes. . . . The dangers of simple prescriptions are that they will not encourage the sustained commitment of the social resources required to continue the unending search for sustainable rural land uses" (Barr and Carey, 1992).

Regional Trends in Agriculture

Australia

European colonization of Australia in the mid-eighteenth century prompted the introduction of European-style agricultural systems onto a land that had previously been manipulated primarily by hunter-gatherer aboriginal communities. Although there is considerable evidence for the controlled use of fire to manipulate plants and animals for food procurement by aboriginals prior to European annexation, there is little evidence for permanent environmental change in a land that was, and still is, subject to numerous and large natural wildfires.

When European settlers arrived, they not only brought old practices to a new land but also harnessed indigenous practices such as firing to clear substantial swaths of Australia's natural vegetation for pasture and cultivation. According to the National Land and Water Resources Audit, some 13 percent of Australia has been cleared of its pre-European vegetation cover. The greatest change has occurred in the southeast and southwest regions of the country, where land use and population settlement have been concentrated. For example, in Victoria and western Australia, where intensive forms of agriculture are practiced, only 37 percent and 56 percent of the total area of native vegetation remains intact, respectively (Australia National Land and Water Resources Audit, *Australia's Native Vegetation,* 2001).

Australia devotes a greater share of its total land area to agriculture— including pastoralism and cropping—than any other land use. Approximately 60 percent of the continent is devoted to one agricultural purpose or another, though the majority of this is natural rangelands and other forms of pasture. Depending on the season, between 20 and 25 million hectares are seeded with crops, while another 94 million hectares of pasturelands are grazed (Australian State of the Environment Committee, 2001). Indeed, livestock production—and especially sheep ranching—has long been a staple of the Australian economy. Ranching is practiced in many parts of Australia, but it is

Cotton harvest in New South Wales, Australia. LANCE NELSON/CORBIS

especially strong in the arid and semiarid rangelands of Australia's dry tropical regions of the northeast and the interior, although pastures in the temperate and high-rainfall zones of the southeast also have large sheep flocks at
much higher grazing intensities. These areas of natural rangeland are able to
sustain large sheep populations, but they are not suited for intensive production of crops or other livestock. Nonetheless, Australia does support a beef
cattle industry that is 20 million head strong. These ranches are widespread
but are especially important in the northern and central regions of Queensland and the Northern Territory. Cattle are reared on a semiextensive basis,
and many are prepared for slaughter in feedlots. Dairy herds rely on rain-fed
pastures and intensive production systems; they are concentrated in Victoria
(60 percent of the country's total dairy herds), but dairy operations are also
present to a lesser degree in New South Wales, Queensland, Tasmania, and
Western Australia. These farms produce nearly 11 billion liters of milk annually, two-thirds of which is exported to the Pacific Rim and other trading
partners (Australia National Land and Water Resources Audit, *Australian Agriculture Assessment 2001*, 2001).

Only 6.5 percent of Australia's land area is used for arable cropping, but this
relatively small area produces large quantities of cereal crops, notably wheat,
rice, potatoes, and cotton. The country's capacity to generate large quantities

Table 5.2 Remaining Natural Vegetation in Areas of Intensive Agriculture in Australia's States

	Area of Native Vegetation Remaining km^2	% Remaining
Australian Capital Territory	1,620	69
New South Wales	470,604	67
Northern Territory	186,629	98
Queensland	772,452	72
South Australia	174,966	64
Tasmania	42,520	80
Victoria	84,541	37
Western Australia	234,423	56

SOURCE: Based on National Land and Water Resources Audit, 2001

of these crops from relatively modest land area reflects the widespread availability and utilization of irrigation networks and fertilizers, as well as investments in the latest in agricultural mechanization and technology. Grain crops are grown in both the north (Queensland) and the south (New South Wales, Victoria, Tasmania, and the southwestern region around Perth), and 75 percent of the grains produced from these regions are exported. Wheat is particularly important in terms of area planted and overall production, though productivity per unit area of land is low, at about 1.8 tons per hectare, in comparison with the average world production of 2.7 tons per hectare. This is largely due to limited water availability and vulnerability to drought. Such constraints have always been imposed by Australia's environment, but yields have increased by a factor of four throughout the twentieth century because of improved farming practices designed to conserve water, such as stubble mulching, crop rotation, and minimum tillage practices (Australia National Land and Water Resources Audit, *Australian Agriculture Assessment 2001*, 2001).

Cotton is produced in central Queensland, central New South Wales, and the border area between those two regions, and its production has increased substantially since the 1960s, when irrigation schemes were first developed. Output has increased markedly in both irrigated and dry-land enterprises, and production in years of normal rainfall now reaches 3 million bales annually. Severe drought conditions were expected to reduce Australia's 2002–2003 cotton crop by as much as half, however, as nearly all of the nation's cotton is grown with the use of irrigated water.

Despite such setbacks, Australia today ranks as the third-largest exporter of cotton in the world, with genetically modified (GM) cotton crops accounting for a steadily greater percentage of the total produced. Indeed, GM cotton is expected to account for about half of the nation's total production in 2002, and it may well take over the entire crop in the near future. Sugar cane is another water-intensive crop favored by Australian growers. Concentrated in the wet tropics of the Queensland coast, effluents generated by these plantations and subsequently deposited in ocean waters have been cited as a health menace to the Great Barrier Reef ecosystem. Other important crops include rice, vegetables, and fruit, including grapes nurtured in the famous vineyards of Western Australia.

Genetically altered crops are also likely to occupy a greater role in the sector. The emergence of GM cotton has been well documented, and government investments in other areas have increased in recent years. In 2002, for instance, the Australian government approved an A$28 million (U.S.$16 million) grant to establish a Cooperative Research Centre for Sugar Industry Innovation through Biotechnology. Advocates of GM foods claim that the development of these crops can dramatically reduce dependence on herbicides and fertilizers that can degrade soil and freshwater resources. For example, the introduction of GM cotton to Australia in the mid-1990s has reduced pesticide spraying by 40 to 60 percent. Moreover, increased productivity associated with GM seeds raises the possibility of increasing productivity without increasing the land area under cultivation, which spares natural habitats from clearing. In addition, the development of drought-resistant and salt-tolerant strains of crops is attractive to a country that is increasingly concerned about its diminishing freshwater supplies, vulnerability to drought, and trends in soil acidity. Applications of biotechnology in animal husbandry, such as development of disease-resistant strains of sheep and cattle, may also prove important. These and other innovations in biotechnology and information technology have the potential to change the face of agriculture not only in Australia but also worldwide in the coming decades (Australia Department of Agriculture, Fisheries and Forestry, 2000).

Enthusiasm for GM (also known as transgenic) crops is not universal, however. Critics of GM foods believe that the full impact of this technology on the environment has not been adequately studied. Potential hazards cited by foes include breeding between GM and non-GM species that creates weed and insect populations resistant to toxins; increased risk of allergic reactions and other negative health effects in humans over time; disappearance of wild species of flora and fauna; and an inability of poor communities in Oceania and elsewhere to purchase GM seeds and crops (Paarlberg, 2000; Pinstrup-Anderson and Schioler, 2001). These concerns have prompted several Australian state governments to consider outright bans on genetically modified commercial food crops.

As Australian ranchers and farmers enter the twenty-first century, major environmental issues confronting them include accelerated rates of soil erosion, acidification, and salinity; natural habitat loss and alteration from grazing and land-clearing; the influx of invasive species; and water pollution caused by the deposition of agrochemicals into rivers, lakes, and marine areas (Australian State of the Environment Committee, 2001). Diminishing soil quality is possibly the paramount concern from an economic and food security perspective. "Although it is the most basic of our agricultural resources, the soil is also our most finite and, in Australia, our most delicate resource" (Lovett and Duggin, 1992). Soil erosion stemming from overgrazing and land clearance for cultivation is problematic throughout Australia, and particularly in its arid interior and northern regions. Moreover, the effects of this have been exacerbated in some locales by drought conditions. Land salinization also afflicts large regions of the Australian countryside, partially because of excessive extraction from groundwater and surface water sources. Approximately 5.7 million hectares of land in Australia are now at risk from salinity, and the size of that area could triple by 2050 (National Land and Water Resources Audit, 2001). Meanwhile, the area of soil affected by acidification has reached an estimated 13 million hectares. This problem, which has arisen because of the draining of coastal soils and the acidification of agricultural soils, could be addressed through lime applications, but ranchers and farmers saddled with thin profit margins are reluctant to make these investments.

From an environmental perspective, meanwhile, land clearance and its repercussions for Australia's flora and fauna are a major concern. For years, conservation efforts in this realm were concentrated in southern and eastern Australia, the site of the country's major population centers and most intensive land use. But as one government report noted: "[T]here is now a growing appreciation among government and the community of the potentially significant effects of altered fire, grazing and hydrological regimes, pests and weeds and mining on biodiversity in the Extensive Land-use Zone in central, western and northern Australia. The pastoral industry covers about 70 percent of the continent, and grazing in arid and semiarid regions is considered partly responsible for the extinction of many plant species and continues to threaten around one-quarter of the plant species listed as threatened" (Australian State of the Environment Committee, 2001).

In light of the concerns raised in recent years about agriculture's impact on the Australian environment, both government establishments and universities are engaged in a wide range of agricultural and related environmental research. Future developments are likely to be influenced by the dissemination of best practices that attempt to reduce environmental impacts while increasing productivity and biotechnology. Examples of best practices include soil and water

---

Introduced Rabbits Overrun Pastoral Australia

Many species of animals have been introduced to Australia since the arrival of Europeans. Some of these species—such as sheep, cattle, and red foxes—were introduced intentionally for breeding or for sport, while others—such as mice—arrived by accident. In either case, introduced species have had a marked effect on Australia's environment and biodiversity. One of the most problematic of all the exotic species found in Australia is the rabbit, which has spread across the continent and taken a serious toll on both pastoral productivity and native flora and fauna.

Rabbits were initially introduced in Tasmania for sport in the early nineteenth century. The creatures proved so adept at reproducing that they soon became pests, prompting Tasmanian wildlife officials to warn mainland Australians against importing rabbits. In 1859, however, sportsmen introduced twenty-four wild gray rabbits to Victoria; within three years, the rabbit population in the region had grown out of control.

Rabbits spread across the Australian continent in waves throughout the remainder of the 1800s, despite attempts to stop them through trapping, shooting, poisoning, and fencing. The species was declared illegal in 1880, at the same time that feral cats were protected in hopes that they would prey upon the rabbits. Still, by the early 1900s rabbits were found in all but the tropical regions of Australia. They were so numerous in some places that farmers would herd them into fenced areas and club them to death by the hundreds.

In 1950, Australia introduced its most effective weapon yet against the rabbit invasion—the myoxomatosis virus. This virus, along with the availability of new poisons, helped reduce rabbit numbers significantly over the next few years. For example, southern Australia showed a 95 percent decrease in rabbit population, which was accompanied by a rapid increase in wool production among sheep farmers. But the rabbits eventually built up resistance to the virus, which did not spread well to dry, inland areas, and their numbers rebounded. The 1969 introduction of the European rabbit flea led to another temporary decline in the rabbit population, but the creatures

(continues)

conservation, including improved use of irrigation water to prevent water logging and soil degradation, and improved use of fertilizers. Many of these models have been embraced in Australia. For example, some ranchers have modified their pastoral grazing patterns to allow natural restoration of erosion-prone areas. In addition, an ambitious national land management program known as Landcare was initiated by the National Farmers' Federation and the

---

soon managed to return in even greater numbers. By the 1990s, the population of rabbits in Australia was estimated at 200 million. Experts noted that the rabbits consumed enough pasturage each year to feed about 4 million cattle (Young, 2000).

Rabbits have caused a variety of environmental problems in Australia. The most severe problems have occurred in pastoral areas, where the creatures have caused tremendous changes in plant communities. Rabbits compete for food with sheep and other livestock in pastures. This added grazing pressure often eliminates native plants and allows less desirable species— including exotic plants and weeds—to take their place. In addition, rabbits eat tree seedlings and buds, reducing tree growth. Furthermore, rabbit grazing and tunneling decrease agricultural productivity and increase soil erosion.

By changing plant communities and eliminating native plants, rabbits have also had a disastrous effect on several of Australia's native animals. For example, competition with rabbits for food helped reduce distribution of the bilby to 20 percent of its original range (ibid.). This small marsupial is now virtually extinct, surviving only in tropical regions where rabbits do not. Rabbits also contributed to the displacement of bettongs, or rat kangaroos, which fed on the seedlings of woody weeds that have subsequently spread unchecked into pasturelands.

Despite the environmental harm caused by introduced rabbits in Australia, some people still resist programs to reduce their numbers. Some rabbit supporters come from the industry that has developed around rabbit fur and meat. Others tend to view rabbits as cute, furry, gentle creatures and are reluctant to acknowledge the damage they cause. Groups such as the Foundation for a Rabbit-Free Australia have tried to increase public support for eradication programs by characterizing rabbits as dangerous pests that threaten native plants and wildlife.

Sources:

Jarman, Peter, and Jeremy Smith. 1992. "The Invaders." In *The Unique Continent*. Edited by Jeremy Smith. Queensland: University of Queensland Press.

Young, Ann. 2000. *Environmental Change in Australia since 1788*. 2d ed. Melbourne: Oxford University Press.

Australian Conservation Foundation in the mid-1990s, and it has spawned several like-minded programs, including the Dune Care, RiverWatch, Bushcare, and Coastcare initiatives.

The full effects of these volunteer land stewardship programs will only be visible with the passage of years, but acceptance of their precepts has been high among targeted groups. For example, in 1999 more than 80 percent of Australian farmers indicated that they had participated in some type of Landcare activity (Australian State of the Environment Committee, 2001).

Moreover, the gap between environmental destruction and environmental sustainability in agriculture is narrower in Australia in some important respects than it is in other regions of the world. Australia already has more than 7.5 million hectares of land under organic management, and it uses much lower levels of pesticides and fertilizers than most other developed countries; thus environmental contamination from those pollutants is not as severe. This phenomenon is undoubtedly due at least in part to the comparatively small size of government subsidies for such expenditures in Australia, but initiatives to further reduce agrochemical use have nonetheless been launched by the horticultural, cotton, grain, and sugar cane industries in recent years (Australian State of the Environment Committee, 2001).

New Zealand

Agriculture is a primary industry and source of income for New Zealand. It contributes 8 percent of the country's GDP (Gross Domestic Product) and employs an estimated 8.3 percent of its workforce. But agriculture is also the dominant cause of alteration and removal of natural vegetation communities. Pasturelands account for the bulk of this loss, a reflection of the importance of livestock to New Zealand's economy.

Nearly half of New Zealand's total land area is now classified as pasture, and this land supports some 57 million animals in free-range agricultural systems. Land used for pasture comprises natural tussock grassland and created pastures that may contain exotic grass and legume species; the latter occupy almost 10 million hectares (about 36 percent of the land area) while the former occupy almost 4 million hectares (approximately 14 percent of the land area). Sheep predominate, but other livestock are also reared in significant numbers, including beef cattle, dairy cattle, pigs, and chickens. Indeed, there are an estimated 17,000 commercial sheep and cattle farms in New Zealand; the average size of these enterprises is 550 hectares, with average holdings of 2,830 head of sheep and 230 beef cattle (New Zealand Ministry of Agriculture and Fisheries, *Sectors/Animals*, 2002).

The export of venison is a thriving industry in New Zealand. COREL

The extensive rearing of animals is a relatively low-energy system, as energy consumption of fossil fuels is minor compared with other forms of agriculture, to say nothing of commercial and industrial sectors. Nevertheless, environmental impacts associated with ranching include modification or removal of natural vegetation and degradation of soil and freshwater sources and processes. In recent years, however, sheep farming and other forms of pastoralism have declined in response to the suspension of some government subsidies and increased government emphasis on agricultural diversification (New Zealand Ministry for the Environment, 1997). However, substantial growth has occurred in deer farming. There is a thriving export trade not only in venison (deer meat), which is a lower-fat alternative to beef, but also in velvet; this latter is the soft skin on the surface of the growing deer antlers, used in traditional Asian medicines. New Zealand now has one of the largest deer industries in the world, and further growth is anticipated (Trade Partners UK, 2002). Investment in dairy farming—and especially intensive, large-scale operations—has also increased. But dairy farming's consumption of energy has risen dramatically, and it is increasingly reliant on artificial nitrogen fertilizers that have been cited as a factor in reduced water quality in rivers and other freshwater sources. Other environmental impacts associated with this intensification include increased trampling and compaction of fragile soils, and increased volumes of animal waste that degrade land and water resources alike.

New Zealand's arable agriculture sector is also energy intensive. Arable cropping dominates the Canterbury Plain west of Christchurch in central South Island, though most farms also carry animal herds. The region's yields—which are well above global averages—reflect high energy inputs through artificial fertilizer use, mechanization, and crop protection chemicals such as herbicides and pesticides. High application rates, though, have been blamed for eutrophication of waterways and soil acidification, and runoff from treated fields has contaminated rivers, wetlands, and coastal areas with chemical agents contained in pesticides, defoliants, and fertilizers. New Zealand also has a large horticulture sector that caters to the home market. For example, apple production is important in Hawke's Bay, North Island, and Nelson, South Island, while vine cultivation is concentrated in Marlborough in the hinterland of Wellington, North Island. Like dairying and cereal cropping, this sector is also energy intensive (ibid.).

Although New Zealand's agricultural profile is changing as the emerging markets of Asia continue to grow, and although other sectors such as tourism and manufacturing continue to develop, New Zealand's economy remains predominantly agricultural in character. The nation's future agricultural productivity is likely to be boosted by biotechnological innovations that include herbicide- and insect-resistant cereals, improved varieties of fruits, and improved animal health. Although field trials of several genetically modified crops have been undertaken, no such crops are yet being grown commercially (New Zealand Ministry for the Environment, 1997).

Papua New Guinea

Agriculture in Papua New Guinea is quite different from that of neighboring Australia and New Zealand. Its physical environment is unique in terms of climate, terrain, and vegetation cover, and it is markedly different in terms of economic development and social conditions. Papua New Guinea's economy is focused on the production and export of primary commodities such as minerals, wood, fish, and agricultural products—primarily coffee, tea, oil palm, cocoa, copra, and rubber. These are produced commercially, either in plantations or by small subsistence landholders. Sweet potato, sago, and banana are the major crops produced on a subsistence basis, but cultivation of taro, maize, and cassava also is substantial. Sweet potato, the most important staple crop, is grown by about 60 percent of the rural population; it occupied 102,000 hectares and generated 480,000 tons in 2000 (UN Food and Agriculture Organization, 2002). Sago and banana are the second and third most important crops and are the primary staples for 10 percent and 8 percent of the rural population, respectively (Allen et al., 2001).

Only a small proportion of Papua New Guinea's land area is used for agriculture. Cropland occupies less than 1.4 percent of the land area and permanent pasture less than 0.4 percent (UN Food and Agriculture Organization, 2002). Factors contributing to the country's light farming presence include rugged topography, which makes access and cultivation difficult and produces high susceptibility to soil erosion, and Papua New Guinea's extensive tropical forests, which have made logging a more lucrative pursuit. Nonetheless, several large estates that cultivate coffee, cocoa, and other products for export do exist. These are usually monocultural in nature, specializing in a single crop that is grown using relatively high inputs of fossil fuels and high numbers of laborers.

Subsistence-based agricultural systems are low-energy-input systems primarily based on swidden or shifting cultivation, whereby small forested areas of one to three hectares are cleared by burning to release land and nutrients for two or three years of crop cultivation; when productivity declines, the family moves on to cultivate another area, leaving forest to reclaim the abandoned cropland. Where land is not left long enough for forest to recolonize, soil erosion and other forms of degradation occur. Population growth is contributing to shortened fallow periods in many areas of the country. This phenomenon is particularly apparent on gently sloping land in the highland provinces, urban hinterlands, and some islands. In some extreme cases, fallow periods are no longer a component of the cropping system (Hanson et al., 2001).

Papua New Guinea's annual 2 percent rate of population increase also indicates that future expansion of agricultural land is probably inevitable, barring an unexpected surge in the productivity of existing agricultural land. Part of the effort to increase food production and improve nutritional standards could involve an increase in livestock. Indeed, increased livestock rearing has been described as a "prerequisite for national food security," provided it is accomplished in a sustainable manner. For example, an emphasis on small animals such as rabbit, geese, and quail would have a much smaller impact on the environment than larger domestic species such as sheep or cattle, provided that operations are developed and maintained in an environmentally sensitive manner (Maika, 2001). Increased productivity through genetically modified crop strains and expanded use of plant-derived pesticides may also be pursued, although Papua New Guinea has undertaken little research activity in these areas to date (Schuhbeck and Bokosou, 2001).

The Remaining Islands of Melanesia

Agriculture is practiced in all of these islands, most of which produce cash crops for export as well as staple crops for home consumption. Sweet potato, coconut, taro, yam, and banana are particularly important staples, while cash crops include coconut, coffee, and cocoa. Agriculture has altered the environment of all these islands, and in most cases it is the primary cause of biodiversity loss and environmental change, especially in relatively flat coastal areas. Moreover, the need to generate cash coupled with rapidly growing populations is putting increasing pressure on island governments to expand existing agricultural systems or increase productivity of existing plots through increased use of fertilizers and other intensification measures known to have a deleterious effect on freshwater and marine water quality.

New Caledonia

More than 12 percent of New Caledonia's total land area (1.858 million hectares) has been converted for agricultural use. About 13,000 hectares are used for the cultivation of arable and permanent crops such as maize, coconut, and coffee, while the remainder (216,000 hectares) are used for permanent pasture. The latter are reserved primarily for the rearing of beef cattle and sheep, although deer farming operations have taken root in recent years and are providing growing volumes of venison for export to Europe. Aquaculture is an expanding presence as well, especially prawn farming (UN Food and Agriculture Organization, 2002).

Vanuatu

The eighty-two islands that compose Vanuatu have a total land area of 1.219 million hectares, with the large islands of Espiritu Santo and Malekule accounting for about half of the total. Mountainous terrain constrains farming through most of the country, but coastal strips are widely cultivated. These areas provide most of the 162,000 hectares of Vanuatu's land that is used for agriculture, with 42,000 hectares used for permanent pasture and 120,000 hectares devoted to the production of arable and permanent crops (ibid.). About 65 percent of Vanuatu's population relies on subsistence agriculture for its livelihood.

The most important cash crops include banana, cocoa, coconut, coffee, and maize. Coconut and cocoa bean are grown in plantations, though their significance has declined in the last decade as the contribution of smallholders has increased. Vanuatu has an active research program on coconut biotechnology with a focus on the production of high-yielding varieties. The dominant subsistence crops are yam and taro. In terms of livestock production, beef cattle predominate, and overgrazing has become a serious problem in some areas. Overall, Vanuatu exports more agricultural commodities than it imports, and islanders enjoy a high level of food security.

A Comprehensive Reform Program (CRP) has recently been established by the Vanuatu government. This initiative aims to promote private-sector involvement in economic activities, of which agriculture is of primary importance, and reduce that of the public sector. This will include new legislation focused on tax changes, the privatization of state-owned enterprises, and the encouragement of foreign investment. The objective is to increase efficiency, growth, and export earnings, as well as to encourage diversification. However, the CRP may do little to reduce the environmental impact of agriculture, which, as currently practiced, is a chief cause of deforestation and soil erosion (Asian Development Bank, 2001).

The Solomon Islands

Although agriculture is a mainstay of the economy of the Solomon Islands, permanent agriculture occupies only about 100,000 hectares (40,000 hectares of pasture and 60,000 hectares of cropland) of the state's total land area of 2.89 million hectares. But shifting agriculture is widely practiced on the Solomon Islands.

The cash crops of coconut, oil palm, and cocoa beans are particularly important in terms of overall land use. Oil palm production is a relatively recent innovation following the success of experimental oil-palm plots on the Guadalcanal plain of the Island of Honiara in the late 1960s. By 2000 some 9,000 hectares were devoted to oil palm production, which has reached 30,000 tons annually. Root crops such as sweet potatoes, yam, and taro that are cultivated in shifting agricultural systems are the most important subsistent crops, while rice is the main cereal produced. In 2000 livestock production accounted for 11,000 head of cattle and 64,000 pigs; the former are raised on permanent pasture, while the latter are reared in smallholder enterprises that also include crop production (UN Food and Agriculture Organization, 2002).

Fiji

Fiji's 300 islands have a total land area of 1.827 million hectares, of which 460,000 hectares are used for agriculture (175,000 hectares of permanent pasture and 285,000 hectares of cropland). The major cash crops are sugar cane and coconuts, while minor cash crops include ginger, kava, cocoa beans, pineapple, and squash. All of these commodities are exported and are the main source of Fiji's income. Fiji's pasturelands support 335,000 head of cattle and 7,000 sheep, and beef and veal also rank as important exports (ibid.).

Subsistence crops include taro, sweet potato, yam, banana, and rice, but sugarcane ranks as the most commercially important crop produced in Fiji's

A man harvests sugar cane in Fiji. JACK FIELDS/CORBIS

fields. It directly employs one out of four members of the country's labor force for production and accounts for 40 percent of the value of its commercial agriculture (Bank of Hawaii, 1996). However, the government is encouraging agricultural diversification in order to protect Fiji from global fluctuations in sugar production and prices. In the wake of the World Summit on Sustainable Development in Johannesburg in 2002, the FAO has been asked to assist the Fiji government in its agricultural program, and especially in efforts to increase rice production and expand its dairy industry.

Fiji is one of the few centers of biotechnological research in the Pacific Islands. A program to collect and disseminate tissue of disease- and pest-resistant varieties of roots and tubers common to the Pacific Islands was established in the 1980s by the South Pacific Commission (SPC). There is also a Sugarcane Research Centre at Lautoka and an ongoing program to produce disease-free kava by the SPC's Plant Protection Service in Suva (Pacific Magazine and Islands Business, 2002).

Micronesia

Of the 2,000 islands that characterize Micronesia, the largest groups are the Federated States of Micronesia and the Marshall Islands. The latter nation relies heavily on copra production, though taro, breadfruit, cocoa, tomato, and melon are also produced in significant volumes. Most agricultural production in the Marshall Islands is on a subsistent basis, and copra and coconut oil are the major agricultural exports. In fact, 7,000 of the island state's 18,000-hectares are given over to coconut production (UN Food and Agriculture Organization, 2002). In contrast, the Federated States of Micronesia have a more diversified agricultural base; 46,000 hectares of a total land area of 70,000 hectares are used for agriculture, with 36,000 hectares of arable and permanent croplands and 10,000 hectares of permanent pasture. Coconut is the dominant crop in terms of area and production, but the main exports are banana, betel nuts, black pepper, and citrus fruits, which are imported to Guam and the Marshall Islands. There are several staple crops, including sweet potatoes and rice. Agriculture ranks as the main cause of deforestation in both the Marshall Islands and the Federated States of Micronesia, and it is a chief cause of soil erosion (UN Environment Programme, 1999).

Other island groups in Micronesia include Palau, where a subsistence-based agriculture sector contributes 12 percent of the island nation's gross domestic product. Farming operations also occupy nearly half of the island's land mass of 46,000 hectares; 12,000 hectares are used for arable and permanent crops and 8,000 hectares are permanent pasture (UN Food and

Agriculture Organization, 2002). Palau's agricultural holdings, which produce coconut, tapioca, taro, and a variety of tropical fruits, have suffered extensive damage at the hands of invasive plant and insect species. For example, two species of fruit flies introduced to Palau in the mid-1990s have decimated mountain apple and carambola fruit crops and have diminished guava and banana productivity; export of these fruits has been banned (Office of Environmental Response and Coordination, 2002).

Polynesia

The largest island groups of Polynesia are the Cook Islands and French Polynesia. Both island states maintain significant subsistence and commercial agriculture sectors. In the Cook Islands, approximately one-third of the land area of 23,000 hectares is used for arable and permanent crops; permanent pasturelands are nonexistent (UN Food and Agriculture Organization, 2002). Approximately 70 percent of households rely on agriculture for their livelihood, but the sector has actually declined slightly in significance in recent years as a result of increased economic activity in the finance, business, and tourism sectors (Cook Islands Ministry of Agriculture, 2002). The commercial sector is focused on exports of tropical fruits such as papaya and mango, while coconuts and sweet potatoes are other important crops. The Cook Islands have also developed a range of niche-market crops for export, including chili, coffee, vanilla, and the nono, a traditional Maori medicine fruit.

The importance of agriculture to the economy of the Cook Islands is reflected in the many research programs that are underway at the Totokoitu Agricultural Research Station, a joint venture between the Cook Islands and New Zealand that is exploring production possibilities of a wide assortment of fruit, vegetable, nut, and root crops. Research also is ongoing on a range of pest and disease eradication initiatives.

In French Polynesia, approximately 10 percent of the 400,000 hectares of land area distributed among its 130 islands is used for agriculture, with agricultural land divided roughly evenly between permanent pastures and croplands (UN Food and Agriculture Organization, 2002). Economically, agriculture is not as important as the growing tourism industry or the sale of Tahitian pearls, but increases in native populations and tourist arrivals have combined to place heavy pressure on intensification and expansion of existing agricultural operations. Already, agriculture is primarily responsible for the loss of lowland and coastal forests, which have been cleared for coconut groves and other forms of cultivation.

Other islands in Polynesia include the Wallis and Futuna group and Pitcairn, where subsistence-based agriculture is a dominant element of the socioeconomic fabric. In the Wallis and Futuna group, one-quarter of the total land area of 20,000 hectares has been converted for arable and permanent crops. There is no permanent pasture, but introduced goats have inflicted considerable damage to the flora of these small islands and shifting cultivation is common, including the use of fire for initial vegetation clearance. Subsistence agriculture on the small island of Pitcairn involves the production of yams, beans, citrus, banana, watermelon, sugar cane, and coconut, all of which have contributed to forest loss.

Tonga

Agriculture is well-developed and extensive in Tonga. Of Tonga's land area of 75,000 hectares, 52,000 are given over to agriculture, with cropland accounting for nearly all of this total (ibid.). Farming has been a longtime mainstay of the economy, but it has undergone substantial change in the last few decades. Whereas coconuts and bananas were once the premier crops, the pumpkin has now emerged as Tonga's most important and profitable agricultural product. In fact, exports of pumpkin crops, primarily to Japan and New Zealand, provide more than half of the kingdom's total export earnings. Production is smallholder-based, with cooperatives facilitating the export trade, but it is also heavily reliant on artificial fertilizers and pesticides, which have given rise to environmental problems such as the eutrophication of aquatic environments. In addition to the aforementioned products, high-value specialty crops include kava and vanilla. Indeed, these crops dominate agriculture on the island of Vava'u, Tonga's second-largest island. In terms of animal production, cattle and pigs are most important.

Samoa

Almost half of Samoa's total land area of 284,000 hectares is used for the production of arable and permanent crops. Coconut is by far the most important commercial crop, while the leading subsistence crop is taro. Tropical fruits that are actively cultivated include papaya, pineapple, and mango, but none rival banana in terms of economic importance. As with so many other Pacific states, Samoan communities rely heavily on agriculture for their livelihoods; fully 65 percent of Samoan households support themselves directly or indirectly in agriculture and related industries. Agriculture operations are based in the coastal plains, which have suffered extensive forest loss as a result (ibid.). This deforestation and subsequent farming activity have dramatically increased sedimentation of coastal reefs, which in turn has produced downturns in the populations of important near-shore fish stocks (UN Environment Programme, 1999).

Sources:

Allen, B. J., R. M. Bourke, and L. Hanson. 2001. "Dimensions of PNG Village Agriculture." In *Food Security for Papua New Guinea*. Edited by R. M. Bourke, M. G. Allen, and J. G. Salisbury. Canberra: ACIAR.

Asian Development Bank. 2001. *Vanuatu: Agriculture and Fisheries Sector Review 2000*. Manila: ADB. Available at www.adb.org.

Australia Department of Agriculture, Fisheries and Forestry. 2000. *Agricultural Biotechnology: What Is happening in Australia in 2000*. Available at www.affa.gov.au (accessed November 18, 2002).

Australia National Land and Water Resources Audit. 2001. *Australian Agriculture Assessment 2001*. Canberra: National Land and Water Resources Audit.

———. 2001. *Australia's Native Vegetation*. Canberra: National Land and Water Resources Audit.

Australian State of the Environment Committee. 2001. *Australia State of the Environment Report 2001*. Canberra: Commonwealth of Australia.

Bank of Hawaii. 1996. "Fiji Economic Report." Available at www.boh.com (accessed November 22, 2002).

Barr, N. F., and J. W. Cary. 1992. *Greening a Brown Land: The Australian Search for Sustainable Land Use*. Melbourne: Macmillan.

Commonwealth of Australia. 2000. *Our Vital Resources—National Action Plan for Salinity and Water Quality in Australia*. Canberra: Environment Australia. Available at http://www.napswq.gov.au/publications/vital_resources.html (accessed August 2002).

Cook Islands Ministry of Agriculture. *Importance of Agricultural Research*. Available at www.cook-islands.gov.ck (accessed December 3, 2002).

DaSilva, E. J., and M. Taylor. 1998. "Island Communities and Biotechnology." *Electronic Journal of Biotechnology* 1.

Economic and Social Commission of Asia and the Pacific. 1995. *Review of the Environment and Development Trends in the South Pacific*. Port Vila, Vanuatu: ESCAP.

Hanson, L. W., et al. 2001. *Mapping Land Resource Potential and Agricultural Pressure in Papua New Guinea*. Technical Report from ACIAR Project ASEM 1996/044. Canberra: Australian National University.

Journeaux, P. 1996. "Trends in New Zealand Agriculture." *New Zealand Journal of Geography* (October).

Lovett, John, and John Duggin. 1992. "Agricultural Side-Effects." In *The Unique Continent*. Edited by Jeremy Smith. St. Lucia, Queensland: University of Queensland Press.

Maika, C. B. 2001. "The Role of Livestock in Food Security for PNG." In R. M. Bourke, M. G. Allen, and J. G. Salisbury, eds. *Food Security for Papua New Guinea*. Canberra: ACIAR.

Mannion, A.M. 1997. *Global Environmental Change: A Natural and Cultural Environmental History.* 2d ed. Harlow: Addison Wesley Longman.

———. 2002. *Dynamic World: Land-cover and Land-use Change.* London: Arnold.

New Zealand Ministry for the Environment. 1997. *The State of New Zealand's Environment 1997.* Wellington: Ministry for the Environment.

New Zealand Ministry of Agriculture and Fisheries. *Sectors/Animals.* Available at www.maf.govt.nz (accessed November 26, 2002).

———. *Sectors/Horticulture.* Available at www.maf.govt.nz (accessed November 26, 2002).

Nunn, P. 1994. *Oceanic Islands.* Oxford, UK: Blackwell.

Office of Environmental Response and Coordination (Republic of Palau). 2002. *National Report to the United Nations Convention to Combat Desertification.* Palau: Office of Environmental Response and Coordination.

Paarlberg, Roger. 2000. "Promise or Peril? Genetically Modified Crops in Developing Countries." *Environment* (January/February).

Pacific Magazine and Islands Business. 2001. *The Answer to Pitcairn's Woes?* Available at www.pacificislands.cc, June 2001 (accessed December 1, 2002).

———. 2002. *Agriculture: SPC Plant Protection Brings in Help to Tackle Kava Dieback.* September. Available at www.pacificislands.cc (accessed November 28, 2002).

Pinstrup-Anderson, Per, and Ebbe Schioler. 2001. *Seeds of Contention: World Hunger and the Global Controversy over GM (Genetically Modified) Crops.* Washington, DC: Johns Hopkins University Press/International Food Policy Research Institute.

Pyne, Steven J. 1998. "Forged in Fire: History, Land, and Anthropogenic Fire." In *Advances in Historical Ecology.* Edited by W. Balée. New York: Columbia University Press.

Schuhbeck, A., and J. Bokosou. 2001. "The Potential of Using Homemade Plant-derived Pesticides to Increase Food Crop Production and Local Food Security." In *Food Security for Papua New Guinea.* Edited by R. M. Bourke, M. G. Allen, and J. G. Salisbury. Canberra: ACIAR.

Singh, D., P. Kaushal, and M. Singh. 2001. "Impacts of Biotechnology on Food Security and Food Quality." In *Food Security for Papua New Guinea.* Edited by R. M. Bourke, M. G. Allen, and J. G. Salisbury. Canberra: ACIAR.

Solomon Islands Economic Report. *III. Economy by Sectors and Major Industries.* Available at www.boh.com (accessed November 28, 2002).

Trade Partners UK. *Agriculture, Horticulture and Fisheries Market in New Zealand.* Available at www.tradepartners.gov.uk (accessed November 15, 2002).

Tupou, S. *Cash Cropping and Squash Pumpkins in Tonga.* Available at http://abc.net.au (accessed December 3, 2002).

UN Environment Programme. *Pacific Islands Environmental Outlook.* Available at www.unep.org, 1999 (accessed December 4, 2002).

UN Food and Agriculture Organization. 2000. *State of the World Fisheries and Aquaculture 2000.* Rome: FAO.

———. 2001. *The State of Food and Agriculture 2001*. Rome: FAO.

———. 2001. *State of the World Fisheries and Aquaculture 2001*. Rome: FAO.

———. *Agricultural statistics (FAOSTAT)*. Available at www.fao.org (accessed November 5, 2002).

U.S. Department of Agriculture. *Census of Agriculture Guam*. Available at www.nass.usda.gov (accessed December 3, 2002).

Willis, R. 2001. "Farming." *Asia Pacific Viewpoint* 42.

Wood, Stanley, Kate Sebastian, and Sara J. Scherr. 2000. *PAGE (Pilot Analysis of Global Ecosystems): Agroecosystems; a Joint Study by the International Food Policy Research Institute (IFPRI) and World Resources Institute (WRI)*. Washington, DC: IFPRI, WRI.

Freshwater
—Angela Casser

Oceania is a region that contains great extremes and variability in climate, rainfall, and freshwater availability. Owing to low population densities throughout many parts of the region, this variability does not pose a significant problem in terms of per capita water availability, although seasonal droughts have created shortages. Regionally, freshwater overabstraction and environmental degradation associated with terrestrial freshwater use poses the greatest environmental risk in Australia, which is the largest, most heavily populated, most economically powerful, and most water-stressed country in the region. But other Pacific Island countries are grappling with troubling trends regarding their freshwater resources as well, and commitment to improved freshwater management is a necessity for the region's future prosperity.

Australia's Freshwater Resources

Water scarcity is a fact of life in many parts of Australia, and numerous regions are experiencing significant social, economic, and ecological problems associated with overabstraction and degradation of freshwater resources. Australia has the most variable precipitation and runoff distribution in the world, ranging from parched desert interior sections that receive minimal rainfall to northeast Queensland and the west-facing slopes of Tasmania and the Australian Alps, all of which receive more than 4,000 mm (157 inches) annually (Smith, 1998). In addition, seasonal variability in rainfall is considerable, providing Australians with an intrinsic understanding that their country is one "of droughts and flooding rains" (McKellar, 1911). This variability has been an important factor in maintaining some of Australia's unique and aquatic ecosystems of amazing biodiversity, such as floodplain wetlands and billabongs (oxbow lakes).

By world standards, Australia's surface runoff and renewable groundwater resources are notably low, representing just over 10 percent of Australia's total rainfall (Smith, 1998). This amount is depleted further when one considers that, of Australia's total surface runoff, only 32 percent can be feasibly diverted for human use (Australian State of the Environment Committee, 2001). This is primarily because the mean annual runoff is highest in the tropical northern areas of Australia, a lightly populated region of pronounced seasonal precipitation disparities where 65 percent of all runoff occurs. Variability of supply is a main reason why this water can not be utilized more efficiently in Australia; the ability to store water in tropical areas is limited, as most runoff occurs after very large rainfall events that require uneconomically large reservoirs to capture water.

In part, the variability experienced in Australia can be attributed to the El Niño–Southern Oscillation weather phenomenon, which brings with it cloudless skies over the parched outback. The El Niño–Southern Oscillation occurs when the eastern Pacific Ocean currents alter and cold water upwelling along the Peruvian coastline in South America ceases (Glantz, 1996). In South America, El Niño is associated with heavy rains and flooding, and the reverse is true on the other side of the Pacific in Australia, where the El Niño event is associated with drought.

The science of the El Niño–Southern Oscillation phenomena is not completely understood, and predicting its return is an inexact pursuit, but it has shown that it can have dire consequences for Australian agriculture and water supplies. In the early twenty-first century, for example, Australia was gripped by a fierce drought blamed on El Niño. The period from April to October 2002 was cited as the driest seven-month period in the country's history, and analysts with the Australian Bureau of Meteorology state that the drought, which has descended on nearly all regions, could rank as the worst and most destructive in Australian history by the time it ends. The government forecaster ABARE has already predicted that the drought will wipe A$5.4 billion from the nation's economy in 2002/2003 (ABARE, 2002), and major cities such as Sydney and Melbourne have been forced to initiate water-use restrictions. Other cities, such as the Australian capital of Canberra, have been threatened by major bush fires roaring through the tinder-dry backcountry.

Some observers believe that global climate change is another factor at work in Australia's 2002 drought. In early 2003, for example, the World Wide Fund for Nature Australia released a study that cited human-induced global warming as a contributor to the nation's water woes. The study, which was endorsed by the government-funded Commonwealth Scientific and Industrial Research Organization (CSIRO), concluded that greenhouse gases and inappropriate crop selection were exacerbating the country's natural vulnerability to drought. It claimed that higher temperatures attributable to global warming were causing marked increases in evaporation rates from Australian soil, waterways, and vegetation (World Wide Fund for Nature Australia, 2003).

Water Use in Australia

Approximately 75 percent of all freshwater consumed in Australia is used in irrigation, which, more than any other single factor, has pushed the country's consumption levels to all-time highs. Indeed, from 1985 to 1996–1997, Australia increased its water use by 65 percent, with surface water accounting for 79 percent of all water extracted and groundwater accounting for the remaining 21 percent (Australian National Land and Water Resources Audit, *Australian Water Resources Assessment,* 2001).

Unfortunately, the geographical distribution of agricultural development in Australia does not reflect the limited availability of freshwater; the nation's major agricultural regions are located within the 80 percent of Australia's land that has an average rainfall of less than 600 mm (24 inches) per year. As a result, irrigation has become the cornerstone of the agricultural economy. Most of this irrigation is concentrated in "Australia's food bowl," the Murray-Darling Basin, which in 1997 accounted for 71 percent (1.472 million hectares) of the total area irrigated in Australia. In addition, the rate of growth in water use for irrigation has surged in some areas of Australia over the past few decades. New South Wales and Queensland, which have large areas within the Murray-Darling Basin, have almost doubled their areas of irrigated land over the last twenty years (Australian State of the Environment Committee, 2001).

These steadily growing rates of extraction from Australian rivers and streams for agriculture and other purposes have had a considerable impact on aquatic ecosystems. More than one-quarter of Australia's river systems are either close to or are already oversubscribed (Australian National Land and Water Resources Audit, *Australian Water Resources Assessment,* 2001). Moreover, nearly 70 percent of the total volume of water extracted from surface waters in Australia is taken from these stressed river systems (Australian State of the Environment Committee, 2001).

These heavy rates of withdrawal from river systems, combined with modifications for water storage, flood alleviation, hydroelectric power, water transport, and other purposes, have appreciably altered the fundamental character of many Australian rivers. A 2002 government survey of Australia's freshwater resources determined that over 85 percent of the country's rivers have been "significantly modified" in terms of their environmental features. New South Wales, South Australia, and Western Australia have the greatest amounts of modified river length (97 percent, 96 percent, and 93 percent, respectively). Further, over 80 percent of the country's total river length was affected by

Figure 6.1 Net Water Consumption by Sector

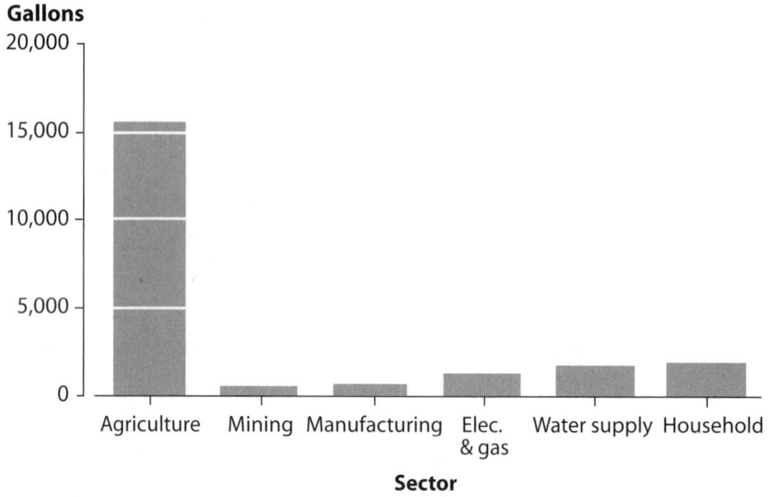

SOURCE: ABS data used with permission from the Australian Bureau of Statistics. http://abs.gov.au. Water Account for Autralia 1993–1994 to 1996–1997 (Cat. No. 4610.0, p. 13)

catchment disturbance, with land uses affecting delivery of sediment, nutrients, and water into systems, and more than 50 percent of the country's river length featured modified habitat (mainly linked to changes in sediment loads that can alter channel morphology). Not surprisingly, this study also reported widespread degradation of aquatic ecosystems associated with these various types of modification and development (Australian National Land and Water Resources Audit, *Australian Water Resources Assessment,* 2001).

Australia's dams have come under particular scrutiny for their environmental impact. Almost all of Australia's major rivers are now dammed and their flows regulated. These projects have created reservoirs that have provided highly valued water security for agricultural and household users. In addition, some dams have a significant hydroelectricity generation function, such as the Snowy River Hydroelectric Scheme. But many large dams in Australia have been faulted for their adverse consequences, such as reduced fishery health, flooding of upstream habitat, and alteration of downstream aquatic habitat. In addition, Australia's agricultural regions are riddled with small to medium on-farm dams, which until recently have not been rigorously regulated. These smaller farm dams are typically located in areas that capture rainfall and runoff, thus preventing normal replenishment of nearby streams. Alone, they are minor obstructions to runoff, but cumulatively they can demonstrate considerable impact on river flow and volume.

Water Conservation in the Murray-Darling Basin

Home to Australia's largest river system, the Murray-Darling Basin is also the country's most productive agricultural region. It covers 14 percent of Australia's total land mass (1,058,590 square kilometers [408,722 square miles]), straddles five states and territories, and supports more than 2 million people and a wide array of fish, reptiles, birds, mammals, and plants. But average rainfall in this region is relatively low, necessitating high rates of water extraction from rivers and groundwater sources for irrigation. As a result, the Murray-Darling Basin has become one of the most water stressed regions of Australia (National Land and Water Resources Audit, 2001; World Wide Fund for Nature Australia, 2001).

Water extraction from the Murray-Darling system dates back to the 1870s, increasing sharply in the 1950s and 1960s. From 1944 to 1994, extraction rates across the basin tripled (Murray-Darling Basin Commission, 2000). The greatest increases in rates of extraction have been in the northern regions of the basin, where water-intensive crops such as cotton and other large-scale enterprises (high-value horticulture, viticulture, rice, and vegetables) have been established. The cumulative impact of these enterprises has been significant. It is estimated that present median annual flow within the basin is only 27 percent of predevelopment flow (ibid.).

During the 1990s it was determined that the increase in water-extraction rates for irrigation in the basin was not sustainable, especially since the region was also experiencing a sharp increase in salinity-induced land degradation, mainly in the lower catchment area. In addition to these problems, wetlands (including several of international importance) and red-gum forests were also experiencing increased stress from altered flood regimes (mainly reduced frequency and intensity), and native fish species were also in severe decline (ibid.).

Other threats to the health and integrity of the watershed were reported as well. Increases in nutrients from agricultural runoff and increased sediment loading from deforestation contributed significantly to a rise in algal blooms throughout the basin, resulting in fish kills and deoxygenation of water. The direst of these events occurred in 1991, when a toxic blue-green (cyanobacteria) algae bloom afflicted a 1,000-kilometer (620-mile) stretch of the Darling River.

The degradation of the Murray-Darling system has also heightened the impact of introduced species such as European carp. Indeed, carp numbers have exploded in many of Australia's rivers, where long sections of still water and a dearth of predators have created ideal conditions for population growth; a study conducted in 1992 reported that overall, 90 percent of the fish samples taken from the Darling River system were carp (Harris, 1992). The carp have had a pronounced impact on riverine environments in the Murray-Darling basin and other regions. Feeding in

(continues)

direct competition with native fish species, they have disrupted the ecological balance in many waterways. Moreover, the feeding habits of carp dislodge vegetation, adding to the suspended-sediment load of already naturally turbid waters (Smith, 1998).

Australian governments have responded to this clear need for action. Since 1985, the Murray-Darling Ministerial Council has operated to facilitate interstate cooperation among Queensland, New South Wales, Australian Capital Territory, Victoria, and South Australia to ensure that a river basin approach to management is encouraged. The boldest measure taken by the Council was the 1995 imposition of "The Cap," a commonwealth and state/territory agreement to limit water extraction from the basin. The Cap is intended to hold the level of water extraction to that of 1993/1994, putting an end to steadily rising rates of consumption. Since this mechanism was imposed, there has been an increase in water trading within the Murray-Darling basin. It is hoped that trading will encourage a shift from "low-return uses" (such as irrigation of water-intensive crops) to "high-return uses" and prompt greater efficiencies in water usage (Murray-Darling Basin Commission, 2002).

But although the Cap has succeeded in slowing the increase in water extraction in the basin, not all parties have met their water conservation commitments. Queensland, for example, has not agreed to recommended Cap levels, and withdrawals from New South Wales's Barwon River have exceeded Cap limits. Conservationists also note that the Cap alone is not capable of restoring already damaged riverine environments. They have called for new investments in aquatic habitat restoration programs and new restrictions on environmentally destructive forms of land-use (Australian State of the Environment Committee, 2001).

Sources:

Australian National Land and Water Resources Audit. 2001. *Australian Catchment, River and Estuary Assessment 2002.* 2 vols. Canberra: National Land and Water Resources Audit.

Australian State of the Environment Committee. 2001. *Australia State of the Environment Report 2001.* Canberra: Commonwealth of Australia.

Harris, J. 1992. *Fish Migration in the Darling River.* Sydney: New South Wales Fisheries.

Murray-Darling Basin Commission. 2000. *Review of the Operation of the Cap: Overview Report of the Murray Darling Basin Commission.* Canberra: MDBC.

———. 2002. *Water Audit Monitoring Report 2000/01: Report of the Murray-Darling Basin Commission on the Cap on Diversions.* Canberra: MDBC.

Smith, D. I. 1998. *Water in Australia: Resources and Management.* Melbourne: Oxford University Press.

World Wide Fund for Nature Australia. 2001. *Greening the 2001 Agenda: Priority Environment Initiatives for Commonwealth Government 2002–2005.* Sydney: WWF Australia.

Reductions in river flow in Australia have had major consequences for river ecology, and there needs to be greater recognition that the ecological health of river basins is important to livelihoods and to the protection of the continent's unique biodiversity. By altering natural patterns of high and low river flows, unsustainable water extraction for human use reduces the amount of water available for dependent animals, plants, and habitat. For example, wetland modifications over the last century have been severe, with many wetlands suffering substantial reductions in area because of changes in flow regimes and inundation areas and reclamation (Kingsford, 2000; Australian State of the Environment Committee, 2001).

Australia's political system, which gives states and territories much of the responsibility for oversight and management of freshwater and other natural resources contained within their borders, complicates efforts to address growing pressures on the continent's rivers, wetlands, and aquifers. "Each state and territory has different approaches to management, to defining environmental needs, and on deciding what is the acceptable health of an aquatic system," acknowledged the authors of one recent environment study. "This is further complicated when a river, wetland or groundwater resource crosses state and territory boundaries. Cross border natural resource management authorities are striving to achieve more integrated processes and outcomes in the management of their respective inland waters and catchments. However, from some issues state or territory interests have overridden what is environmentally sustainable for the whole catchment" (Australian State of the Environment Committee, 2001).

In recent years, however, there has been a greater effort to incorporate environmental considerations into the management of rivers and other freshwater resources. By mid-2000, 13 percent of Australian river systems had operational environmental flow allocations, and state and commonwealth governments have pledged their commitment to restoring more natural environmental flows to many of Australia's degraded rivers, including the Snowy River watershed (Australian National Land and Water Resources Audit, *Australian Water Resources Assessment,* 2001). In addition, so-called "whole-of-catchment" management schemes have been successfully launched in places like Australia's Lake Eyre Basin. Finally, state and federal agencies are exploring a variety of reforms meant to reduce water consumption, including charging for the full cost of supplying water, reallocation of water to highest value crops, and reduced reliance on water-intensive crops (Australian State of the Environment Committee, 2001).

Pollution of Australia's Freshwater Resources

National inventories on pollution of Australia's freshwater resources are incomplete, apart from point-source pollution in known contaminated areas such as derelict mines. It is also very difficult to discuss water quality in terms of Australian rivers because under natural conditions they tend to have much higher loads of suspended particles than other regions, and therefore, even under natural conditions, many Australian rivers exceed the recommended suspended sediment limits for drinking water (Smith, 1998). But known pollutant sources of significance include pesticides and fertilizers used in agriculture; oil and heavy metals; and waste from human settlements and livestock operations.

In some regions, contamination has reached the point that aquatic ecosystems and drinking water safety have been endangered. One increasingly notorious manifestation of degraded waterways is toxic algal blooms (such as blue-green algae, or cyanobacteria), which now appear with regularity throughout Australia. For example, in 1991 the Barwon and Darling rivers in New South Wales were beleaguered by a toxic algal bloom that stretched for 1,000 kilometers (620 miles). Elsewhere in New South Wales, blue-green algal blooms have erupted in the Hawkesbury-Nepean River and in many inland lakes and reservoirs. And in Western Australia, rivers such as the Blackwood, Vasse, Serpentine, and Swan-Canning have all been regularly damaged by blue-green algal blooms since 1996. As the Australian government now acknowledges, nutrient levels are now high enough to support algal blooms in most river systems of the economically vital Murray-Darling Basin and numerous coastal river systems in Victoria, New South Wales, Queensland, and Western Australia (Australian State of the Environment Committee, 2001).

Cyanobacteria occur naturally throughout Australia, but they pose significant health and environmental problems when there are population explosions, most of which are attributable to anthropogenic influences. Australia's naturally low-gradient, low-flow rivers have had their flows further depleted through overextraction. This has created an ideal incubator for blue-green algal blooms, which occur most frequently in still waters. Another factor has been the introduction of plant nutrients, nitrogen, and phosphorus from farming, inadequate sewage treatment, and other human sources. These algal blooms can result in eutrophication, a condition in which excess organic nutrients from fertilizers and waste deplete a body of water's supply of oxygen, which in turn can devastate resident aquatic life.

Most pollutants entering Australia's inland waters are from non–point sources such as pesticides used in agriculture, particularly cotton, rice, sugar cane, and horticultural crops. Since 1990, at least twenty fish kills in New South Wales have been linked to pesticides, and analysts are concerned that pesticide use is likely to increase at least over the short term. Excessive sedimentation stemming from timber operations, including the construction of

Figure 6.2 Tons of Nitrogen Discharged Annually in Australia

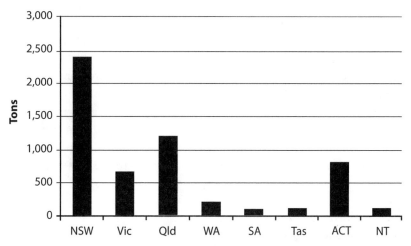

SOURCE: Australian State of the Environment Committee. 2001. *Australia State of the Environment 2001.* Independent Report to the Commonwealth Minister for the Environment and Heritage. CSIRO Publishing on behalf of the Department of the Environment and Heritage. Copyright Commonwealth of Australia reproduced by permission.

Figure 6.3 Tons of Phosphorous Discharged by Australia's Inland Sewage Treatment Plants Each Year

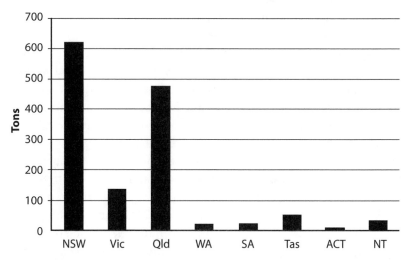

SOURCE: Australian State of the Environment Committee. 2001. *Australia State of the Environment 2001.* Independent Report to the Commonwealth Minister for the Environment and Heritage. CSIRO Publishing on behalf of the Department of the Environment and Heritage. Copyright Commonwealth of Australia reproduced by permission.

logging roads, has also been faulted for causing serious erosion problems that have compromised water quality and ecosystem integrity in some rivers and streams. In addition, acidification attributed to discharges from mining sites, agricultural activities, and disturbance of soils with high acid content have created high levels of water acidity in some inland waters of Victoria and New South Wales. Other pollutants, such as oil and heavy metals from industrial operations, mining, and urban areas, have caused localized damage, but authorities in some states and territories have made significant strides in imposing more stringent pollution parameters for some industries and in implementing stormwater management plans for catchments (watersheds) with large urban populations (Australian State of the Environment Committee, 2001).

Salinity—A Major Challenge for Australia's Environmental Future

Salinity of dryland areas and freshwater resources represents possibly the most significant, damaging, and urgent environmental dilemma facing Australia today. Freshwater systems in Australia threatened by rising salinity levels include the Murray-Darling Basin and major catchments in Western Australia and South Australia. Australia has naturally saline groundwater in many areas, reminiscent of ancient marine environments. Poor environmental management practices, particularly relating to irrigation and inappropriate clearing of vegetation, have contributed to the widespread rise of this saline groundwater to the surface; left unchecked these practices can eventually render large areas of land unusable.

Although salinity does arise naturally, salinity mobilized through anthropogenic activities exhibits the most damaging and widespread damage. Broadly, these can be characterized as "irrigation" and "dryland" salinities. Irrigation salinity occurs when the natural level of the groundwater table is raised by irrigation. Saline groundwater is able to reach the surface following this artificial recharge, particularly in low-lying areas and regions with shallow groundwater tables. Once the salt has been mobilized to the surface, the productive capacity of the land is irreversibly damaged.

Dryland salinity occurs as a result of clearing native vegetation for pasture or shallow-rooted crops and pastures. Shallow-rooted plants can only utilize water in the upper part of the soil profile, with the rest passing through to recharge groundwater. These shallow-rooted crops and pastures also tend to evapotranspire less than larger native vegetative cover. This combination of factors produces greater levels of water infiltration that can sometimes bring saline groundwater tables to the surface, putting an end to the land's agricultural productivity (Smith, 1998).

Trees killed and soil scalded by dryland salinity, NSW. IAN PATERSON/PHOTOLIBRARY/PICTUREQUEST

Indications of excess salinity are already evident in many areas of Australia. An estimated 5 million hectares of land have already been affected by salinity, and some forecasts have stated that up to 17 million hectares could be affected by 2050. Much of the presently salt-affected or potentially salt-affected areas are in the most agriculturally productive regions of Australia. The area damaged by salinity to date represents about 4.5 percent of present cultivated land, and estimated current costs include $130 million annually in lost agricultural production; $100 million annually in damage to infrastructure, and at least $40 million in loss of environmental assets (Land and Water Resources Research and Development Corporation, 1998; Australian National Land and Water Resources Audit, *Australian Water Resources Assessment,* 2001).

Inland lakes and rivers have been harmed by salinity as well. Across the continent, eighty ecologically significant wetlands have already been affected by salinity, and the number of salinity-degraded wetlands is expected to rise in the coming years. Managers of river systems in western Victoria and southwest Western Australia are also grappling with rising salinity levels, as are many of the cities and towns of South Australia and New South Wales, where drinking water supplies are now in jeopardy because of salinization. In Adelaide, for instance, scientists contend that drinking water could exceed safety guidelines for salinity 40 percent of the year by 2020 if rising salinity in the Murray River is not curbed. Given the ecological importance of inland waters as habitat and sources of food and water, it is clear that rising salinity levels must be addressed in a decisive manner to ensure that Australia's aquatic and terrestrial biodiversity is protected.

Australia's Dwindling Groundwater Resources

Freshwater stresses are not confined only to surface waters in Australia. Groundwater use increased by 90 percent across Australia between 1985 and 1996/1997. More than half (51 percent) of the freshwater extracted from Australia's aquifers is utilized for crop irrigation, while the remaining 49 percent is divided between urban/industrial use (32 percent) and rural use and livestock care (17 percent) (Australian State of the Environment Committee, 2001).

The end use of groundwater depends on regional priorities and economic orientations. In eastern and southern Australia, more than 60 percent of groundwater withdrawals are made for irrigation, while Western Australia devotes 72 percent of its groundwater extractions to household use, factory operations, and other urban and industrial purposes (Perth's heavy reliance on groundwater resources for its freshwater needs is a major factor in this high percentage). All told, an estimated 4 million people in Australia depend partially or totally on groundwater for their domestic water supply (ibid.). In many locales, however, authorities are concerned that groundwater resources are being drained at a rate far beyond the level of natural recharge. The chief culprits in this "drawing down" of water tables are urban centers and irrigation-dependent agricultural operations. Specific regions at risk of exhausting their aquifers at present rates of consumption include aquifers along the nation's eastern coast, aquifers in the Murray-Darling and Perth basins, and the Great Artesian Basin, one of the largest and most economically important groundwater basins in the world.

The Great Artesian Basin is located in the arid Central-Eastern region of Australia. Covering an area of 1,711,000 square kilometers (661,000 square miles), with an estimated 64,900 cubic kilometers of stored water, the Great Artesian Basin underlies approximately one-fifth of Australia's total land area. It extends beneath the arid and semiarid regions of Queensland, New South Wales, South Australia, and the Northern Territory, extending as far south as Lake Eyre depression, the terminus of the overlying surface drainage basin. At its deepest, the Great Artesian Basin reaches a maximum depth of 3,000 meters (9,800 feet). This water is an ancient resource, with formation of some southwestern portions of the basin dating back an estimated 2 million years (Department of Natural Resources and Mines, 2002).

In the most arid areas of the Great Artesian Basin, the overlying surface hydrology consists of ephemeral rivers and creeks that flow only seasonally or during periods of significant precipitation. Yet in the late nineteenth century, European settlers utilized this area for grazing cattle and sheep by tapping into

Excess salinity is a major problem in many regions of Australia. IAN PATERSON/PHOTOLIBRARY/
PICTUREQUEST

the massive Great Artesian Basin aquifer. The Great Artesian Basin, as its name suggests, consists of *artesian* water—groundwater under pressure. Because of this pressure, the water will flow freely without needing to be manually pumped once bores are drilled.

Over time, much of the land area covering the basin became enormously productive farmland. But many users have been negligent in their stewardship of the resource. For example, many of the bores used to tap into the Great Artesian Basin remained uncapped, and some are still uncapped, allowing water from the subterranean depths to gush wastefully out over the arid land-scape. In addition, expanding populations and agricultural development have prompted the drilling of myriad new bores to reach the basin's precious water. Indeed, thousands of kilometers of bore drains have been excavated through-out the basin to distribute water to privately owned sheep and cattle herds. These bore drains are small, open channels that can extend 100 kilometers or more. Overall, almost 34,000 kilometers of bore drains have been excavated in Queensland and New South Wales and are presently being utilized. But be-cause these bore drains are open channels, up to 95 percent of the water is wasted through evaporation and seepage, and infestations of invasive woody weeds such as prickly acacia in and around bore drains have proliferated as a consequence of uncontrolled flow. Poorly maintained bore drains have also created artificial "green" areas in the countryside that have been cited as a fac-tor in the explosive growth of kangaroos and rabbits, which have by their sheer numbers altered some regional ecosystems and damaged agricultural productivity. Erosion problems are another common malady in drain areas, and there have been reports of incidents in which animal health has suffered from exposure to high concentrations of minerals (such as sodium and fluo-ride) left behind after evaporation of aquifer water (Great Artesian Basin Consultative Council, 2000).

A number of Australian government initiatives aimed at addressing this problem have been initiated. The Great Artesian Basin Sustainability Initiative (GABSI) is a jointly funded initiative of the commonwealth (federal) and state governments and pastoral bore owners aimed at protecting and preserving groundwater pressure throughout the Great Artesian Basin. The approach taken is a rehabilitative one that emphasizes capping or replacement of bores, drains, and water distribution infrastructure with more efficient materials (ibid.). For Australia as a whole, meanwhile, the country's recent National Water Reforms Framework includes a number of provisions for groundwater, but further reforms to groundwater use and allocation are badly needed in most states and territories.

Freshwater in New Zealand

In comparison to Australia, New Zealand is blessed with an abundant supply of freshwater. Indeed, its average precipitation is more than three times that of the Australian continent, providing the country with ample freshwater re-sources to accommodate its relatively small population of 3.78 million. In fact, New Zealand uses a mere 1 percent of its 196.69 cubic kilometer total re-newable freshwater resource annually (UN Food and Agriculture Organiza-tion, 2002).

Restoring a Legendary River

The Snowy River is one of the most famous natural landmarks on the Australian continent. Until the mid-twentieth century, this wild river ran unfettered from its origins in Eastern Australia's Snowy Mountains, part of the Great Dividing Range that separates the east coast from the rest of the continent, to the sea. Australian songs and stories are threaded with paeans to the river's untamed character, most notably in A. B. Patterson's famous poem "The Man from Snowy River" and a critically acclaimed film of the same name.

In 1949, however, the Snowy River became the centerpiece of one of the most ambitious freshwater diversion schemes of the twentieth century. This project—The Snowy Mountains Hydro-Electric Scheme—aimed to redirect Snowy River water to the arid west side of the Great Dividing Range, where growing agricultural operations were clamoring for water for irrigation. Over the course of the next quarter-century (1949 to 1974), more than 100,000 workers carved giant tunnels through the mountains, built sixteen dams, and constructed massive pipelines and aqueducts for the project. By the time construction was completed, the Scheme had the capacity to pump 1.8 trillion gallons of water from the Snowy River through the Great Dividing Range and into the Murray and Murrumbidgee rivers, where it was used for hydroelectric power generation and crop irrigation. This infusion of water opened new areas for agricultural development, and today the Snowy Mountain Hydro-Electric Scheme accounts for more than 82 percent of hydroelectric power generation in Australia. Indeed, it is an important power source for households, shops, and factories in Melbourne, Sydney, and Canberra (Snowy Water Inquiry, 1998).

But the project also wreaked wrenching ecological changes on the Snowy River. Water volume in the river was reduced to 1 percent of its former might by the diversions. This diminished flow drastically reduced the river's capacity to dilute chemical runoff from farming and industrial operations. In addition, water-starved sections of the river downstream from the diversion have seen marked deterioration of ecosystems and major changes to the character of the river channel. For example, river flows became too weak to clear vegetation from taking root or move sediments deposited in the riverbed. As a result, downstream sections of the Snowy have narrowed down and silted, with detrimental effects to fish and other dependent species. Finally, downstream communities noted that the Snowy's diminished flow has reduced recreational options that might otherwise be pursued, such as fishing, camping, canoeing, and rafting (Pigram, 1998).

For many years, the sorry state of the Snowy River has been a source of

(continues)

anger and distress for Australian environmental groups. Indeed, a multitude of campaigns to restore the Snowy River to a semblance of its former glory have been launched by local and national environmental groups over the years. In 2002 those efforts finally came to fruition with the launch of a joint Victoria/New South Wales program to dramatically increase the river's flow. Ultimately, this ten-year, AU$300 million initiative aimed to return 21 percent of the Snowy's natural average flow to the river, with an ultimate goal of increasing the volume to 28 percent of its prediversion flow.

Officials associated with the project claim that the impact on irrigation operations will be minimal, for the restoration scheme emphasizes water savings projects such as paying for repairs of leaky pipelines, reduction of evaporation losses stemming from inefficient water storage infrastructure, and improved water inventory systems to monitor water use and highlight points at which water is being needlessly lost. Ranchers and farmers dependent on the diversions are skeptical of these assurances, and concerns have been raised about the potential impact of restoration on hydroelectric power generation capacity as well. But Australian conservationists and fishermen are ecstatic with the plan. Indeed, Australian Conservation Foundation president Peter Garrett hailed the measure as "a historic turnaround in the health of the Snowy" and claimed that "it symbolizes a major shift in our nation's treatment of its rivers."

Sources:
Jones, Mathew. 2000. "The Snowy Flows Again!" *Habitat Australia* 28 (December).
Pigram, John J. 1998. "Options for Rehabilitation of Australia's Snowy River." Armidale, Australia: Center for Water Policy Research.
Snowy Water Inquiry. 1998. *Final Report: Snowy Water Inquiry.* Sydney: Snowy Water Inquiry.
Victoria Department of Natural Resources and Environment. n.d. *Snowy River Journal.* Available at http://www.nre.vic.gov.au (accessed February 2003).

This embarrassment of freshwater riches is due in part to the country's rugged, mountainous character. In fact, the Maori name for New Zealand, *Aotearoa,* literally means "the land of the long white cloud," an indication of topography's influence on New Zealand's hydrology. The high Southern Alps on the South Island are a particularly important influence on distribution of precipitation. Other influential factors include prevailing westerly winds, ocean currents that carry saturated air to both islands, and the country's latitudinal position between warm subtropical waters and cool sub-Antarctic waters. The only areas of New Zealand subject to occasional shortages of freshwater are the so-called rain shadow regions on the eastern side of New Zealand's mountain ranges. In these regions, higher population densities (both human and livestock) coupled with periodic dry spells can affect urban and rural water supplies, agricultural production, and hydroelectricity generation. For example, in places such as Central Otago, east of the Southern Alps, average rainfall is about 350 millimeters (14 inches) annually; by contrast, regions west of the Alps such as Fiordland and Westland receive an average rainfall of more than 6,000 millimeters (236 inches) a year, with some locales occasionally exceeding 13,000 millimeters (512 inches) annually (New Zealand Ministry for the Environment, 1997).

In fact, water is so abundant across most of New Zealand that flooding is a major concern for agriculture, industry, and urban populations alike. Floods can occur in any season and in all regions of the country, and the severity of these events has increased since the arrival of European settlement because of land-clearing activities that have removed forests and other vegetation that absorbed excess water. Despite extensive river and catchment control schemes, damage from flooding is estimated to cost at least NZ$125 million annually (ibid.).

By world standards, the state of New Zealand's freshwater is excellent both in terms of quality and quantity; the Pupu Springs that feed the Waikoropupu River near Takaka in the South Island have been described as possibly the clearest freshwater in the world (Smith, 1998). Unlike Australia, which has naturally high sediment loading in rivers, New Zealand's rivers have low concentrations of dissolved materials, and are low in nutrients.

But while New Zealand generally has very high quality freshwater, this quality varies naturally according to the geology of the catchment and streamflow volume. In addition, water quality has been increasingly influenced by anthropogenic activities, and varies according to surrounding land use. As a general trend, water quality is higher in mountain streams and in sparsely developed areas throughout much of the South Island and the upper reaches of most North Island rivers. The quality declines measurably in lowland streams and rivers, particularly in pasture-dominated catchments where livestock degrade riparian habitat and deposit large volumes of waste into waterways (Hoare and Rowe, 1992). In some localized areas, degradation of rivers and streams has been sufficient to make water unsuitable for drinking or recreational use, and it has damaged the health of resident fish species and aquatic ecosystems (New Zealand Ministry for the Environment, 1997).

New Zealand has reported positive trends in reducing pollution of rivers and coastal waters from sewage plants, industrial facilities, factories, and other "point sources" (specific sites) over the past three decades. These gains have been attributed to increased environmental awareness and improvements in waste disposal and treatment programs.

Another source of water pollution, urban stormwater, has also been the focus of increased attention. Indeed, urban stormwater runoff has periodically caused serious problems in New Zealand's largest city, Auckland, and other metropolitan centers. Stormwater has polluted estuaries and harbors with sediment and toxic substances, including heavy metals from industrial activities and oil from buses and automobiles. At times, stormwater has also infiltrated and flooded sewerage systems (Auckland Regional Council, 1995).

In a process of reclamation to secure more agricultural land, wetland areas in New Zealand have been reduced by about 85 percent in the last century and a half, from nearly 700,000 hectares to about 100,000 hectares (Cromarty and Scott, 1996). Many of the remaining wetlands, including many that are significant repositories of floral and faunal biodiversity, are at a persistent risk of degradation from further reclamation activities, pollution, grazing, and introduced species of plants. Invasive species of plants, fish, and other animals are a growing concern in wetlands and rivers as well.

Dams have also altered the character of many waterways in New Zealand. More than 400 dams with reservoir storage capacities greater than 18,500 cubic meters have been constructed throughout New Zealand. Although these dams were built for purposes including water storage, domestic and industrial supply, and floodwater mitigation, the larger dams were constructed expressly for power generation. Indeed, fully 98 percent of the water that is harnessed for human use in New Zealand is utilized to generate electricity (New Zealand Ministry for the Environment, 1997).

This emphasis on hydroelectric energy has made New Zealand far less dependent on oil and other energy sources that contribute to air pollution, greenhouse gases, and other environmental problems when consumed. However, critics believe that large dam developments in New Zealand have wreaked major alterations on hydrologic regimes, with consequential depletion of water quality and quantity. They note that large dams create significant barriers to fish movements, including migration, which has diminished some fish populations and altered some aquatic ecosystems. Dams have also transformed entire watershed areas by flooding large valleys and raising the natural level of lakes. Some large hydroelectric dam developments in Australia, such as the Snowy River Hydroelectric Scheme, have reduced the flow of some major rivers to a virtual trickle. Other dam developments that have dramatically altered the hydrology of New Zealand's rivers and lakes include the Benmore Dam in the Waitaki headwaters, which has radically transformed downstream freshwater environments; the Manapouri power station, which

Hydro electricity station, Snowy Mountains, NSW. PAUL NEVIN/PHOTOLIBRARY/PICTUREQUEST

receives half of the flow of Southland's Waiau River via a diversion canal; and dams on Otago's Clutha, Waitaki, and Waipori rivers and the North Island's Waikato River (ibid.).

New Zealand also contains extensive groundwater aquifers, including underwater basins throughout some of the country's most agriculturally productive districts—the Canterbury Plains, Marlborough and Tasman districts, Hutt Valley, Manawatu, Hawke's Bay, the Bay of Plenty, the Waikato and Hauraki lowlands, and South Auckland. Notably, these areas are east of the Southern Alps and typically drier than the western portions of the South Island and are located within areas prone to surface water shortages or seasonal fluctuations in river flows and rainfall. At times of low supply, these groundwater reserves become an important source of supply. Overall, approximately 40 percent of New Zealand's freshwater supplies are now drawn from groundwater. Consequently, groundwater levels have fallen in most of New Zealand's flood plains, as withdrawal is not rigorously regulated (ibid.; Hunt and Bibby, 1992).

The use of coastal groundwater aquifers has led in some circumstances to seawater intrusion. In 1990, seawater intruded 600 meters (1,960 feet) into a shallow gravel aquifer at Lower Moutere near Nelson (northern South Island) after irrigation caused groundwater levels to drop. To address this situation, water use restrictions were imposed. This quick action enabled natural recharge from rainfall to replenish the aquifer. In other circumstances, however, seawater intrusion can last for many years (as has been the case in aquifers on the Heretaunga and Waimea plains and on the Coromandel Peninsula). To prevent such occurrences in the major urban center of Christchurch, the largest city on the South Island, yearly "safe yields" (withdrawal limits) have been imposed for the artesian aquifers.

Freshwater Supply in
Oceania's Pacific Island States

The twenty-two countries and territories of the Pacific islands region contain approximately 550,000 square kilometers (212,400 square miles) of land that support approximately 7.5 million inhabitants. The numerous small island states and territories of the South Pacific are similar both in their tropical climatic character and in their limited freshwater resources. The independent island states—Papua New Guinea, Fiji, Kiribati, the Marshall Islands, Nauru, Samoa, the Solomon Islands, Tonga, Tuvalu, and Vanuatu—do not have strong water-monitoring systems in place. But it is increasingly clear that on many of these far-flung isles, pressure on finite freshwater resources is becoming problematic. After all, many of these countries are bereft of rivers or freshwater lakes, relying entirely on a fragile groundwater lens floating on top of the sea's salt water. Fiji, for example, is composed of more than 300 islands, but only a handful of larger islands contain river systems or freshwater lakes of any size or volume.

In recent years, numerous Pacific Island states have cited water supply and storage issues and groundwater pollution as significant security concerns. Countries including Papua New Guinea and Samoa suffered through significant droughts in the late 1990s, and many nations have compromised their all-important groundwater aquifers through inadequate waste disposal systems and unsustainable rates of withdrawal (South Pacific Regional Environment Programme, 1998; Loerzel, 1998). In response to these trends, international organizations have urged the nations of Oceania to carefully monitor all pumping from the freshwater lens in order to mitigate unsustainable withdrawals, salt water contamination, and contamination from chemicals, dissolved salts, and other threats to water quality. "Once the lens, which is in a dynamic state of equilibrium, is contaminated (by saltwater intrusion, for example), the delicate balance between fresh and salt water may take years to reestablish in certain situations. If the problem is from a land-based source (pesticides or leachate, for example), the problem may persist much longer" (UN Environment Programme, 1999).

Entering the late 1990s, access to safe drinking water was variable throughout the region. Four countries—Niue, Tokelau, Tonga, and Tuvalu—reported being able to provide access to safe water to all of their inhabitants. Conversely, only 30 percent of the people of the Federated States of Micronesia had access to safe water, and only 23 percent of the population in Papua New Guinea—by far the largest country by land area and population in Oceania, excluding Australia and New Zealand—enjoyed access to water of good quality. In other states, water quality tends to be worst in flooded riverine and estuarine environments, and questions about water supply reliability (through periods of drought, for example) persist for a number of states (UN Development Programme, 1996).

Given the rising pressure on freshwater resources from growing populations in places like Fiji, Papua New Guinea, and the Solomon Islands, maintaining the health and vitality of freshwater ecosystems that do exist has become an even more difficult task. For example, many freshwater wetlands containing numerous endemic plant and animal species have been cleared to make way for growing populations or have been compromised by pollution emissions from new industrial, logging, and agricultural activities. These various forces are manifesting themselves across the South Pacific, from Tonga, where relatively high standards of living have spurred rising demand for water, to Fiji, where extensive use of fertilizers and pesticides by sugar cane plantations has degraded rivers and aquifers. In water-rich Papua New Guinea, meanwhile, where numerous rivers and extensive wetlands are complemented by more than 5,000 freshwater lakes, subsistence agriculture is the largest single economic activity. Most of the crops are rain-fed, which means that there is little need for irrigation. This dynamic is a major factor in the country's low per capita freshwater consumption rate (UN Food and Agriculture Organization, 2002). However, many freshwater resources have been adversely affected by mining wastes, large scale commercial agriculture, and untreated human waste. In addition, the expansion of logging practices has increased runoff volumes and sediment loads in rivers, and human interference has also been associated with the introduction of aquatic weeds and other invasive species that have disrupted natural ecosystems.

As the countries of Oceania venture deeper into the twenty-first century, freshwater protection and conservation are expected to become increasingly pressing issues. Historical shortfalls by governments in investment in urban sanitation, monitoring of water quality, and assessment of the environmental impact of major infrastructure developments (such as tourist resorts) could prove disastrous if local, national, and regional authorities do not dedicate themselves to dramatic improvements in their freshwater stewardship. Specific issues requiring significant progress in the near term include better watershed management, reductions in deforestation rates, improved public awareness of wise water use and management, reforms in agricultural water use for irrigation and other activities, and improvements in waste disposal (UN Environment Programme, 1999).

Sources:

ABARE (Australian Bureau of Agricultural and Resource Economics). 2002. "Australian Crop Report: Special Drought Issue." Canberra: Commonwealth of Australia, October 29.

Auckland Regional Council. 1995. "The Environmental Impacts of Urban Stormwater Run-off." ARC Environment Technical Publication No. 53. Auckland: Auckland Regional Council.

Australian National Land and Water Resources Audit. 2001. *Australian Catchment, River and Estuary Assessment 2002.* 2 vols. Canberra: National Land and Water Resources Audit.

———. 2001. *Australian Dryland Salinity Assessment 2000.* Canberra: National Land and Water Resources Audit.

———. 2001. *Australian Water Resources Assessment 2000.* Canberra: National Land and Water Resources Audit.

Australian State of the Environment Committee. 2001. *Australia State of the Environment Report 2001.* Canberra: Commonwealth of Australia.

Bibby, H. M., T. G. Caldwell, and T. H. Webb. 1995. "Geophysical Evidence on the Structure of the Taupo Volcanic Zone and Its Hydrothermal Circulation." *Journal of Volcanology and Geothermal Research* 68.

Campbell, A. 1994. *Landcare: Communities Shaping the Land and the Future.* Sydney: Allen and Unwin.

Cave, M. P., J. T. Lumb, and L. Clelland. 1993. *Geothermal Resources of New Zealand.* Wellington: Ministry of Commerce.

Cooper, A. B. 1992. *Rural Impacts on Water Resources.* Auckland: IIR Wastewater Management, Treatment and Technology Conference.

Cromarty, P., and D. A. Scott. 1996. *A Directory of Wetlands in New Zealand.* Wellington: Department of Conservation.

Department of Natural Resources and Mines. 2002. *The Great Artesian Basin, Facts and Figures.* Brisbane: State of Queensland.

Duncan, M. J. 1992. "Flow Regimes of New Zealand Rivers." In *Waters of New Zealand.* Edited by M. P. Mosley. Wellington: New Zealand Hydrological Society.

Freestone, H. J. 1992. "Hydrology and Large Water Projects." In *Waters of New Zealand.* Edited by M. P. Mosley. Wellington: New Zealand Hydrological Society.

Glantz, M. H. 1996. *Currents of Change: El Nino's Impact on Climate and Society.* Cambridge, UK: Cambridge University Press.

Great Artesian Basin Consultative Council. 1998. *Great Artesian Basin Resource Study Summary, Great Artesian Basin.* Brisbane: GABCC.

———. 2000. *Great Artesian Basin Strategic Management Plan.* Brisbane: GABCC.

Habermehl, M. A. 1982. "Springs in the Great Artesian Basin, Australia—Their Origin and Nature." Bureau of Mineral Resources, Geology & Geophysics, Australia Report No. 235.

Harris, J. 1992. *Fish Migration in the Darling River.* Sydney: New South Wales Fisheries.

Hillier, J. 1996. *The Great Artesian Basin: Management of Water Resources after 100 Years of Development.* Sydney: Geological Society of Australia.

Hoare, R. A., and L. K. Rowe, 1992. "Water Quality." In *Waters of New Zealand.* Edited by M. P. Mosley. Wellington: New Zealand Hydrological Society.

Hunt, B. G., H. B. Gordon, and H. L. Davies. 1995. "Impact of the Greenhouse Effect on Sea Ice Characteristics and Snow Accumulation in the Polar Regions." *International Journal of Climatology* 15.

Hunt, T. M., and H. M. Bibby. 1992. "Geothermal Hydrology." In *Waters of New Zealand.* Edited by M. P. Mosley. Wellington: New Zealand Hydrological Society.

Kingsford, R. T. 2000. "Ecological Impacts of Dams, Water Diversions and River Management on Floodplain Wetlands in Australia." *Austral Ecology 2000* 25.

Land and Water Resources Research and Development Corporation. 1998. *National Dryland Salinity Program: Management Plan 1998–2003.* Canberra: LWR-RDC.

Loerzel, A. 1998. *Protect Our Source of Life: Clean Water.* GEPA Supplement to *Pacific Daily News,* April 17.

McConchie, J. A. 1992. "Urban Hydrology." In *Waters of New Zealand.* Edited by M. P. Mosley. Wellington: New Zealand Hydrological Society.

McKellar, D. 1911. "My Country." In *The Closed Door and Other Verses.* Melbourne: Specialty Press.

Murray-Darling Basin Commission. 2000. *Review of the Operation of the Cap: Overview Report of the Murray-Darling Basin Commission.* Canberra: MDBC.

———. 2002. *Water Audit Monitoring Report 2000/01: Report of the Murray-Darling Basin Commission on the Cap on Diversions.* Canberra: MDBC.

Natural Environment Research Council. *British Antarctic Survey, 2002.* 2002. Available at www.antarctica.ac.uk (accessed January 2003).

New Zealand Ministry for the Environment. 1997. *The State of New Zealand's Environment 1997.* Wellington: Ministry for the Environment.

Smith, D. I. 1998. *Water in Australia: Resources and Management.* Melbourne: Oxford University Press.

Smith, D. J. 1998. "The World's Clearest Fresh Water?" *Water and Atmosphere* 1, no. 2.

South Pacific Regional Environment Programme. 1998. *Overview of Threats and Management Regimes for International Waters of the Pacific Region.* Apia, Western Samoa: SPREP.

———. 1998. *Coastal Management Profiles: A Directory of Pacific Island Governments and Non Government Agencies with Coastal Management Related Responsibilities.* Apia, Western Samoa: SPREP.

UN Development Programme. 1996. *The State of Human Settlements and Urbanization in the Pacific Islands.* Suva: UNDP.

UN Environment Programme. 1999. *Global Environment Outlook 2000.* London: Earthscan.

UN Food and Agriculture Organization. "AQUASTAT Information System on Water in Agriculture: Review of Water Resource Statistics by Country." Available at www.fao.org/waicent/faoinfo/agricult/agl/aglw/aquastat/water_res/index.htm (accessed December 2002).

World Resources Institute. 2002. EarthTrends Website Statistical Database. Available at www.earthtrends.wri.org (accessed December 2002).

World Wide Fund for Nature Australia. 2001. *Greening the 2001 Agenda: Priority Environment Initiatives for Commonwealth Government 2002–2005.* Sydney: WWF Australia.

———. 2003. *Global Warming Contributes to Australia's Worst Drought.* Sydney: WWF Australia.

Oceans and
Coastal Areas

The marine resources under the jurisdiction of Australia, New Zealand, and the other South Pacific Islands collectively known as Oceania dwarf the terrestrial holdings of the states in this region. Indeed, these island nations—many of them scattered archipelagos themselves—are separated from one another by vast expanses of ocean. In total, the South Pacific's twenty-four island states and territories include over 10,000 islands sprinkled over more than 40 million square kilometers (15.4 million square miles) of ocean. Many of these islands are virtual specks on the ocean surface. The Republic of the Marshall Islands alone contains more than 1,100 islands scattered across 1,210,000 kilometers(750,000 miles) of the central Pacific, but their combined land area is no larger than that of the District of Columbia (Woodard, 2000). But the same marine environment that isolates these nations and territories also serves as the region's common bond. It provides the people of the South Pacific with vital transportation, food, and economic activity, and it has profoundly influenced cultural identities and traditions in the region over many millennia.

Shared dependence on the ocean and its resources gives Australia and other South Pacific states a significant stake in preserving the environmental health of the sea, from estuaries and other coastal areas to coral reefs and deep-water regions. But at the dawn of the twenty-first century, the waters of the South Pacific are under severe stress from an array of ecological pressures including persistent overfishing, escalating levels of water pollution, and runaway coastal development. Moreover, the region's governments are grappling with the specter of global warming, which, if not meaningfully addressed by industrialized nations half a world away, could produce rising sea levels capable of engulfing several states of Oceania and partially submerging portions of many other inhabited islands.

Pacific Island Nations
Control Large Swaths of Ocean

The South Pacific's island states and territories are usually divided into three culturally and geographically distinct subregions: Micronesia (including Palau, Guam, Kiribati, Nauru, the Northern Mariana Islands, the Marshall Islands, and the Federated States of Micronesia), Melanesia (including New Guinea, Vanuatu, New Caledonia, Fiji, the Solomon Islands, and parts of Papua New Guinea), and Polynesia (including New Zealand, Tuvalu, Tonga, Samoa, Wallis and Futuna, French Polynesia, Pitcairn Island, and the Cook Islands). All told, the South Pacific Islands region includes nine independent nations (Fiji, Kiribati, Nauru, Papua New Guinea, Solomon Islands, Tonga, Tuvalu, Vanuatu, and Samoa), six self-governing entities that maintain some association with their former colonial power (Cook Islands, Niue, Federated States of Micronesia, Palau, Northern Mariana Islands), and eight territories, associated with the United States (American Samoa, Guam, and the Northern Marianas), France (New Caledonia, Wallis and Futuna, and French Polynesia), New Zealand (Tokelau), and the United Kingdom (Pitcairn Island). Australia is sometimes lumped in with the rest of Oceania, but it is more often defined as a separate region of the world in recognition of its greater size, unique geographical and cultural characteristics, and economic stature.

Under the UN Convention on the Law of the Sea, which came into force in 1994, all coastal nations have sovereign control over the waters and seafloor that lie up to 12 miles (19.4 kilometers) off their shores, as well as dominion over seas extending 200 miles (323 kilometers) from inhabitable land. The latter area is known as an Exclusive Economic Zone, or EEZ, and this element of the global treaty provides even the smallest South Pacific Island nation with sovereign rights to explore, conserve, exploit, and manage the natural resources contained within significant expanses of sea. The thirty-three islands that constitute the tiny Micronesian nation of Kiribati, for example, have a total land area of only 313 square miles (811 square kilometers), but these islands extend across about 2,400 miles (3,900 kilometers) of ocean, enabling the country to claim the world's eleventh-largest EEZ, at approximately 1 million square miles (more than 3 million square kilometers) (Howe, 1994). All told, the total EEZ area for the states and territories of Oceania, excluding Australia and New Zealand, is 30.6 million square kilometers (11.8 million square miles), about one-sixth of the earth's total surface area (South Pacific Regional Environment Programme, 1998).

Over the years, the nations of Oceania have occasionally used the combined size of their EEZs as leverage in international negotiations on fisheries management and other marine issues. In the 1980s, several nations of Oceania operating under the organizational banner of the South Pacific Forum used their extensive legal jurisdiction over waters coveted by international fishing fleets to nudge larger, industrialized nations toward an international ban on driftnetting, a fishing practice long condemned by environmentalists and scientists because it entangles and kills large numbers of birds, marine mammals, and other "by-catch" (nontarget species). First, the island nations united to forbid the use, possession, and transit of driftnets longer than 2.5 kilometers (1.5 miles) in the waters of member states. They then successfully lobbied the United Nations for passage of an international moratorium on driftnetting that went into effect in December 1992 (Weber, 1994).

But the nations of Oceania have not always spoken with a unified voice on marine issues, in part because of the region's singular island cultures and the stunning variety of languages spoken (an estimated 1,200 distinct languages are spoken in Oceania, including 700 in Papua New Guinea alone). In addition, Oceania has extremely limited economic and political clout on the world stage in nonmarine areas. These factors have diluted the island states' influence in the creation and implementation of international ocean policies.

In contrast, Australia and New Zealand—possessed of significant terrestrial holdings, comparatively large, wealthy, and educated populations, and huge EEZs of their own—have exercised much greater influence over the marine resources of the South Pacific. Australia and New Zealand hold the world's third- and fourth-largest exclusive economic zones, respectively, with Australia claiming 4.8 million square kilometers (1.854 million square miles) of ocean and New Zealand 4.64 million square kilometers (1.793 million square miles) (each nation has about 6 percent of the global EEZ total) (South Pacific Regional Environment Programme, 1998). Australia and New Zealand also have a combined population of more than 23.5 million people, while the other states and territories of the Pacific Islands have only 7.5 million residents among them (Secretariat of the Pacific Community, 1998). In addition, Australia and New Zealand have a combined land area of 8 million square kilometers (3.1 million square miles). The other states and territories of Oceania have a total land area of only 550,979 square kilometers (212,733 square miles), 84 percent of which is accounted for by Papua New Guinea.

Australia and New Zealand also are the South Pacific's lone nations with modern economies; the other countries of Oceania are in varying stages of economic development, but none are remotely in the same league as Australia. On most island states, poverty and heavy dependence on foreign aid are long-standing realities, and environmental degradation is pervasive because of heavy use of pesticides, unsustainable rates of deforestation, poorly planned coastal development, and untreated releases of municipal and industrial effluents. All of these activities have had a deleterious impact on the quality of the coastal waters upon which islanders depend so much for food and jobs. "Our land to sea ratio is generally so small that, with the possible exception of the largest land masses of Papua New Guinea, all our islands are wholly coastal in character," explained the South Pacific Regional Environment Programme. "This means that the whole island influences, or is influenced by, marine coastal and near-shore activities and processes. It also means that a natural or anthropogenic disaster such as a cyclone or a pollution accident often affects the entire society and economy of an island" (South Pacific Regional Environment Programme, 1998).

Fisheries

Overfishing in Australia and New Zealand

The South Pacific is one of the world's largest swaths of ocean, but it provides only about 2 percent of the globe's total fishery production in terms of weight (UN Food and Agriculture Organization, 2002). Nestled next to the productive, shallow waters of the Tasman Sea and island states to the north, New Zealand possesses the region's single largest commercial fishery. In the mid-1990s the nation's fleet accounted for about 70 percent of the total marine capture registered by the combined fishing industries of Australia and New Zealand.

But while Australia is not among the world leaders in commercial fishing—it ranks only around fiftieth in the world in tonnage of fish caught annually (about 200,000 tons a year) despite having the globe's third-largest EEZ—its catch has a relatively high monetary value because it is heavily skewed toward the harvest and export of expensive seafood such as oysters, scallops, lobster, and tuna. In addition, saltwater sport fishing ranks as one of Australia's most popular outdoor pursuits. The Australian government estimates that about 25 percent of the nation's populace is actively engaged in the sport, and it estimates that about 30,000 tons of seafood are harvested by sportfishers each year (Commonwealth of Australia, 1998).

The modest size of the fisheries located off Australia's shores is attributed to the continent's smallish continental shelf and a relative dearth of nutrients upon which marine species feed. Australia's few rivers deliver low nutrient loads to coastal waters, and offshore currents do not deliver upwellings of nutrient-rich deep waters. Of those marine species that do exist in Australian waters, however, many are unique to that part of the world. In the nation's southern temperate waters, as much as 80 percent of the species are endemic—not found anywhere else (ibid.).

Figure 7.1 World Capture Fisheries and Aquaculture Production

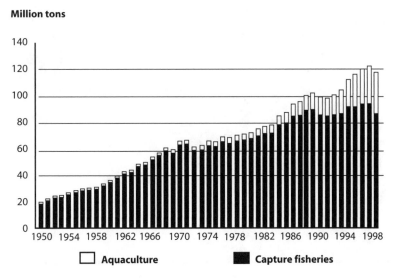

Million tons

SOURCE: UN Food and Agriculture Organization

Both New Zealand and Australia are harvesting some fish species at rates near or exceeding levels of sustainability. Efforts to relieve pressure on stressed fisheries have ranged from catch quotas to licensing restrictions, but in many cases these steps have been taken only after evidence of dramatic declines in fish populations becomes impossible to ignore. Moreover, attempts to rein in the fishing industry are complicated by the potential economic repercussions on fishing communities. In Australia, for instance, marine industries contribute about Aus$30 billion a year—8 percent of the country's gross domestic product—and account for about 7 percent of the country's total export value (ibid.).

Some analysts have touted aquaculture as a means of relieving fishing pressure on wild species. Numerous farms producing oysters, pearls, trout, and ornamental fish have already been established, and the industry has enjoyed particularly strong growth in rural areas. In 1990, Australia's aquaculture production was valued at Aus$200 million. By 1996, it had nearly doubled, and it is projected to reach Aus$1.4 billion by 2005 (ibid.). But as other observers note, the environmental implications associated with these operations are not insignificant. They include loss of estuaries utilized by wild species for feeding and breeding, contamination of near-shore waters with chemicals and waste from penned fish, loss of genetic diversity in farmed species, and damage to wild stocks that breed with escapees from aquaculture operations (Zann, 1995).

Subsistence fishermen on Ifaluk Atoll in the Caroline Islands. ANDERS RYMAN/CORBIS

Fishing Sustains the Island Nations of Oceania

Contemporary fishing practices in the sovereign waters of the island states of Oceania take wildly different forms. On numerous islands, subsistence fishermen ply their trade in much the same way as did their ancestors. They roam out to near-shore fishing grounds (typically shallow-water shelves or coral reefs) each morning in primitive dugout boats or massive double-outrigger canoes, then slip back to shore at day's end, their nets weighed down with the fish that feed their families and pay for clothing and other necessities. Indeed, many of Oceania's communities rely on marine fisheries as their primary source of protein. But the South Pacific is also patrolled by hundreds of deep-sea fishing vessels, with flags from nearly two dozen countries fluttering over decks bristling with modern fishing accoutrements. Indeed, some South Pacific states now earn more from access fees, paid by deep-water foreign fishing fleets that wish to harvest within their territorial waters, than they do from any other economic sector (Hinrichsen, 1998; UN Food and Agriculture Organization, 2002).

Most of the foreign fishing fleets that crisscross the South Pacific are pursuing tuna. The Pacific Islands region is the most productive tuna fishing area in the world, accounting for approximately one-third of all harvested tuna. The economic value of this fish eclipses that of all other fisheries in the region.

According to the South Pacific Regional Environment Programme, the total regional tuna catch in 1995 was valued at U.S.$1.7 billion, six times the value of all other Pacific Island fisheries combined. In Oceania, the amount of tuna caught is more than nine times that of all other fisheries combined. Yet only 7 percent of the annual tuna catch is taken by vessels flying flags of one of the Oceania states; the remaining 93 percent is harvested by fleets hailing from China, Japan, Taiwan, Australia, the Philippines, South Korea, the United States, and other nations. This distribution is a major reason why less than 0.25 percent of the international tuna catch enters the domestic food supply of Pacific Island states (South Pacific Regional Environment Programme, 1998).

Certainly, the access fees that the Pacific Islands charge for tuna fishing rights are an important boon to their economies. In fact, these fees represented about 10 percent of the combined GDP of Pacific Island countries in the mid-1990s. But access license fees charged in the mid-1990s amounted to less than 4 percent of the total value of the regional tuna catch, which means that foreign fishing industries are pocketing most of the money generated by the harvest of tuna stocks (ibid.).

Some tuna populations in the South Pacific have dropped significantly in recent years, a development attributed primarily to years of overzealous harvesting. Southern bluefish tuna populations, for instance, declined precipitously in the mid-1980s, and environmentalists continue to classify the species as critically endangered. Signs of unsustainable fishing are evident in skipjack and albacore fisheries as well (UN Food and Agriculture Organization, 2002). But fishing pressure on tuna stocks remains very strong. The Japanese fleet, for instance, continues to harvest and import large volumes of sashimi-grade bluefin and bigeye tuna from the waters of Oceania. These species are sold in Japan for as much as U.S.$50,000 a fish for use in making sashimi, a popular dish of thinly sliced raw fish. The size of Japan's tuna harvests has drawn fire from environmental groups and some marine scientists, who claim that overfishing of tuna and other top predators is triggering major changes in the region's marine ecosystems. For its part, the Japanese fishing industry contends that southern bluefin tuna populations have been underestimated, and it continues to press for higher catch quotas.

Indications that tuna and other stocks are being harvested at unsustainable rates have not escaped the notice of the governments of the Pacific Islands. In fact, these states have historically displayed a conservationist approach to marine species management, in part because of their own limited capacity for deep-water fishing, but also because of entrenched traditions of local resource ownership and deeply felt awareness of the importance of sustainable fishing practices in preserving community stability (Preston, 1997; South Pacific

Table 7.1 Tuna Catch by Major Species in the Secretariat of the Pacific
Community Statistical Area

Year	Skipjack	Catch (thousands of tons) Yellowfin	Albacore	Bigeye	Total
1976	167.5	62.0	30.0	42.8	302.4
1977	200.2	73.6	35.9	41.1	350.8
1978	230.0	86.0	30.4	27.9	374.3
1979	186.4	82.7	25.4	39.1	333.7
1980	211.8	104.5	39.8	41.6	397.7
1981	254.6	110.2	31.1	28.2	424.2
1982	266.6	111.2	28.8	29.0	435.6
1983	426.1	141.3	20.2	26.5	614.1
1984	434.8	129.4	19.6	32.2	616.0
1985	367.3	124.6	27.3	40.5	559.6
1986	431.1	126.4	32.5	34.5	624.4
1987	406.9	183.2	23.7	40.7	654.5
1988	541.6	127.9	33.2	35.7	738.3
1989	531.3	181.2	47.5	34.2	794.2
1990	589.3	202.8	31.0	52.1	875.2
1991	759.1	229.3	24.6	36.7	1,049.6
1992	686.4	275.4	41.2	44.0	1,047.0
1993	535.8	284.3	34.3	49.4	903.8
1994	663.2	263.4	38.5	59.3	1,024.4
1995	666.8	215.8	38.3	37.3	958.2

SOURCE: Secretariat of the Pacific Community, 2000

Regional Environment Programme, 1998). But Oceania's island states have
limited resources to conserve, manage, and study their marine resources. For
example, the Pacific Island states have little power to repel foreign fleets that
illegally swoop across maritime boundaries and conduct harvesting operations in sovereign waters. They also have only meager resources to enforce
fishing regulations on catch quotas and fishing practices. As a result, fishermen continue to use explosives, cyanide, bleach, and other destructive tools
on fish-rich coral reefs off the waters of American Samoa, Fiji, the Marshall
Islands, the Federated States of Micronesia, and other regions of Oceania with
little fear of punishment.

Finally, pressures to make fishery management decisions for short-term
economic gain are growing across Oceania, as native peoples look to garner a
greater share of the riches being pulled out of the sea. Indigenous commercial
tuna-fishing vessels are proliferating in the Pacific Islands, with Fiji, the
Solomon Islands, and American Samoa all now maintaining their own deep-

water fleets. "As the region's small island states and territories evolve into modern economies, their traditional fisheries management systems are crumbling. Worse, as those traditional methods of coastal governance—based on clan and community enforcement—collapse, they leave no viable enforcement mechanisms in place" (Hinrichsen, 1998).

Marine Pollution in the South Pacific

Australia and the other nations of the South Pacific region oversee large sections of ocean and coastline in which relatively pristine conditions still prevail. But other marine ecosystems of the region—and especially those systems adjacent to coastal population centers—have suffered considerable damage as a result of human activity. Indignities visited upon these fragile waters every day include partially treated or untreated sewage; agricultural pesticides and fertilizers; livestock waste; sediments generated by mining, forestry, farming, and coastal dredging; airborne pollutants from automobiles, mining operations, and power plants; discharges of heavy metals and other pollutants from industrial facilities; seepage from landfills; and discharges of cooling water from power plants and industrial sites that destroy temperature-sensitive sedentary species such as corals.

Water Quality in Australia Linked to Population Pressure

Much of Australia's coastline is lightly populated and undeveloped. In these regions, the environmental condition of bays, estuaries, and near-shore reef areas is excellent. But marine conditions near coastal metropolitan areas—where about 85 percent of all Australians live—have deteriorated markedly over the past three decades. In these areas, long stretches of coastline have been sacrificed to make way for marinas, residential developments, and commercial activities. Moreover, these rapidly expanding cities generate ever-greater amounts of trash, sewage, and other pollutants that eventually infiltrate and degrade near-shore marine habitats. As a result, pollution from heavy metals, municipal waste, and other contaminants has become so severe in some urban estuaries and bays that conditions constitute a public safety concern. "Public health may be at risk from high concentrations of faecal coliform and enterococcal bacteria in estuarine and coastal waters, either through contact recreation (especially swimming) or consumption of contaminated seafood," admitted the Australian government. "Along some beaches (e.g., in the Sydney harbour) and under certain conditions (following heavy rains or sewage system overflows), beach users risk a range of illnesses such as carditis, conjunctivitis, hepatitis, and skin and wound infections" (Commonwealth of Australia, 1998).

During the 1990s, Australia did make substantial gains in upgrading sewage treatment plants, treating and reusing stormwater and wastewater, and implementing coastal water quality monitoring programs. After years of inaction and equivocation, Australia also produced a comprehensive national oceans policy in 1998. This policy hinges on the formation of regional marine plans that will be binding on all governmental agencies. It includes a multitude of specific goals as well, from reviewing ocean transport regulations and the environmental impact of aquaculture operations to seeking greater international conservation protection for the great white shark (ibid.).

But despite this increased attention from federal authorities, "the quality of estuarine coastal and inshore waters has not improved over the past five years on a national basis. Water quality has improved in specific localities and regions, such as coastal waters off Sydney [but] more than half of Australia's estuaries are modified and are not in good condition as a result of the pressures caused by human settlements. Fragmentation of responsibilities for estuary management [between local, provincial, and national agencies] is delaying improvements to the condition of estuaries" (Australian State of the Environment Committee, 2001).

The latter factor is a particularly vexing obstacle to greater habitat protection. In 1989, Australia's federal government agreed to pass regulatory responsibility for the first three nautical miles offshore to state governments (responsibility for waters further offshore—the nation's EEZ—remained with federal authorities). But responsibility for many local land use decisions (beachfront development, restrictions on commercial or recreational activity, implementation of nature conservation areas) is often passed down to the municipal level, albeit within broad state planning parameters. Many municipal boards are decidedly prodevelopment in their outlook, making it difficult for environmentalists and other proconservation constituencies to realize even modest preservation goals.

Further inland, meanwhile, widespread clearing of land for agriculture has generated massive runoffs of sediments and nutrients that are ultimately deposited in fragile estuaries, causing eutrophication and other problems. Indeed, toxic algae blooms erupted with increasing frequency and severity along the shores of both Australia and New Zealand during the 1990s. In addition, pollutants carried by air and water from Australia's extensive mining operations have contributed to the degradation of coastal waters. All told, land-based pollution is believed to contribute up to 80 percent of all marine pollution entering Australian waters (Zann, 1996; Australian State of the Environment Committee, 2001).

Another problem bedeviling sections of Australia's coastline is deposition of trash, much of it nonbiodegradable in nature. "Australia's beaches are increasingly littered with plastic bottles, plastic bags, tangled fishing lines, nets and other rubbish. Litter comes from 'tourist trash' left by beach-goers or is washed there. The latter comes from land litter washed from catchments and stormwater drains, from ships' garbage, from discarded fishing gear from anglers and fishing boats, and from remote sources far across the ocean. Urban beaches are worst affected, but even the most remote coastal and island beaches are not free from litter" (Zann, 1995).

Australia's dependence on sea transport for trade has also impacted near-shore waters. Approximately 97 percent of Australia's total trade volume is transported via marine shipping, with most goods carried by foreign shipping services. This situation has made Australian waters particularly vulnerable to alien species that accompany these vessels in their ballast waters or on the outside of hulls. Studies indicate that at least 200 species of foreign origin have been introduced into Australia's seas in this manner, and while the Australian government acknowledges that "many of these species slip quietly and unnoticed into our marine systems, forming small populations that do not interfere with the ecosystem," it notes that "some of these species cause dramatic changes and threaten entire habitat types, and some cause toxic algal blooms that threaten oyster and mussel fisheries and the health of those who eat affected shellfish" (Commonwealth of Australia, 1998). In recognition of this threat, Australia has taken a leading role in international efforts to combat the introduction of exotic species in marine areas.

Finally, Australia utilizes marine transport as the primary vehicle for exporting oil, and it maintains significant offshore oil exploration and drilling facilities. Indeed, offshore petroleum operations generate approximately $8 billion annually, contribute $2.4 billion in tax revenue each year, and account for 85 percent of the country's petroleum consumption (ibid.). In both of these areas, Australia has a very good safety and environmental record. The nation's offshore oil exploration and drilling operations have lost only an estimated 800 barrels of oil to the sea, and while three major tanker spills (defined as over 1,000 tons) have been recorded in Australian waters over the years, none appear to have caused major or permanent ecological damage. Indeed, the leading source of marine oil pollution in Australia is oil-laced materials that enter the sea from sewage and drainage systems.Nonetheless, the possibility of a major spill accident from offshore facilities or a tanker mishap troubles many Australians, for even a minor spill could devastate fragile marine habitats such as near-shore coral reefs, which can trap oil slicks in species-rich

Australia's Great Barrier Reef is under threat from record warm temperatures, overfishing, and pollution.
REUTERS NEWMEDIA INC./CORBIS

near-shore areas. The environmental repercussions associated with major oil contamination events are so great that Australian law strictly forbids oil and gas exploration in and around the Great Barrier Reef, the continent's most famous natural treasure. Nonetheless, oil pollution remains a threat to this and other areas. "Every year 200 tankers carrying over 100,000 tons of oil, and 1800 ships with up to 5000 tons of fuel oil, travel along the inner route between the coast and the outer [Great Barrier] Reef. A large spill could not move out to open ocean, and limited wave activity means that it would not disperse well by natural agitation. It could ruin the reef life and the beauty of the reef over large areas" (Young, 2000).

Among the nations of Oceania, disposal of raw sewage and other waste materials has been a perennial problem, and one that appears to be worsening. Few states or territories have effective sewage treatment facilities, and regulations governing industrial releases of pollutants are inadequate. As a result, the coastlines around nearly every urban center in the Pacific are strewn with untreated sewage, municipal wastes, and household refuse (Hinrichsen, 1998). Countries and territories such as Fiji, New Caledonia, Guam, and Papua New Guinea have fouled large sections of their coastlines with industrial pollutants, visiting particularly severe damage on estuaries and bays that are essential components of marine ecosystems. Fiji's heavily populated Suva Harbor, for example, has been transformed into a toxic mix of heavy metals, untreated sewage, and chemical effluents. Some of these pollutants enter the harbor directly, while others leach into the waterway from the Suva city dump, which is situated directly next to the harbor. These pollutants, trapped in the port area by an offshore reef that severely limits exchange of harbor water with that of the open sea, have made consumption of local shellfish and fish a serious health issue (Cripps, 1992; Sheppard, 2000).

Other pollution problems defy easy answers as well, for they are deeply interwoven into the socioeconomic dynamics of the islands. For example, litter is discarded indiscriminately, with little regard for the environment or aesthetic beauty, by residents of many island states. As a result, trash is an unfortunate presence on countless beaches, mangroves, and other natural areas in Oceania. This entrenched acceptance of pollution as a "natural" state of affairs within societal mores makes ecologically sound personal and business behavior tremendously difficult to institute. In addition, many South Pacific states continue to make extensive use of chemicals that are banned or heavily regulated in other parts of the world. For example, use of the pesticide DDT has been outlawed in many other areas of the world because of its deadly impact on wildlife and concerns about public safety. But DDT and other hazardous chemicals are widely utilized across much of the South Pacific, with few restrictions on their implementation or disposal.

Reefs and Other Marine Resources

The South Pacific is home to some of the world's greatest concentrations of ecologically significant marine treasures. Australia's coastal waters, for instance, have the largest seagrass and coral reef systems on the planet, and its shoreline holds the world's third-largest area of mangrove forest. But increased pollution emissions from industry and agriculture, coupled with wholesale land conversions, both inland and along coastal areas, have dramatically escalated pressure on these resources (Wilkinson, 2000). The marine resources of the states and territories of Oceania are also at risk, their integrity jeopardized by pollution generated by increasingly urbanized populations with limited financial and institutional ability to implement effective marine protection mechanisms. "Urbanization is a trend that the South Pacific shares with virtually every other region of the world," observed one expert. "But small islands, with limited space and resources, can least afford the damaging effects of crowded coasts" (Hinrichsen, 1998).

Reefs of the South Pacific

Coral reefs constitute the single most important and extensive of the various types of marine ecosystems in the South Pacific. A vital source of breeding, nursery, feeding, and shelter habitat for fish and shellfish caught for sport, subsistence, and commercial purposes, reefs also generate economic activity in a host of other ways, from attracting international tourists to providing coasts with protection from severe weather events (South Pacific Regional Environment Programme, 1998).

In the mid-1990s approximately 70 percent of the South Pacific's coral reef resources—believed to be about 15 percent of the world total—were classified as being in good or excellent condition. But the remaining 30 percent, including sections of internationally famous reef systems such as Australia's Great Barrier Reef, had been degraded to one extent or another by runoff pollution, sedimentation, overfishing, coral mining, and fishing with cyanide or other environmentally destructive tools (Jameson, 1995; Wilkinson, 2000). Since then, the amount of reef area believed to be under imminent threat from human activity has continued to increase.

Virtually no region of Oceania still boasts pristine reef resources. On the Solomon Islands, for instance, large-scale—and largely unregulated—logging and mining operations have virtually destroyed near-shore coral reefs and other habitat vital for fish and shellfish stocks, and the outlook for stemming this abuse is grim (as of 1996 more than four dozen mining companies were exploiting mineral deposits in the islands). Elsewhere, in the Mariana Islands, a 1996 survey revealed that more than 90 percent of the archipelago's coral reefs were in poor to fair condition, with less than 50 percent of the reefs still showing live coral cover. And in Tahiti, the main island of French Polynesia, the region's coral reefs have been abused by a multitude of destructive human activities, including overfishing, mining and dredging, coastal development, and heavy discharges of raw sewage and industrial waste (Grigg, 1996; Wilkinson, 2000).

The greatest of the South Pacific's reef systems is Australia's Great Barrier Reef, and it too is under stress from human activities. Composed of approximately 2,900 distinct reefs and 940 islands, the Great Barrier Reef stretches for about 2,500 kilometers (1550 miles) off the shoreline of western Australia. The single largest system of coral reefs on the planet, it is believed to hold more than 400 species of coral, 4,000 species of molluscs, 1,500 species of fish, 6 species of turtles, 35 species of sea birds, and 23 species of sea mammals (Zann, 1996).

Much of the Great Barrier Reef remains in good shape, with marine ecosystems functioning without major disturbances from human activities. Oil drilling and mining activities are banned throughout the reef's waters, and as the centerpiece of Australia's extensive system of marine parks, activities in and around the reef are closely regulated and monitored. But concerns about the long-term health of the Great Barrier Reef have intensified in recent years. Water quality in some inshore areas has declined markedly, eroded by massive conversions of land to agricultural use, which in turn has increased discharges of sediments and nutrients into the sea. Overfishing of reef species and introductions of exotic species from passing ships have also been blamed for upsetting the balance of delicate reef ecosystems. The crown-of-thorns starfish has also emerged as a deadly threat to the reef in recent decades. Periodic population explosions of this creature, which devours the coral polyps that build reefs, have damaged nearly 20 percent of the Great Barrier Reef over the past thirty years (ibid.).

Environmentalists and scientists also have expressed serious concern about a possible recurrence of a 1998 "coral bleaching" episode that damaged coral reefs around the world ("bleaching" is a process wherein reefs lose the algae upon which they depend for their survival). Attributed to unusually high ocean temperatures and intense solar radiation, the 1998 outbreak affected 87 percent of the system's inner reefs and 28 percent of its offshore reefs.

In recent years, somber warnings about the possible future of the Great Barrier Reef have proliferated. A 2001 World Wide Fund for Nature study reported that the inshore coral and seagrass meadows of the Great Barrier Reef were under particular stress, claiming that 28 million tons of sediment flowed into the waters of the Great Barrier Reef each year, the equivalent of 3.5 million dump trucks emptying soil onto the reef. The report blamed this trend on the wholesale changes taking place in the reef's catchment area, stating that nearly 77 percent of the catchment had been converted to grazing land, leaving only 11 percent of the land as undeveloped wilderness. It also charged that up to 80 percent of freshwater wetlands, which filter pollution runoff before contaminants enter the reef area, have been lost on account of cane growing—which produces high concentrations of nitrates—and other coastal development (World Wide Fund for Nature, 2001). One year later, the Australian Institute of Marine Science issued a report that echoed many of the WWF's findings. The Australian Institute of Marine Science study bluntly warned that large expanses of the Great Barrier Reef were slowly choking to death on fertilizer and pesticide-laden runoff created by the clearance of wetlands and forests for agricultural purposes along Australia's western coast. "Terrestrial runoff may have serious indirect and long-term impacts when acting in combination with storms, coral bleaching or crown of thorns starfish outbreaks," it concluded (Australian Institute of Marine Science, 2001).

Flora and Fauna under Stress in South Pacific Waters

Australia and Oceania possess some of the world's greatest tracts of seagrasses and mangroves. Australia's waters contain the largest expanses of seagrasses on the globe, and mangrove forests adorn the shorelines of numerous South Pacific islands. Both seagrasses and mangroves are significant ecological assets. Mangroves, which are especially prevalent in the western reaches of Oceania, contribute to coastal water quality by acting as a sink for sediments, nutrients, pollutants, and contaminants that can damage marine ecosystems. They also serve as a buffer against cyclones and other severe weather events, and play an important role as breeding, feeding, and shelter habitat for a variety of marine species. Seagrasses, which also exist in greater abundance in western Oceania, also provide food, shelter, and breeding habitat for many species, including endangered dugong and sea turtle species. In addition, seagrass beds aid in stabilizing coastal lands and help maintain coastal water quality by filtering nutrients.

Still, these linchpins of the South Pacific's coastal ecosystems are in jeopardy in some areas. Countless mangroves have been cut down across the region to make way for new commercial and residential construction, while numerous other stands are dying because of sustained and intensive exposure to hazardous chemicals and other pollutants. Seagrass beds have also been depleted by sewage and sediment from urban runoff. These discharges create toxic blooms that crowd out seagrasses and other marine life, leaving barren seafloor. Loss of seagrasses is a growing problem in many developing South Pacific states, but it is also apparent in the waters of Australia. Indeed, localized depletion of seagrass beds is evident all around the continent, from Cockburn Sound in Western Australia to South Australia's Gulf of St. Vincent (Young, 2000). Inevitably, these losses have harmed marine wildlife. For example, the loss of seagrass beds has been cited as a significant factor in the dramatic downturns in populations of loggerhead turtles and dugongs in Australian waters.

Despite these problems, however, the South Pacific continues to boast a high level of marine biodiversity, especially in near-shore waters. The region contains globally significant populations of numerous rare and endangered species, including whales, sharks, marine turtles, giant clams, dugongs, and crustaceans. In addition, the region nourishes important populations of sea lions, fur seals, tuna, marlin, swordfish, and other creatures, including terns, cormorants, albatrosses, and other seabirds.

Many of these species are thriving, in part because conservation efforts have increased in recent years. But human activities still affect wildlife populations in a variety of unintended ways, and in some cases the impact has been significant. For example, mesh netting erected near swimming areas to keep out dangerous species of sharks has been implicated in the deaths of large numbers of dolphins, dugongs, and gray nurse sharks, which are now imperiled (Australian State of the Environment Committee, 2001). Elsewhere, trawling by fishing vessels has been blamed for steady declines in green and loggerhead turtle populations in northern Australia.

Marine Protected Areas in Australia and Oceania

Creatures that make their home in Australian waters have benefited enormously from that nation's extensive system of marine parks. Indeed, Australia is the global leader in this regard. In the mid-1990s, it held about one-quarter of the total number of marine parks in the world (Zann, 1995), and during the late 1990s state, territorial, and commonwealth governments passed a flurry of legislation establishing several new protected areas. By the close of the twentieth century, Australia had formally designated 190 marine protected areas (MPAs) covering 60 million hectares (Australian State of the Environment Committee, 2001), and in 2002 it announced plans to create a new 6.5 million hectare reserve around the Heard Island and McDonald

Islands group, located 4,500 kilometers (2,790 miles) southwest of the mainland and 1,000 kilometers (620 miles) north of Antarctica. Formal protection of this sub-Antarctic island group, which maintains pristine ecosystems that support charismatic albatross, seal, and penguin species, will create the globe's largest fully protected marine reserve.

The crown jewel of Australia's MPA system, though, is Great Barrier Reef Marine Park. Currently the largest marine park in the world—it covers an area larger than the United Kingdom—it protects most of the reef's sprawling length. This region first received formal protection from the Australian government in 1975, when proposals to establish offshore oil drilling and mining operations on the reef sparked public outrage. Today, it is managed as a multiple-use park, with sections cordoned off exclusive for marine preservation, scientific research, light tourism, and some types of commercial fishing.

Elsewhere in the South Pacific, the level of meaningful protection for marine areas varies considerably. Some island states and territories have established conservation areas of laudable size and number to protect reefs, beaches, mangrove forests, and other ecological treasures from development or exploitation. In recent years, five Pacific Island nations have even declared their EEZs to be whale sanctuaries (South Pacific Regional Environment Programme, 2002). But other nations of Oceania have not yet established significant protections for any of their coastal or marine resources.

Climate Change Models
Suggest a Bleak Future for Oceania

Global warming has emerged as one of the world's most pressing environmental issues. But whereas the impact of climate change associated with global warming may bring wrenching change to the ecosystems, economies, and demographic characteristics of the industrialized nations of Europe, North America, and other parts of the world, it threatens to constitute a truly cataclysmic event in the South Pacific. Scientists believe that if greenhouse gas emissions continue to increase, spurring incremental but steady increases in the earth's temperature, sea levels will rise as the poles' massive ice sheets melt and shrink. Under climate change models of the Intergovernmental Panel on Climate Change (IPCC), global average temperatures and sea levels will rise significantly from 1990 to 2100. According to IPCC models, temperatures are projected to rise by 1.4 degrees Celsius (3 degrees Fahrenheit) to 5.8 degrees Celsius (12.5 degrees Fahrenheit), and sea levels will rise from 0.1 meter (3.9 inches) to 0.9 meter (35.5 inches) (Intergovernmental Panel on Climate Change, 2001).

A worldwide rise in sea level of even modest proportions would increase Oceania's vulnerability to storms, which may become more frequent in a warming world. Hurricanes and other storms will be more likely to infiltrate deep inland, poisoning already limited croplands and freshwater supplies with salt. Moreover, essential infrastructure—homes, businesses, fishing vessels and canneries, and so forth—may become more vulnerable to storms of even moderate strength.

Even more significantly, rising sea levels would claim a significant percentage of the total land area of the South Pacific states, and totally submerge many islands altogether. "For many small-island states, sea-level rise will not be simply expensive but apocalyptic, a most biblical end to their land, culture, and history. A 3-foot rise would consume much, but not all, of the Federated States of Micronesia and the Solomon Islands in the Pacific and the Maldives in the Indian Ocean. It would completely submerge at least three nations that consist entirely of atolls: the Marshalls, Kiribati, and Tuvalu. . . . Not surprisingly, the governments of small island states attach greater urgency to climate change issues than most countries" (Woodard, 2000).

Already, the threat of global warming has attracted serious attention from Oceania's states and territories. A number of South Pacific nations have joined with other island countries around the world to form a diplomatic block called the Association of Small Island States in order to lobby industrialized nations like the United States, China, and India to reduce their greenhouse gas emissions. In addition, several South Pacific states are already diverting funds that would normally be spent on education and health care toward climate-change preparation programs (ibid.).

In some areas of Oceania, these preparations include the creation of evacuation plans. According to a 1992 study of the National Oceanic and Atmospheric Administration, saving the Marshall Islands from rising sea levels and storms would require the entire output of the Marshallese economy over at least a century. In a warming world, peoples such as the Marshallese will have no option but to relocate. "Retreat may take the form of Marshallese moving to least vulnerable areas within or among atolls in the country, with Majuro Atoll being developed as the ultimate safe haven for the nation," stated NOAA. "Full retreat of the entire population of Majuro Atoll and the Marshall Islands must be considered in planning for worse case [sea-rise] and climate change scenarios" (Holthus, 1992).

If sea levels do rise significantly as a result of global warming, mass relocations of affected peoples will almost surely be implemented, preventing serious loss of human life. Already, New Zealand's government is openly studying ways in which it might incorporate refugees from imperiled states into its population with a minimum of economic and social disruption. But if the peoples of Oceania are ultimately forced to abandon their homelands, their cultures will ultimately be lost under the waves as well.

Sources:

Acharya, Anjali. 1995. "Small Islands: Awash in a Sea of Troubles." *World Watch* (November–December).

Anderson, Ian. 1996. "Return of the Coral Eaters." *New Scientist* (February 3).

Australian Fisheries Management Authority. 2001. *Annual Report 2000.* Canberra: AFMA.

Australian Institute of Marine Science. 2001. "Long-Term Monitoring of the Great Barrier Reef: Status Report No. 5." AIMS, CRC Reef Research Centre, and the Great Barrier Reef Marine Park Authority, November.

Australian State of the Environment Committee. 2001. *Australia State of the Environment Report 2001.* Canberra: Commonwealth of Australia.

Bleakley, Chris. 1997. *Review of Critical Marine Habitats and Species in the Pacific Islands Region.* Apia, Samoa: Strategic Action Programme for International Waters of the Pacific Islands Region.

Commonwealth of Australia. 1998. *Australia's Oceans Policy.* 2 vols. Canberra: Commonwealth of Australia.

Cripps, K. 1992. "Survey of Point Sources of Industrial Pollution Entering the Port Waters of Suva." Suva: Ports Authority of Fiji.

Grigg, Richard, and Charles Birkeland. 1996. *Status of Coral Reefs in the Pacific.* Sydney: Scientific Committee on Coral Reefs of the Pacific Science Association.

Hinrichsen, Don. 1998. *Coastal Waters of the World: Trends, Threats, and Strategies.* Washington, DC: Island Press.

Holthus, P., et al. 1992. *Vulnerability Assessment of Accelerated Sea Level Rise: Case Study: Majuro Atoll, Marshall Islands.* Apia, Western Samoa: SPREP.

Howe, K. R., Robert C. Kiste, and Brij V. Lal. 1994. *Tides of History: The Pacific Islands in the Twentieth Century.* Honolulu: University of Hawaii Press.

Intergovernmental Panel on Climate Change. 1998. *The Regional Impacts of Climate Change: An Assessment of Vulnerability.* Geneva: IPCC.

———. 2001. *Climate Change 2001: Mitigation, Impacts, Adaptation, and Vulnerability: Summaries for Policymakers.* Geneva: IPCC.

Jameson, Stephen, John McManus, and Mark Spalding. 1995. *State of the Reefs: Regional and Global Perspectives.* Washington, DC: National Oceanic and Atmospheric Administration.

Organization for Economic Co-operation and Development. 1998. *Environmental Performance Reviews: Australia.* Paris: OECD.

Nickerson, Colin. 1994. "Stripping the Sea's Life." *Boston Sunday Globe,* April 17.

Preston, Garry L. 1997. *Review of Fishery Management Issues and Regimes in the Pacific Islands Region.* Apia, Samoa: Strategic Action Programme for International Waters of the Pacific Islands Region.

Secretariat of the Pacific Community. 1998. *Pacific Island Populations.* Noumea: SPC.

Sheppard, Charles, ed. 2000. *Seas at the Millennium: An Environmental Evaluation.* 3 vols. Oxford: Pergamon.

South Pacific Regional Environment Programme. 1998. *Changing Climate and Sea Levels Affect Pacific Countries.* Apia, Samoa: SPREP.

————. 1998. *Strategic Action Programme for International Waters of the Pacific Islands Region.* Apia, Samoa: SPREP.

————. 2002. *Action Strategy for Nature Conservation in the Pacific Islands Region, 2003–2007.* Apia, Samoa: SPREP.

UN Environment Programme. 1999. *Global Environment Outlook 2000.* London: Earthscan.

UN Food and Agriculture Organization. 1997. *Fisheries and Aquaculture in the South Pacific: Situation and Outlook in 1996.* Rome: FAO.

————. 2002. *State of World Fisheries and Aquaculture 2002.* Rome: FAO.

Wachenfield, D. R., J. K. Oliver, and J. I. Morrissey. 1998. *State of the Great Barrier Reef World Heritage Area 1998.* Townsville: Great Barrier Reef Marine Park Authority.

Weber, Peter. 1993. *Abandoned Seas: Reversing the Decline of the Oceans.* World Watch Paper No. 116. Washington, DC: World Watch Institute.

————. 1994. *Net Loss: Fish, Jobs, and the Marine Environment.* World Watch Paper No. 120. Washington, DC: World Watch Institute.

Whitty, Julia. 2001. "Shoals of Time." *Harper's Magazine,* January.

Wilkinson, Clive, ed. 2000. *Status of Coral Reefs of the World: 2000.* Townsville: Australian Institute of Marine Science.

Woodard, Colin. 2000. *Ocean's End: Travels through Endangered Seas.* New York: Basic.

World Resources Institute. 2000. *World Resources 2000–2001, People and Ecosystems: The Fraying Web of Life.* Washington, DC: World Resources Institute.

World Wide Fund for Nature. 2001. *Great Barrier Reef Pollution Report Card.* WWF.

Young, Ann. 2000. *Environmental Change in Australia since 1788.* 2d ed. South Melbourne: Oxford University Press.

Zann, Leon P., ed. 1995. *Our Sea, Our Future: State of the Marine Environment Report for Australia.* Canberra: Department of the Environment, Sport and Territories.

————. 1996. *The State of the Marine Environment Report for Australia: Technical Summary.* Canberra: Department of the Environment, Sport and Territories.

8

Energy and Transportation

Australia, New Zealand, and the rest of Oceania—twenty-two nations and territories sprawled across a 30-million-square-kilometer (11.6-million-square-mile) section of the southern Pacific Ocean—have exhibited increased interest in pursuing renewable energy technologies over the past two decades. But while New Zealand and, to a lesser degree, Australia have made some progress in increasing their energy consumption levels from hydroelectric, wind, sun, and other renewable energy sources, the region's energy infrastructure—including burgeoning transport systems in Australia and New Zealand—and its economic prosperity remain heavily dependent on coal and oil, fossil fuels that have been blamed for degrading wildlife habitat, damaging biodiversity, compromising human health, and contributing to global climate change.

Energy Use and Its Impact on the Environment

Humankind's ability to harness energy to meet its basic needs and socioeconomic aspirations is an essential component of today's modern world. Indeed, energy is the foundation upon which modern industrial civilizations from the United States to Europe to Australia have been built, and the manipulation of energy—whether it comes from wood, hydroelectric installations, nuclear facilities, natural gas, oil, coal, or renewables—continues to provide people around the world with the capacity to keep their families warm and fed and able to pursue their livelihoods.

However, while energy use is enormously beneficial to individuals, communities, and nations, the pursuit and consumption of energy is not without its drawbacks, especially in ecological terms. Energy use has a host of direct and indirect impacts on the environment. "The indirect impacts arise from the things that plentiful energy enables us to do, such as driving to or through sensitive ecosystems (creating vehicle and visitor impacts in forests and sand dunes), modifying landscapes, clearing forests and draining wetlands (made easier by heavy machinery), generating noise (from machinery and sound equipment), and generating hazardous wastes (from manufacturing processes)," observed the New Zealand Ministry for the Environment. "Other indirect impacts arise from the mining, manufacture and energy use that go into constructing power stations, turbines, generators and associated energy-extraction technology" (New Zealand Ministry for the Environment, 1997). Most forms of energy use—and certainly the ones that dominate today's energy picture—also have significant *direct* impacts on the environment. These impacts accumulate at all stages of the energy use cycle—extraction, storage, transport, and consumption. Specific environmental problems associated with the use of energy include degradation of the atmosphere (most notably through emissions of greenhouse gases responsible for global climate change), air pollution, water pollution, soil pollution, and habitat alteration and destruction (and associated diminishment of biodiversity), all of which influence the health and welfare of human communities.

Continued heavy dependence on fossil fuels—oil, coal, and natural gas—has emerged as a source of particular concern in the past half-century. These energy sources underpin much of the global economy today, but apprehensions about dwindling fossil fuel supplies and the ecological impact of locating, extracting, transporting, and consuming these resources are considerable. For example, extraction and transport of coal—Australia's main energy source—has been implicated in the degradation and erosion of fragile soils; the fragmentation and destruction of species-rich habitats such as forests and meadowlands; and the contamination of rivers, streams, and aquifers (through wastewater discharges, toxic tailings, and landscape changes). At the consumption end, meanwhile, the consequences of coal consumption include heavy emissions of air pollutants and carbon dioxide, the main heat-trapping "greenhouse gas" responsible for global climate change, and discharges of warm, chemical-laced wastewater that undermine the ecological integrity of watersheds.

Fossil fuel extraction and delivery operations have also come under fire for their impact on the world's air, land, and water resources. Critics in the environmental and scientific communities contend that drilling rigs, roadways, pipelines, and other infrastructure used to tap and deliver oil and gas carve up wildlife habitat, contaminate fragile rivers and aquifers with industrial pollutants, and diminish the wilderness character of undeveloped areas. And while natural gas consumption does not degrade surrounding air or water, airborne emissions from automobiles and other oil-dependent sectors continue to generate air pollutants and greenhouse gases responsible for global warming.

Figure 8.1 Total Consumer Energy by Fuel in New Zealand, 2001

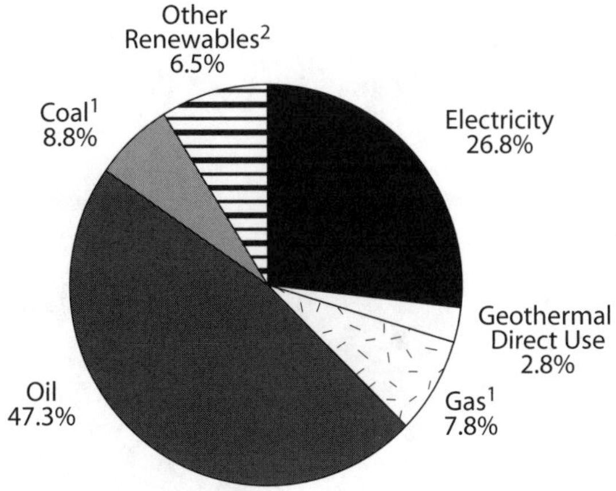

SOURCE: UN Food and Agriculture Organization

NOTES: 1. Excludes cogeneration. 2. Includes direct use of biogas, industrial waste, and wood.

Technological innovations and public policy adjustments have enabled developed nations to blunt the ecological impact of fossil fuel use in some ways, such as reducing emissions of air pollutants from coal-fired power plants and automobiles. But many environmentalists, scientists, policy-makers, and community leaders believe that preservation of the earth's land, water, and air resources will require a much greater investment in and dedication to renewable energy technology.

Australia Remains
Heavily Dependent on Coal and Oil

Energy Use in Australia

Australia is the only country in the South Pacific/Oceania region with internationally significant reserves of fossil fuels. In 2001, Australia had 8.3 percent of the world's proved coal reserves (approximately 82 billion tons). No other nation in Oceania had more than 0.1 percent of the planet's coal reserves (BP, 2002). Australia's consumption of coal rose steadily throughout the 1990s, jumping by 10 million tons of oil equivalent from 1991 to 2001, when it consumed 47.6 million tons of oil equivalent (about 2.1 percent of the world total) (ibid.). But the presence of extensive coal beds and low population densities have nonetheless enabled the country to maintain its station as the world's largest exporter of coal, with most shipments delivered to rapidly growing economies in Southeast Asia.

In terms of oil, Australia has 3.5 thousand million barrels in proved oil reserves, approximately 0.3 percent of the global total. In 2001 the country

Coal mining operation in Ravensworth, Australia. COREL

consumed 845 thousand barrels (38.1 million tons of oil), about 1 percent of worldwide consumption. Australia also has about 90 trillion cubic feet of proved natural gas reserves, approximately 1.6 percent of global reserves. A net importer of natural gas, Australia consumed 22.5 billion cubic meters of natural gas in 2001, 6 percent of the world total. In terms of hydroelectric power, Australia accounted for only 0.7 percent of world consumption in 2001 (3.9 million tons of oil equivalent) (ibid.).

Australia currently has no nuclear power facilities in operation. Australia flirted with developing a nuclear power program in the late 1960s and early 1970s, but it was eventually abandoned; Australian authorities have voiced official opposition to nuclear energy ever since. Public opposition to nuclear power is strong as well, but not universal. Proponents of nuclear energy have urged Australian policy-makers and communities to reconsider their utility as an energy source. They note that the technology could reduce Australia's heavy dependence on coal-fired electricity plants, which have contributed to the country's status as the second biggest air polluter on the planet by per capita measurement. Antinuclear conservation organizations, though, reject claims that nuclear energy is an appropriate response to air pollution and climate change problems created by consumption of coal and other fossil fuels. They charge that waste disposal and security concerns associated with nuclear energy programs would place the environment and human communities in too much jeopardy.

All told, coal accounts for about 70 percent of Australia's total energy production, with another 27 percent roughly divided between oil and natural gas and the remaining 3 percent generated by hydroelectric facilities and renewable energy sources. Coal is also the single greatest energy source consumed in Australia, accounting for 40 to 45 percent of total consumption in recent years. Oil (and natural gas liquid) provides another 35 percent of Australia's total energy consumption, with most of the consumption taking place in the gasoline-hungry transport sector. Natural gas satisfies another 15 to 20 percent of Australia's total energy needs, while "green" power (renewables) accounts for roughly 6 percent of annual energy consumption. Overall, Australia's large coal industry enables it to export nearly five times as much energy as it imports (International Energy Agency, 2002). In addition, some experts forecast that Australian coal exports could double by 2015 as industrial and household demand for electricity surges in Asian nations that are experiencing rapid increases in population and economic growth. This is an alarming scenario to supporters of the Kyoto Protocol, a UN-sponsored agreement designed to reduce emissions of greenhouse gases responsible for global climate change. Australia, however, has refused to ratify Kyoto and is instead urging a course that emphasizes voluntary measures to reduce emissions.

Trends in Energy Consumption

Not surprisingly, Australia's steadily growing population and robust economic development have produced increases in energy consumption. But according to many indicators, energy consumption across Australia is actually outpacing population and economic growth rates. For example, end-use consumption of energy by Australia's residential sector surged by 60 percent from 1975 to 1999, even though the country posted an overall population increase of only 35 percent during that period (Australian State of the Environment Committee, 2001). Today, Australia ranks among the world leaders in energy use per capita. Moreover, "'[b]usiness as usual' projections indicate that this growth is expected to continue unless significant policy and practice changes occur. Over the past 25 years, renewable energy consumption has increased by only 50 percent, much less than the growth in fossil fuel use" (ibid.).

One factor in Australia's high per capita energy consumption is the country's energy pricing structure. The cost of gasoline and electricity in Australia is lower than in most other parts of the world. In fact, from 1997 to 1999, Australia was the only country in which electricity prices declined (Energy Efficiency and Conservation Authority, 2001). These low energy prices give

Australian households and industries only limited economic incentive to conserve or improve energy consumption efficiency. Indeed, the average Australian household spends only 3 percent of its budget on energy (Australian State of the Environment Committee, 2001).

The industry and transport sectors (both private and commercial) account for most (85 percent) of Australia's total energy consumption, and current population, demographic, and economic trends suggest that demand for energy in these areas will continue to rise. Energy consumption by Australian households (excluding transportation) amounts to less than 15 percent of the country's total, though it should be noted that much of the energy used by industry and commercial sectors is consumed for the purpose of providing goods and services for individuals and families. That caveat aside, household energy use per capita has actually risen at a slower rate than other sectors—15 percent from 1975 to 1999—despite increased use of appliances, growing "quality of life" demands, and declining household size (declining household size tends to increase energy use per capita because each home has many appliances and heats a dwelling, regardless of the number of people living there) (ibid.). Analysts note that energy use in the residential sector would be much higher were it not for the introduction of various energy-efficiency programs specifically targeted at residential users, such as those governing the sale and use of major appliances.

Australia has declared a Mandatory Renewable Energy Target (MRET) that requires electricity suppliers to produce an additional 2 percent of their electricity from renewable sources—excluding hydropower—by 2010. If that goal is reached, this added renewable energy capacity will be able to provide for the residential electricity needs of 4 million people, about 20 percent of the country's current population. The MRET, coupled with various subsidies and other schemes to encourage investment in renewables, reflects a widely held belief that "green" energy will play an increasingly important role in the twenty-first century. But in late 2002, Australia's federal government announced its intention to scrap funding for the Australian Centre for Renewable Energy (ACRE), a major cog in research and development in solar and fuel cell technologies, while at the same time granting almost $70 million to a major mining company engaged in research on "geo-sequestration," a technology that aims to store carbon dioxide underground. Around the same time, the Council of Australian Governments (COAG) called for the abolishment of the MRET, even though it is the commonwealth's only mandatory greenhouse pollution policy and the centerpiece of national efforts to encourage investment in renewable technologies. COAG recommended replacing the MRET program with a national emissions trading scheme. A review of the

Figure 8.2 Residential Electricity Prices in Australia and Selected Countries, January 1999

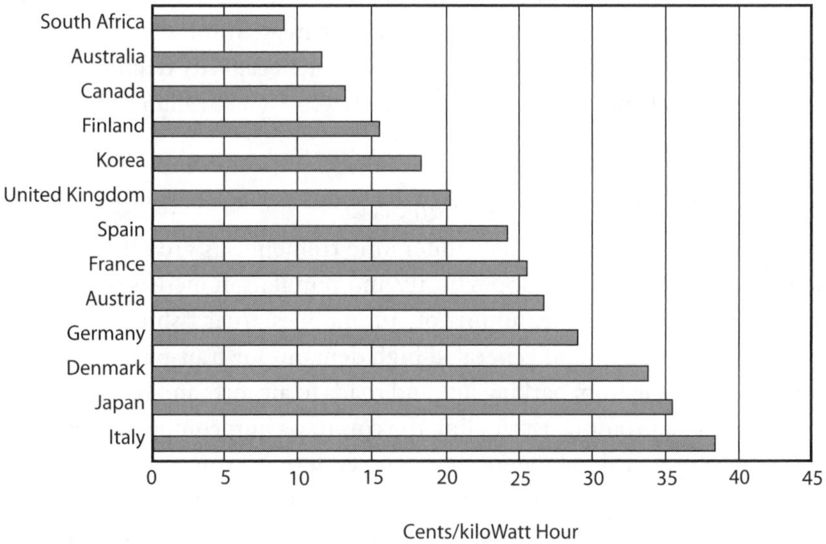

Cents/kiloWatt Hour

SOURCE: Electricity Supply Association of Australia

MRET legislation is scheduled to take place in 2003. Opponents hope to kill it outright; advocates are hoping to further bolster it by increasing the targeted renewable energy goal from 2 percent to 5 or even 10 percent.

"Clearly, the projected trends of ongoing growth in energy use from fossil fuels are inconsistent with the achievement of Australia's environmental goals," acknowledged one major commonwealth-sponsored study (ibid.). But within Australia, opinions vary about the most appropriate path to take in reducing fossil fuel dependence. Members of the environmental community have urged the implementation of an assortment of measures to reduce fossil fuel energy use, from new efficiency programs to changes in pricing structure. But their overarching contention is that Australia must significantly boost the amount of energy it generates from renewable sources. "Australia is a sunburnt country that is also windswept and girt by sea, and therefore has huge potential sources of renewable energy," declared the environmental report *A Continent in Reverse,* sponsored by a consortium of sixteen environmental groups (Christoff, 2002). In recent years, though, the commonwealth has emphasized efficiency gains over reductions in fossil fuel dependence as the most appropriate course of action. "Although there is scope to reduce energy losses in the energy supply system, and to switch to energy sources with lower environmental impacts, more efficient use of energy at the point of consumption is often the most cost-effective means of reducing environmental impacts of energy. For example, buying a more energy-efficient refrigerator can cut energy use for food storage by 30 percent or more. This not only cuts the household's energy bill, but also allows savings to be made throughout the energy supply chain, by reducing the energy supply system capacity required and the amount of coal burned to generate electricity" (Australian State of the Environment Committee, 2001).

Australia's Swelling Transportation Sector

Australia's transport sector has undergone tremendous growth in the last half-century, as economic opportunity and population increases have produced historic highs in the number of automobiles, trucks, ships, and planes crisscrossing its lands and generated high demand for transportation infrastructure (ranging from parking lots and roads to airports and harbors).

Major transportation arteries link the country's burgeoning metropolitan areas concentrated along the southern and eastern coastlines, and Australia's railroad yards, harbors, and airports all bustle with commercial activity.

Not surprisingly, the fuel needs of the transport sector (both individual and commercial) account for a significant amount of Australia's total energy consumption—40 percent or so in recent years (Organization for Economic Cooperation and Development, 2002). Road transport alone is responsible for about 30 percent of Australia's energy consumption annually. In addition, road transport may very well account for a greater share of Australia's overall energy consumption in coming decades, because of very high rates of car ownership, heavy investment in commercial truck transport systems, and ever-growing reliance on private transport (rather than public transit systems) to reach workplaces, grocery stores and shops, and recreational destinations that are growing ever more distant from one another because of the growth in metropolitan boundaries. In the late 1990s, the average Australian road vehicle traveled nearly 15,000 kilometers (9,300 miles) a year, with passenger vehicles (cars, trucks, and motorcycles) accounting for nearly 80 of total travel. Nearly one-quarter of all mileage generated by passenger vehicles was for commuting purposes, a reflection of the increasing distances that separate home and workplace across the continent (Australian Bureau of Statistics, 2000).

This dynamic of increased motor vehicle numbers on the road and growing travel distances are having a host of impacts on Australian quality of life. The widespread availability of cars and improvements in road networks provide communities with increased mobility, which in turn enables individuals and families to access a wide array of community offerings, including lucrative employment opportunities far from home, access to markets for business, and access to a cornucopia of social, recreational, shopping, and personal services. But there are also negative impacts from increased motor travel in both the social and environmental realms. In Melbourne, Sydney, and other cities, traffic congestion is a problem that seems to worsen by the week. Traffic slowdowns and gridlock not only irk commuters but also impose significant costs on business productivity and efficiency and exacerbate the road sector's emissions of chemicals that degrade air quality and contribute to climate change. Indeed, from an environmental perspective, congestion is a major contributor to vehicle emissions. Fuel consumption per vehicle under congested traffic conditions is approximately twice that registered under noncongested conditions. Therefore, congestion has the potential to double the output of greenhouse gas emissions from a stream of vehicle traffic (Australian Bureau of Statistics, 2001).

At this point, the cost of gasoline in Australia is relatively low by international standards. Only the United States and Canada have posted lower gasoline prices in recent years. This abundance of comparatively inexpensive gasoline has provided Australians with little financial incentive to curb their travel, and it remains an obstacle to new investment in public transport, which remains largely limited to inner-city cores.

New Zealand Relies on Renewable/Nonrenewable Mix

New Zealand's Energy Sector

New Zealand harnesses energy from a myriad of sources. It remains dependent on nonrenewables for about two-thirds of the nation's energy supply. Oil provides approximately one-third of its total primary energy supply, because of the gasoline needs of its transport sector. Imported oil accounts for 30 percent of New Zealand's total energy supply, while indigenous oil accounts for less than 3 percent of the nation's energy supply (Ministry of Economic Development, 2003). Reliance on natural gas, meanwhile, has increased over the past two decades as a result of the discovery of new reserves and the belief that it has fewer environmental drawbacks than oil or coal. It currently accounts for less than 30 percent of energy use, but analysts believe that its share of the country's energy market could increase in coming years. Coal, meanwhile, accounts for only about 7 percent of the country's energy.

New Zealand supplements its nonrenewable energy sources with a very strong hydroelectric scheme. Energy generated from the hydroelectric facilities that gird its numerous rivers accounts for around 20 to 25 percent of the country's energy production and consumption annually, including 70 to 80 percent of its total electricity (Energy Efficiency and Conservation Authority, 2001), depending on water supplies and electricity demand. Indeed, New Zealand has used its wealth of rivers and streams to surpass neighboring Australia in the sheer amount of energy derived from hydropower, and it accounts for about 0.8 percent of world hydropower consumption (5 million tons of oil equivalent) (BP, 2002). Other energy sources include geothermal steam, firewood, solar heating, and wind power. Nuclear energy is not utilized in New Zealand, and prospects for investment in this technology in the future are dim, given widespread popular skepticism about its safety and its impact on the environment.

New Zealand's investments in geothermal energy and hydroelectric systems have enabled it to pull about one-third of its total energy supply from renewable sources (water in both of these cases). But environmentalists, scientists, and policy-makers contend that renewable energy could become an even bigger contributor in the future, if New Zealand is willing to invest in other green energy options, including wind power, biofuels, solar power, and ocean tides and waves (the energy of which could be harnessed by turbine systems similar to those in place at hydro power stations) (New Zealand Ministry for the Environment, 2001).

Energy consumption has increased across the board in New Zealand in recent years, with residential, commercial, transport, agricultural, and industrial sectors all posting spikes in their energy requirements. But the greatest growth since 1980 has been in the transport sector, which now accounts for 35 to 40 percent of all energy used. By contrast, industry, residential, and commercial sectors report steadily rising energy needs, but the rate of growth pales beside that of the fast-expanding transport sector, so industry, residential, and commercial sectors all account for slightly smaller shares of New Zealand's total energy consumption than in past decades (New Zealand Ministry for the Environment, 1997). "Overall New Zealand's energy consumption has increased markedly since the 1950s," admitted one government report. "From the early 1980s to the early 1990s it climbed more steeply than ever before. Although the population rose by only 17 percent between 1974 and 1995, energy consumption increased by 53 percent" as a result of new investment in the smelting, petrochemicals, and steel-making industries (ibid.).

Investing in Green Sources of Power

In the last quarter-century, New Zealand has implemented a number of reforms and initiatives in the energy sector. In the late 1980s the federal government consciously decided to divest itself of many direct responsibilities in the energy sector. In subsequent years it reduced its involvement by transferring energy generation, transmission, and exploration efforts to the private sector, by deregulating energy markets, and by introducing a royalties regime to encourage international investment in oil and gas exploration. Under these reforms, much of the responsibility for regulating activities in the energy industry devolved to local authorities who assumed primary responsibility for enforcing pertinent laws and regulations and ensuring that energy producers avoid, mitigate, or remedy any and all environmental impacts associated with exploration, transport, and production activities (ibid.).

The federal government, meanwhile, remains heavily involved in efforts to realize greater energy efficiencies in New Zealand homes and businesses. "At the consumer end, a considerable amount of our daily energy consumption is wasteful or plain unnecessary," declared the Ministry for the Environment. "This applies to both businesses and domestic households. Electricity, for example, however generated, is a relatively expensive form of energy, in money and in natural resources. Minimizing its use is therefore a good way of saving costs and the environment. Local power supply authorities are now offering energy efficiency advice and services. . . . Some large industrial sites are now installing co-generation power plants to harness energy from their waste materials while others are trying to make savings in other ways, such as making greater use of insulation, natural light, or longlife fluorescent bulbs" (ibid.). Toward this goal of greater energy efficiency, New Zealand has launched a variety of programs under the Ministry for the Environment's Cleaner Production Programme and the Energy Efficiency and Conservation Authority, a small government agency created in 1992 with a clear mandate to find ways for New Zealanders to use energy in a more sustainable manner (Energy Efficiency and Conservation Authority, 2002).

New Zealand acknowledges that its energy needs will almost certainly increase in the coming decades, given current trends in population growth, economic activity, and living standards. With this in mind, it remains interested in discovering and developing new oil and gas fields, introducing additional dams and geothermal stations, and pursuing advantageous trade agreements for the import of oil, natural gas, and other nonrenewables.

But New Zealand is also engaged in a concerted effort to bolster its energy security and reduce environmental problems associated with other types of energy through the promotion of renewable energy sources. Toward this end, the country recently passed the Energy Efficiency and Conservation Act (EECA) 2000, a landmark piece of legislation with a two-pronged emphasis on (1) promoting energy efficiency and energy conservation, and (2) moving New Zealand toward a sustainable energy future through increased investment in renewable energy systems and technologies. One year later, the country announced the launch of its National Energy Efficiency and Conservation Strategy, the creation of which was mandated by the EECA 2000 legislation. "[It] dominates the recent energy management landscape," declared the EECA. "New Zealand was not the first nation to adopt such a comprehensive template for energy management, but we believe that we are better placed than many other nations when it comes to producing the positive results we seek." The Strategy includes fifty-seven specific targets/goals influencing all sectors of New Zealand society, from energy generators, importers, wholesalers, and retailers to government agencies, local authorities, community groups, and end-users (both business and residential) with an eye toward increasing energy efficiency in all sectors and expanding the role of renewable energy in meeting the nation's energy needs (ibid.).

Studies undertaken by the New Zealand government have concluded that renewables with the greatest promise are small hydroelectric installations, biofuels, and wind power. The government has identified more than 170 river sites across the North and South Islands that could be outfitted with weirs or dams used by small power stations, with the bulk of these sites located in the more heavily populated North Island. Support for further investment in hydroelectric power, however, is complicated by debate over the environmental advantages and drawbacks of hydroelectricity. In earlier decades, harnessing the might of New Zealand's wild rivers to provide "clean energy"—energy that does not pollute the air with greenhouse gases and other pollutants generated by fossil fuel consumption—was widely popular and regarded as environmentally benign. But the environmental impact of existing and proposed new hydroelectric plants can be significant. For example, dams in New Zealand (and elsewhere) have been faulted for disrupting natural river behavior, destroying riverine ecosystems, and flooding species-rich upstream habitat.

New Zealand may ultimately display greater enthusiasm for biofuel technology and wind power. It has been estimated that if New Zealand converted 1 million hectares of pasture land to plantations of fuel crops, the annual energy yield could equal 85 percent of the nation's current primary energy supply. Similarly, studies indicate that wind farms could generate up to 30 percent of the country's current electricity consumption if all potential sites were developed (Energy Efficiency and Conservation Authority and Centre for Advanced Engineering, 1996; New Zealand Ministry for the Environment, 1997).

Certainly, the country is ideally situated geographically to reap the benefits of wind power, which produces no greenhouse gases or other pollutants. Strong winds and sea breezes are a daily fact of life across New Zealand, inasmuch as the country lies squarely in the path of the southern hemisphere's prevailing northwesterly winds. In recent years, scientists have identified at least a dozen sites distributed across the North and South Islands that are well-suited for wind farms. In addition, wind power is comparatively inexpensive to install because farms do not require major alterations of landscape for construction purposes. This gives wind farms considerable flexibility in size and scope, and perhaps even more important, leaves only a faint—and temporary—ecological footprint on the land. Only 1 percent of the land on which a wind farm is built is actually taken up by the turbines, leaving the remaining 99 percent of land area available for farming and other economic activities. Moreover, wind farms do not leave behind mines, dams, wells, and other infrastructure, unlike operations to capture conventional fossil fuels. Instead, windmills can be dismantled without leaving major scars on the landscape (Energy Efficiency and Conservation Authority and Centre for Advanced Engineering, 1996). The chief environmental drawback associated with wind farms is bird mortality, especially in areas where birds congregate or along migratory corridors. Otherwise, the main complaints leveled against wind power are aesthetic ones. Noise levels from turbines can be high in the immediate vicinity, and some people do not like to see the natural splendor of the landscape marred by rows of towering windmills trailing off to the horizon.

Others signs of heightened commitment to more sustainable energy use are proliferating across New Zealand as well. For instance, in 2001 drought conditions across large parts of New Zealand sparked water shortages that threatened some hydroelectric operations. But a government-sponsored conservation program helped city and rural dwellers alike weather the shortfall. "Two positives emerged from the experience. Many householders and companies came to rapidly understand the value of energy efficiency and conservation measures. A potential loss of supply put the issue into sharp focus. Also the electricity industry realised it was ill-prepared for a dry season, and has since acted to prepare contingency plans" (Energy Efficiency and Conservation Authority, 2002). In 2002, meanwhile, New Zealand passed minimum energy performance standards and mandatory labeling schemes for a variety of domestic appliances, then followed that up with a proposal to implement a carbon tax targeted at fossil fuel consumption. Most recently, in early 2003, the New Zealand government announced that it will support the development of two proposed wind farms by giving them Kyoto Protocol climate change "carbon" credits for the clean energy they will produce. "Electricity from these wind farms would avoid some gas or coal-fired generation, with its associated greenhouse gas emissions," explained

Energy Minister Pete Hodgson. "That is clearly in New Zealand's interests but the initial costs mean that the wind farms would probably not proceed without the credits the government is offering." Hodgson said that the wind farms could deliver emission reductions of up to 1 million tons of carbon dioxide over the protocol's first commitment period of 2008–2012.

Transport Sector Presents Challenges

At the beginning of the twenty-first century, New Zealand maintained approximately 82,000 kilometers of local roads and another 10,700 kilometers of state highways. These arteries of commerce and recreation are supplemented by a 4,000-kilometer (2,500-mile) rail network, thirteen commercial ports, and twenty-seven airports (including seven international airports). This modern transportation system has brought New Zealand's citizenry myriad socioeconomic benefits, but many of its elements—from roadways and other transportation infrastructure to the vehicles themselves—can have adverse effects for human health and the environment. Road systems contribute to the fragmentation or outright elimination of species-rich habitat, and they provide corridors for the spread of invasive pests and weeds into fragile natural areas. Emissions generated by cars, trucks, boats, locomotives, and airplanes pollute the air and water, and disposal of the 30 million liters of used oil generated every year is a vexing problem. In fact, each year, domestic transport contributes more than 40 percent of New Zealand's total carbon dioxide emissions and accounts for 40 percent of the country's total energy use (New Zealand Ministry for the Environment. "Transport." n.d.).

The challenge of reining in transportation's impact on the environment is likely to become even more daunting in the coming years. Transport energy demand grew at an average rate of 3.6 percent annually from 1991 to 2000, and there are few indications that the sector's appetite for fuel has been slaked. In addition, New Zealand's national government currently invests more than $1.6 billion annually in land transport alone, primarily through its National Land Transport Fund. However, pressures to relieve congestion in its largest cities could spur additional expenditures in new roads leading into areas that have thus far been spared development. New Zealand's growing attraction as an international tourism destination (international visitor arrivals have risen from 530,000 in 1985 to more than 2 million annually) has also produced higher emissions from ships and airplanes, and has been cited as a factor in increased traffic congestion in the country's larger cities.

In addition, New Zealand's motor vehicle fleet—already one of the largest in the world per capita—continues to grow. From 1990 to 1999, the number

This wind turbine generator supplies power to Wellington, New Zealand. PAUL A. SOUDERS/CORBIS

of registered private motor vehicles in the country jumped 26 percent, and from 2000 to 2015, the number of motor vehicles is expected to swell from 2.5 million to 3.1 million (ibid.). By contrast, public transit systems remain largely an afterthought in the New Zealand transport landscape. In the late 1990s only 2.2 percent of travel in New Zealand was made by bus and only 0.25 percent by rail.

Given these patterns, the environmental community and other interested constituencies have urged policy-makers to increase their investment in alternative fuels and public transit. Citing the success of urban rail systems in Auckland and Wellington, and the popularity of commuter ferry services in Auckland (3.6 million passengers a year), these advocates assert that increased funding for maintenance, expansion, and other customer service improvements would make mass transit options—whether bus, rail, or ferry—much more attractive to commuters, tourists, and shoppers. But this vision of mass transit as a more visible and vibrant part of the country's social and economic landscape can not be realized without the support of the public. And thus far, most New Zealanders have shown little inclination to park their automobiles, trucks, and motorcycles in favor of a bus or ferry, even though they have a deserved international reputation as environmentally enlightened citizens in such realms as habitat protection and biodiversity conservation.

Oceania Relies on
Outside Sources for Energy

Most Pacific Island Countries (PICs) do not produce any oil or natural gas and are thus dependent on imports of fuel for most of their energy needs. These imports are supplemented, especially in rural households, with wood that is used for basic heating and cooking purposes. A few states have river resources that could enable them to generate hydroelectric power, but thus far only Fiji and Papua New Guinea have made these types of investments.

Energy consumption among all the South Pacific states and territories is quite low by international standards, both in terms of total consumption and per capita consumption. For example, per capita energy use in the United States in the 1990s was approximately thirty-five times greater than in Papua New Guinea and more than nineteen times that of Fiji. Energy efficiency in the region is also low, as states and territories composed of multiple inhabited islands and atolls located many miles apart struggle to disperse energy resources to individual communities in a cost-effective manner.

Given the archipelago character of many states and territories in this region of the world—and the extremely small land area of most PICs—shipping networks understandably reign as the dominant element in most regional transport sectors. Indeed, many Pacific Island states maintain well-established and extensive systems for marine transport of cargo and passengers to and from the region's numerous inhabited islands. Among those PICs that have airports, they are almost invariably located in the same city as the country's most commercially important port. Fiji is the lone exception to this rule of thumb.

Many observers have urged Oceania to reduce its reliance on imports of oil and other nonrenewable fuels by developing green energy schemes. After all, Pacific Island states have extremely limited budgetary resources, and when they shoulder the financial burden of transporting energy resources to their shores, even less money is left for already inadequate health and education programs. In addition, dependence on foreign oil and biomass diminishes the quality of the region's air and water resources and triggers localized degradation of forest resources around settlements. Investment in renewables, on the other hand, could produce benefits in job creation, improved energy security, and more money for health and education programs, as well as reducing the strain on water and land resources upon which many Pacific Islanders continue to depend for their subsistence livelihoods. "It is an exasperating picture, particularly when the alternative is so attractive," admitted one analysis

(UN Development Programme, 1996). But if Oceania is to make progress in harnessing its wealth of wind and sun resources for energy, major regulatory and financial reforms will have to be implemented and community involvement and support will need to be nurtured.

Sources:

Australian Bureau of Resource Economics. 1999. *Getting Energy and Greenhouse Gases into Perspective.* Canberra: ABARE.

Australian Bureau of Statistics. 1997. *Australian Transport and the Environment.* Canberra: ABS.

———. 2000. *Survey of Motor Vehicle Use 2000.* Canberra: ABS.

———. 2001. *Australia's Environment: Issues and Trends 2001.* Canberra: ABS.

———. 2003. *Year Book Australia.* Canberra: ABS. Available at http://www.abs.gov.au (accessed March 2003).

Australian State of the Environment Committee. 2001. *Australia State of the Environment Report 2001.* Canberra: Commonwealth of Australia.

BP. 2002. *BP Statistical Review of World Energy 2002.* London: Group Media and Publications.

Christoff, Peter. 2002. "Australia: A Continent in Reverse." Report prepared for nineteen environmental and conservation groups in response to *WSSD-Australian Assessment Report.* Australia.

Energy Efficiency and Conservation Authority. 2001. *National Energy Efficiency and Conservation Strategy: Towards a Sustainable Energy Future.* Canberra: EECA.

———. 2002. *Annual Report of the Energy Efficiency and Conservation Authority.* Canberra: EECA.

Energy Efficiency and Conservation Authority and Centre for Advanced Engineering. 1996. *New and Emerging Renewable Energy Opportunities in New Zealand.* Christchurch: EECA and CAE.

Hopkins, Andrea. 2001. "Australia's Brush with Nuclear Power 'Ground Zero.'" *PlanetArk,* August 7. Available at http://www.planetark.org/dailynewsstory.cfm?newsid=11916 (accessed August 2002).

International Energy Agency. 2002. *Energy Balances of Organization for Economic Cooperation and Development (OECD) Countries, 1999–2000.* Paris: IEA.

———. 2002. *World Energy Outlook 2002.* Paris: IEA.

Ministry of Economic Development. 2003. "Energy Data File 2003." Wellington.

Krockenberger, Michael. 2002. "The State of Our Environment." *Habitat Australia* 30 (June).

New Zealand Ministry for the Environment. n.d. "Transport." Available at http://www.mfe.govt.nz/issues/transport (accessed March 2003).

———. 1997. *The State of New Zealand's Environment.* Wellington: Ministry for the Environment.

————. 2001. *National Energy Efficiency and Conservation Strategy.* Wellington: Ministry for the Environment.

UN Development Programme. 1996. *The State of Human Settlements and Urbanization in the Pacific Islands.* Suva: UNDP.

————. 2000. *Energy as a Tool for Sustainable Development for African, Caribbean, and Pacific Countries.* New York: UNDP.

————. 2000. *World Energy Assessment: Energy and the Challenge of Sustainability.* New York: UNDP.

UN Environment Programme. 1999. *Pacific Islands Environment Outlook.* Available at www.unep.org (accessed December 2002).

World Wide Fund for Nature Australia. 2001. *Greening the 2001 Agenda: Priority Environmental Initiatives for Commonwealth Government 2002–2005.* Sydney: WWF-Australia.

Air Quality
and the Atmosphere

Most people in Oceania enjoy very clean air by international standards. The high air quality in the region—which includes the continent nation of Australia as well as New Zealand, Papua New Guinea, and another twenty-one countries and territories dispersed across more than 40 million square kilometers (15.5 million square miles) of the South Pacific Ocean—rests on several factors. One is the region's geographic isolation, which limits its exposure to transboundary emissions from other countries. Another ingredient in Oceania's high air quality record is its comparatively modest reliance on heavy industry and manufacturing. Indeed, many Pacific Island states have virtually no industrial component, instead relying on agriculture and tourism for their livelihoods. Finally, population levels are light, especially in the largest countries—Australia, Papua New Guinea, and New Zealand. As a result of this blend of mitigating factors, the only places with significant air quality concerns are some major metropolitan areas (limited mostly to Australia) and some localized areas where mining and other industrial activities are concentrated.

But although air quality is very high across most of Oceania, the region is engaged in a grim struggle to come to terms with possible implications of global warming. Leaders and citizens of many Pacific Island states note that Oceania accounts for only a tiny sliver of the planet's total emissions of greenhouse gases. But this also means that they have little control over steadily rising emissions generated overseas. Barring a dramatic curtailment of emission levels, these gases are forecast to bring about rising sea levels and wreak major changes in weather patterns during coming decades. For some nations of the South Pacific, their very existence is in doubt if these manifestations of climate change come to pass. Nonetheless, gloomy scenarios of island submersion have not convinced neighboring Australia—one of the planet's largest

greenhouse gas producers per capita—to reconsider its opposition to the
Kyoto Protocol, an international agreement designed to reduce greenhouse
emissions by industrialized countries.

Air Pollution in Oceania

Urban Concerns Mar Australia's
Record of High Air Quality

Isolated from other industrialized nations by virtue of its location in the
South Pacific, Australia receives only minimal concentrations of air pollutants
from other nations. This has spared the nation from acid rain—which has
wreaked significant damage on forests and lakes in North America and
Europe—and other common manifestations of transboundary pollution. In
addition, large swaths of the Australian countryside experience little or no automobile use or industrial activity. Air quality in these areas is often exceptional by international standards, though heavy brushfires and high rates of
wind erosion periodically reduce quality in some rural settings. But while
much of the continent is free of air quality problems, those areas that have the
greatest concentrations of people—the fast-growing cities and suburbs of
Australia's southern and eastern quadrants—also have the greatest accumula-
tions of airborne pollutants. In these metropolitan areas, particulate matter
from industrial activity and motor vehicles, ground-level ozone created by industrial and automobile emissions, and pollutants associated with indoor activities (such as cigarette smoking) have all diminished air quality.

Trends regarding some of these air quality issues are encouraging. For example, incidents in which tropospheric (ground-level) ozone levels have exceeded
safety guidelines declined markedly in the 1980s and 1990s in Sydney and
Melbourne, the country's two largest cities. This is a welcome development, for
ozone in the lower atmosphere acts as a poison, killing trees and other vegetation and damaging the respiratory system of humans and other life forms. It
also has been identified as a greenhouse gas that contributes to global climate
change. But Australia's progress in using new pollution technologies and emission controls to reduce its volume of "ozone precursors"—substances that increase the level of ozone and associated smog—may be jeopardized by steadily
rising rates of automobile and truck use and ownership. "It is possible that as
vehicle usage and numbers continue to rise, the sheer quantity of emissions
may again lead to ozone episodes," acknowledged one study (Australian State
of the Environment Committee, 2001).

Already, cars and trucks are the major emitters of air pollutants in urban
Australia, contributing more than 75 percent of the country's carbon monox-

ide emissions and most of the organic compounds (ibid.). Motor vehicles are also a primary source of sulfur dioxide and nitrogen dioxide, along with coal consumption (as in coal-fired power plants) and specific industrial operations (such as oil refineries and fertilizer manufacturing facilities). Both sulfur dioxide and nitrogen dioxide are respiratory irritants that, in sufficiently high concentrations, also have corrosive properties capable of damaging buildings and plants alike. Government standards for the presence of these pollutants are rarely exceeded, even in urban areas, but the health impact of their interactions with other air pollutants, such as particulate matter and ozone precursors, is not completely understood. Studies such as the Melbourne Mortality Study have indicated that the combined effects of these pollutants can trigger increased mortality in urban centers (Environmental Protection Authority, Victoria, 2000).

Australia has taken some effective measures to reduce sulfur dioxide pollution in recent years. Once a scourge of its larger cities because of Australia's heavy—and continuing—reliance on coal for much of its heating and electricity needs, emissions have declined considerably as a result of new practices in mining operations and power plants. For example, many processing facilities began converting sulfur dioxide into sulfuric acid instead of releasing it into the atmosphere. As a result of these and other steps, total emissions of sulfur dioxide in Australia decreased by almost one-third between 1995 and 2000, despite a jump in mineral processing activity (Australian State of the Environment Committee, 2001). In addition, Australia's passage of the National Fuel Quality Standards Act 2000 will further reduce sulfur content in diesel fuel, which is commonly used throughout the country. Still, high levels of sulfur dioxide persist in some regions with substantial industrial operations, especially those with a heavy mineral extraction or processing component. For example, highly concentrated mineral processing communities such as Port Pirie and Mount Isa continue to contain unsafe levels of sulfur dioxide in the air (ibid.). In rural regions of Australia, meanwhile, the paramount air quality issue is management of airborne particulate matter, such as those contained in haze, windblown dust (from mining and agricultural activities), agricultural sprays, wood smoke, smoke from bushfires, and mining industry particle emissions.

Over the past decade, Australia has taken several steps to improve its monitoring of air quality and address known problems. In 1997 it passed new measures designed to substantially reduce emissions of pollutants from cars and trucks (also a focus of the National Fuel Quality Standards Act 2000), and two years later it declared its intention to harmonize Australian vehicle emission standards with existing and emerging European standards, which are the most stringent in the world. In 1998, meanwhile, the country finalized a set of national air quality standards applicable to all states and territories. Advocates of these uniform standards, codified in the National Environment Protection Measure (NEPM) for ambient air quality, say that they will provide a reporting framework that will allow scientists and policy-makers to compare air quality across the country. The year 1998 also marked the creation of the National Pollutant Inventory, a database designed to provide the community, industry, and government with information on the types and amounts of chemicals being emitted into the environment (ibid.).

New Zealand Air Quality
a Source of National Pride

The people of New Zealand have some of the cleanest air on the planet. Whether speaking of remote forested valleys untouched by human development or the settlements that sprout along the country's rugged coastlines, air pollution is low when compared with other points of the globe. Some of the factors contributing to these conditions are providential in nature, such as the country's isolation and exposure to stiff westerly winds that constantly cleanse its valleys and mountain ranges of contaminants before they become too concentrated. Other factors in New Zealand's clean air are more prosaic, such as its relatively low human population, its modest and highly regulated industrial sector, and its bounty of carbon-storing forests. "The country's main revenues come from outdoor industries such as agriculture, horticulture, forestry, fishing, and tourism," observed the Ministry for the Environment. "Except for isolated incidents of spray drift (spraying of pesticides on fields in windy conditions) or controlled burn-offs, air pollution generated by these industries [is] generally low and localized. By world standards, then, New Zealand has low concentrations of most urban air pollutants such as smoke, photochemical smog, and sulphur dioxide" (New Zealand Ministry for the Environment, *The State of New Zealand's Environment*, 1997).

But while it is universally acknowledged that New Zealand's air has been spared much of the pollution that bedevils others countries, quantitative assessments of the country's air quality are lacking. Indeed, monitoring activity has historically been sporadic—and usually prompted by specific perceived problems. Simply put, New Zealand's political leadership and general population have historically not felt the need to regularly monitor air pollution levels in the country.

In recent years, however, recognition of the need for improved monitoring is growing. In the 1990s, for example, the country made significant investments in air pollution research for Christchurch and other metropolitan areas. This research has uncovered significant air quality problems in some urban locations, especially metropolitan "traffic corridors" (Fisher and Thompson, 1996). In fact, air quality has emerged as an issue of serious concern in Christchurch, which lies on the east coast of New Zealand's South Island (the country is composed of two main islands—North and South Island—and numerous smaller islands). Tucked away in a low-lying basin surrounded by the Southern Alps and high hills, Christchurch is susceptible to wintertime temperature inversions, in which a layer of warm air traps cool air—and pollution generated by motor vehicles and domestic fires—in the valley. Other areas of New Zealand, including Dunedin and the Hutt Valley, are also vulnerable to this phenomenon (New Zealand Ministry for the Environment, *The State of New Zealand's Environment*, 1997).

In these localized areas, nationwide trends such as heavy automobile use and frequent wintertime use of open fires and wood burners have had measurable ecological consequences. New Zealand's rate of vehicle ownership is among the highest in the world, with nearly one car for every two people living in the country (450 cars per 1,000 people). Trucks and other vehicles further boost the nation's motor vehicle ownership rate to about 700 vehicles per 1,000 people. The world average, by contrast, is about 84 vehicles per 1,000 people (World Bank, 1999). Many of these vehicles are older models that fail to meet national and international air quality guidelines for emissions of carbon monoxide and other substances. For example, from 1993 to 1995, the Canterbury Regional Council undertook an emission testing program of cars and trucks in Christchurch. Of the more than 40,000 vehicles tested, more than 17,000 (41 percent of the total) failed to meet the program's emission guidelines (Kuschel and Fisher, 1996). Another contributing factor to higher rates of private automobile use and associated increases in emissions from the sector has been the withering of public transport in the country. Indeed, the percentage of New Zealanders taking public transport has declined dramatically since the 1980s. New Zealand has had greater success in reining in emissions from manufacturing factories, processing facilities, and other components of its industrial base. Indeed, emissions from industry have proven much easier to monitor and control than the diffuse and dispersed emissions from households (the primary site of wintertime wood burning) and vehicles.

Air quality management initiatives in New Zealand over the past thirty years have been predicated on two distinct pieces of legislation. The country's first major pollution control legislation was the 1972 Clean Air Act, which regulated emissions from a host of industrial and trade processes. But this law was limited in scope and reach, and the Ministry for the Environment has acknowledged

Pollution from traffic congestion is a growing problem in Sydney, Australia. JOHN VANHASSELT/CORBIS

that while it "may have prevented some situations from getting worse, it cannot be credited with bringing about the main improvements in air quality which occurred during the 1970s and 1980s." Instead, these gains were in large part the result of progressive reductions in lead emissions from cars and trucks. In 1991 the Clean Air Act was discarded in favor of the mechanisms contained within the 1991 Resource Management Act (RMA), which emphasizes sustainable management of New Zealand's natural resources. Under the RMA, much of the responsibility for air quality and air pollution abatement has been handed down to regional authorities (New Zealand Ministry for the Environment, *The State of New Zealand's Environment*, 1997).

Air Quality in Oceania

Historically, air quality in the Pacific Island States that compose Oceania has been perceived as superior to that in most other regions of the world, though a dearth of monitoring and research activity makes quantification impossible. So-called smokestack industries in most of these countries are nonexistent, and pressure on air quality from motor vehicles has traditionally been of little concern because the small size of most of these countries (and the modest economic resources of their peoples) precluded the creation of significant roadway infrastructure or high rates of motor vehicle ownership. Finally, few parts of the South Pacific are heavily urbanized, although levels of migration to towns and cities have risen over the past two decades.

Nonetheless, air quality has been compromised in some parts of some countries. Clearance of forests and vegetation through controlled fires has been blamed for episodes of localized air pollution, and larger urban areas such as Apia, Port Moresby, and Suva have experienced forms of development that have eroded air quality, such as poorly regulated industrialization and road-building that has driven increased use of private motor vehicles for transportation. In most of the countries of Oceania, pollution standards and regulation of emissions from cars, factories, or agricultural activities are minimal or wholly absent (UN Environment Programme, 1999).

Oceania and the Ozone Layer

Worldwide concerns about stratospheric ozone loss—the so-called hole in the earth's ozone layer—have had particular resonance in Oceania. Some countries in the region are relatively close to Antarctica, where ozone loss has been most apparent. For example, ozone cover over New Zealand has decreased by an estimated 5 to 7 percent since the mid-1970s, with an accompanying 6 to 9 percent rise in cancer-causing forms of ultraviolet radiation (New Zealand Ministry for the Environment, *The State of New Zealand's Environment*, 1997).

Researchers note that continued ozone loss would allow higher levels of ultraviolet radiation to reach the earth's surface, which would in turn trigger higher rates of skin cancer in humans in New Zealand, Australia—already home to the world's highest rates of skin cancer—and elsewhere. Other harmful effects associated with increased exposure to ultraviolet radiation include declines in plankton, a keystone species in oceans around the world, and damage to natural forests, vegetation, and a host of different food crops. In essence, significant thinning and loss of the ozone layer raised the specter of wrenching changes to the health and character of ecosystems around the globe.

Fortunately, the international community reacted decisively to the dangers of stratospheric ozone loss. When the hole in the ozone layer was detected in the 1980s, the world's governments responded by hammering out the Montreal Protocol on Substances that Deplete the Ozone Layer, which has now been signed by more than 165 nations. Signatories to this protocol—which has been periodically revised in response to scientific findings on atmospheric growth rates of ozone-depleting chemicals and on measurements of ozone destruction—agreed to eliminate most production of ozone-depleting anthropogenic substances, most notably chlorofluorocarbons (CFCs), which are chlorine-laced chemicals that were common ingredients in refrigerants and aerosol sprays. In accordance with the protocol, Australia, New Zealand, and other developed countries eliminated their production and use of almost all CFCs by 1996; as a consequence, global consumption of CFCs fell from 1.1 million tons to 160,000 tons between 1986 and 1996 (UN Environment Programme, 1998). Production and use of CFCs and other ozone-depleting substances by developing countries is scheduled to cease (with a few exceptions) by 2010. In addition, in 1995 more than one hundred nations agreed to end their use of methyl bromide, a pesticide that was another significant factor in ozone depletion. As a result of these and other multilateral environmental agreements, total production and generation of ozone-depleting substances has declined by as much as 90 percent over the past fifteen years (Australian State of the Environment Committee, 2001).

This reaction to stratospheric ozone loss, which proceeded in the mid-latitudes (Tropic of Capricorn to the Antarctic Circle) at a rate of 2 to 5 percent per decade from the 1950s through the 1980s, has had gratifying results. Concentrations of CFCs, methyl bromide, and other ozone-depleting substances—which had boosted concentrations of chlorine in the atmosphere by more than 600 percent above natural levels—are all stabilizing or declining, and the seasonal ozone holes that have rent the atmosphere over the earth's polar regions in past years appear to be trending downward in size (World Meteorological Organization, 1998). Continued vigilance is necessary, however, to counter emerging obstacles to recovery such as the international black market trade in CFCs. "The potential impact of stratospheric ozone depletion means there is no room for complacency," commented the UN Environment Programme. "[But] the cooperative measures that followed the identification of the problem remain an outstanding and encouraging example of the ability of the international community to act in unison in protecting the global environment" (UN Environment Programme, 1999).

Full recovery of the stratospheric ozone layer is still expected to take decades, however. Ozone-depleting substances continue to exist in the upper atmosphere, and further increases in health problems related to high exposure to ultraviolet radiation have been forecast for the short term, since emissions from earlier years are still working their way through the atmosphere. In addition, scientists report that incipient global climate change could significantly delay the healing process, pushing back full recovery for a century or more (UN Environment Programme, 2000; World Meteorological Organization, 1998).

Casting Greenhouse Gas Reductions as a Moral Issue

As evidence of global climate change accumulates, political leaders in Oceania have mounted a lobbying effort to convince the rest of the world to make major reductions in their consumption of fossil fuels responsible for the bulk of greenhouse gases. At the 1998 Kyoto Climate Summit, for example, President Kinza Clodumar of the Republic of Nauru sought to place the global warming threat to Oceania's small island states in starkly moral terms: "We submit, respectfully, that the willful destruction of entire countries and cultures with foreknowledge would represent an unspeakable crime against humanity. No nation has the right to place its own misconstrued national interest before the physical and cultural survival of whole countries. The crime is cultural genocide. It must not be tolerated by the family of nations. The crime is no less when it is perpetuated slowly by the emission of invisible gases. My plea is not merely an urgent request on behalf of island nations and cultures; it is also a heartfelt warning to the entire family of nations. Small island states provide not only a moral compass; we are also a barometer of broader visitations wisely heeded by all."

Sources:

Clodumar, Kinza. 1998. "Global Warming, Rising Tides, and Cultural Genocide." *Earth Island Journal* 13 (summer).

Global Climate Change: The End for Oceania?

Airborne pollution has long been recognized as a potentially deadly threat to the earth's flora and fauna, including humans. But historically, these impacts were triggered by ingestion of the pollutants contained in emissions from industrial processes, motor vehicle operation, fires (both prescribed fires and wildfires), and other sources. More recently, however, the scientific community has determined that many of these same airborne pollutants are transforming the planet's atmosphere so that it takes on greater insulating properties. This "greenhouse effect," in which the sun's heat is trapped in the atmosphere under a growing blanket of emissions known as "greenhouse gases," poses a potentially major threat to world ecosystems and the people, animals, and plants that depend on those systems for their survival.

The main source of these gases—which include carbon dioxide, nitrous oxide, and CFCs—is anthropogenic activity, specifically the burning of oil, gas, and coal to operate cars, trucks, airplanes, factories, and power plants. This burning of fossil fuel generates huge quantities of carbon dioxide, the main greenhouse gas. Lesser sources of greenhouse gases include methane emissions from livestock and landfills, nitrous oxides from agricultural fields, emissions of fluorinated gases from industry, emissions of carbon dioxide from volcanic activity, and releases of carbon dioxide from carbon-storing forests subjected to "slash-and-burn" deforestation.

According to the 2,500-member Intergovernmental Panel on Climate Change (IPCC), a group operating under the joint sponsorship of the United Nations and the World Meteorological Organization, evidence of climate change attributable to human activities is already proliferating around the planet, with rapid melting of polar ice caps and record-breaking temperatures the most noteworthy manifestations. According to the IPCC, which stands as the world's most authoritative source on global warming, nine of the world's ten hottest years in recorded history occurred between 1990 and 2000 (Intergovernmental Panel on Climate Change, *Climate Change 2001: The Scientific Basis*, 2001).

If left unchecked, the earth's accelerating retention of greenhouse gases in the atmosphere will fundamentally transform the planet and its natural ecosystems. And while some of these sweeping changes may prove beneficial in certain respects to some regions (by transforming arid and semiarid areas into more productive farmland, for example), many of the consequences are expected to be devastating for people, flora, and fauna around the world. The single greatest element in this transformation will be rising temperatures. The IPCC has forecast that the planet will warm by a stunning 1.4 to 5.8 degrees Celsius (2.5 to 10 degrees Fahrenheit) over the course of the twenty-first century without major reductions in greenhouse gas emissions. Probable repercussions of this warming of the planet include increasingly severe and numerous storms, altered rain and snowfall patterns that will bring greater incidence of flooding and drought, inundation of islands and coastal areas from rising sea levels (precipitated by melting glaciers and polar ice caps), expansion of malaria and other tropical diseases into previously temperate zones, and possible mass extinctions of species of mammals, birds, reptiles, amphibians, fish, and plants (Intergovernmental Panel on Climate Change, *Climate Change 2001: Summaries for Policymakers,* 2001).

Scientists believe that the severity of many of these changes can be blunted if countries take prompt action now. Indeed, the decisive international response to the stratospheric ozone loss issue has been cited as a model for crafting future climate policy (Downie, 1995). To date, however, the main international responses to this brewing crisis have been the 1992 UN Framework Convention on Climate Change (UNFCCC) and the 1997 Kyoto Protocol. The latter is a UN-brokered agreement that calls on developed nations to reduce their emissions of greenhouse gases to at least 5 percent below 1990 emissions levels by 2012. The protocol enters into force when it has been ratified by at least fifty-five parties to the convention, including developed countries accounting for at least 55 percent of total carbon dioxide emissions in 1990. But the future of the Kyoto Protocol, which even supporters acknowledge is only a first step in addressing global climate change, is uncertain. The United States, which ranks as the world's leading producer of greenhouse gases, has decided not to ratify the treaty, citing economic hardship and the exclusion of developing countries. In addition, some nations have experienced great difficulty in reaching emission reduction goals.

In the South Pacific, meanwhile, reactions to the global warming issue have been starkly different. Australia and New Zealand have parted ways on Kyoto, with the latter ratifying the protocol in late 2002 and the former joining the United States in opposition. And the nations of Oceania? They watch the debates over global warming and appropriate responses with foreboding and anxiety, fully cognizant that rising sea levels could submerge part or all of their countries under the ocean waves.

Australia and the Global Warming Issue

Among industrialized nations, Australia is the world's largest emitter of greenhouse gases responsible for global warming on a per capita basis. Its emissions of 27.9 tons of greenhouse gases (in carbon dioxide equivalent) per capita far outstrip per capita emissions from any other country (the next highest per capita emitter is Canada, at 22.2 tons). In addition, Australia's per capita emission rate is more than double the average of 12.8 tons for all industrialized countries (UN Framework Convention on Climate Change, 2003).

In terms of total emissions of greenhouse gases by volume, Australia ranks far behind countries such as the United States, which alone accounts for about one-quarter of all emissions implicated in global warming. But Australia does rank seventh in total emissions among industrialized nations, behind only the United States, Japan, Russia, Germany, the United Kingdom, and Canada, and its total emissions are more than that posted by Italy and France, countries with three times Australia's population (UN Framework Convention on Climate Change, 2003).

Australia's high rate of greenhouse gas generation is directly attributable to its abundant storehouses of coal and other fossil fuels. Indeed, Australia is the planet's leading exporter of coal—consumption of which is a major contributor to air pollution and global warming—yet it still possesses enough of this and other fossil fuels to keep its electricity and gasoline prices among the lowest in the world. Armed with high energy supplies and few pricing incentives for resource conservation, Australia has become a profligate consumer, with the energy sector—power stations and transportation—accounting for almost 80 percent of its greenhouse emissions (Australian Bureau of Statistics, 2001).

Australia has managed to make modest reductions in its per capita emissions in recent years. From 1990 to 1999, per capita emissions declined by approximately 3 percent. But this overall decline masked a surge in emissions at the end of the decade. Australian emissions fell sharply in the early 1990s because of anemic economic conditions that diminished investment in industrial activity and land clearing (which reduces capacity to absorb carbon in forests). But Australia emerged from recession in the mid-1990s and since that time has registered considerable growth in emissions, especially from its energy sectors. Changes to the country's electricity market in the late 1990s also exacerbated this trend, as utilities made greater use of brown coal at the expense of black coal and natural gas (Turton and Hamilton, 2002).

Moreover, environmentalists note that modest gains in per capita emissions are of limited comfort since total emissions in Australia continue to rise. The total growth in emissions has been the subject of considerable debate— the Australian government has claimed that it anticipates an 11 percent rise from 1990 levels in greenhouse gases by 2012, while studies mounted by conservation and environmental groups contend that the country's emissions of greenhouse gases rose by more than 17 percent during the 1990s alone; they predict 30 percent growth from 1990 levels by 2012 (Environment Australia, 2002; Christoff, 2002). In making its claims, the latter constituency relies on the government's own data, such as forecasts that emissions from electricity production could rise by more than 40 percent between 1990 and 2010 (Australian Bureau of Resource Economics, 1999).

Australia has acknowledged that global climate change is a reality, and it claims that reduction of greenhouse gas emissions is a priority. But the nation continues to export vast quantities of coal to Asia, where air pollution abatement technologies are still being introduced. In addition, it has announced that it will not ratify the Kyoto climate change treaty aimed at cutting emissions of greenhouse gases blamed for global climate change.

To environmentalists, Australia's spurning of Kyoto symbolized a startling metamorphosis in the country's attitude toward the global warming issue. In the early 1990s, Australia was an enthusiastic supporter of the UN Framework Convention on Climate Change (UNFCCC), one of the major outcomes of the 1992 Rio Summit. During this period, the country's leadership vowed that it would make all necessary investments of money and other resources to return national greenhouse emissions to 1990 levels. Since that time, however, environmentalists contend that "Australia's domestic and international stance on this issue has deteriorated remarkably" (Christoff, 2002).

"Successive national governments (Labor and Coalition) have refused to legislate clear targets for domestic greenhouse gas emissions reduction. More significantly (at Kyoto), the Howard Government refused to accept any mandatory emissions reduction target in the protocol then under negotiation. It argued that even the modest (and ecologically minimal) average target of 5 percent would be against the national (economic) interest. Australia's pressure on the fragile negotiations, and its threat to break ranks and withdraw altogether, resulted in its being rewarded with a special target—a targeted *increase* in emissions, by 8 percent from 1990 levels, by 2012" (Christoff, 1998). Despite this special accommodation, Australia eventually decided to opt out of the treaty, claiming that its implementation would take an unacceptable toll on the country's economy.

During the 1990s, Australia's commonwealth government did unveil a variety of measures ostensibly designed to reduce the continent nation's greenhouse emissions. These included the 1992 National Greenhouse Response Strategy, the 1995 Greenhouse Challenge Program, and the 1998 National Greenhouse Strategy. But all of these programs sought to reduce emissions through voluntary participation, and as one study noted, the country's emission trends make it clear that "none has had any substantial success in tackling core issues dealing with unrestrained expansion of fossil fuel based economic development" (Christoff, 2002). In July 2002, Australia announced the U.S.-Australia Climate Action Partnership with the United States, a scheme to develop a carbon trading market outside the Kyoto Protocol framework. But critics in the environmental community denounced the partnership, noting that its voluntary framework does not penalize either party if it fails to make quantifiable reductions in greenhouse gas emissions.

If forecasts by most members of the scientific community come to pass, global climate change will have an enormous impact on the Australian continent in the twenty-first century. Most of the country will experience warming of 0.4 to 2.0 degrees Celsius (0.7 to 3.5 degrees Fahrenheit) by 2030, and by 1.1 to 6.0 degrees Celsius (2 to 11 degrees Fahrenheit) by 2070. Increased vulnerability to drought and severe storm events that trigger floods are also likely, with both trends affecting agriculture, industrial activity, and infrastructure (roadways, buildings). Considerable investments of time, money, and other resources will likely be necessary to ensure sustainability in these sectors, and some demographic groups—particularly indigenous peoples in some regions—have low institutional capacity and financial resources to adapt (Intergovernmental Panel on Climate Change, *Climate Change 2001: Mitigation, Impacts, Adaptation, and Vulnerability,* 2001).

In addition, increases in temperature and exposure to droughts and floods will likely have a transformative effect on the savanna ecosystem of tropical Australia, with species composition undergoing considerable change. "Some species with restricted climatic niches and which are unable to migrate due to fragmentation of the landscape, soil differences, or topography could become endangered or extinct," stated the IPCC. Australian ecosystems that are particularly vulnerable to climate change include coral reefs, arid and semi-arid habitats in southwest and inland Australia, alpine systems (such as the Southern Alps), and freshwater wetlands in coastal zones. Moreover, more frequent invasions by tropical pests, weeds, and infectious diseases are likely results of changing weather patterns, Finally, sea level rise associated with global warming could endanger many developed coastal areas, where Australia's population is concentrated. Residential housing, ports, bridges, and business centers could all suffer extensive and permanent damage from land encroachment, coastal erosion, storm surges, and wind damage (Australian State of the Environment Committee, 2001; Intergovernmental Panel on Climate Change, *Climate Change 2001: Mitigation, Impacts, Adaptation, and Vulnerability,* 2001).

New Zealand and Global Warming

Unlike its continental neighbor to the west, New Zealand has determined that the Kyoto Protocol is an appropriate mechanism by which the developed world can begin addressing global warming. In late 2002, New Zealand formally ratified the Kyoto Protocol, committing itself to a 5 percent reduction in its 1990-level emissions of greenhouse gases by 2012.

New Zealand's recognition that the country's "geographical isolation . . . affords no sanctuary" from the threat of global warming is reflected in assessments of its own historical emissions performance: "Although New Zealand has a relatively small population, we, like the people in other developed countries, make a disproportionate contribution to greenhouse gas emissions," observed the Ministry for the Environment. "In 1993, New Zealand's 3.5 million people represented only 0.06 percent of the world's population, but our contribution to all human-related carbon dioxide emissions was closer to 0.10 percent and our per capita share of methane emissions was ten times the global average. The reasons for this are emissions from livestock and fossil fuel use" (New Zealand Ministry for the Environment, *The State of New Zealand's Environment,* 1997).

Indeed, New Zealand ranks seventh in the world among industrialized countries in terms of total per capita greenhouse gas emissions, at 14.4 tons of carbon dioxide equivalent, which is higher than the 12.8-ton average for all industrialized countries (UN Framework Convention on Climate Change, 2003). Most of the country's greenhouse gas emissions are carbon dioxide (from cars and trucks, electricity generation, and the petrochemical, steel, and diary industries) and methane (generated by its 50 million sheep and cattle), which provide products responsible for about one-third of the country's total export earnings. The volume of methane generated in New Zealand declined slightly during the 1990s, but emissions of carbon dioxide and several other greenhouse gases, including carbon monoxide, sulfur dioxide, nitrogen oxides, and hydrofluorocarbons, increased during the same time period, pushing overall greenhouse gas emission levels to historic highs (New Zealand Ministry for the Environment, *The State of New Zealand's Environment,* 1997).

New Zealand, though, appears determined to meet its Kyoto obligations. One of the major weapons at New Zealand's disposal in the battle against global warming is its large pavilions of unbroken forest land. At the beginning of the twenty-first century, it was estimated that about half of the country's emissions of carbon dioxide stemming from human activity are absorbed by its forests, which act as a "sink" for carbon. These and other forests around the world have been formally recognized by the Kyoto Protocol as assets to be considered in figuring national emission levels.

The total area of New Zealand under forest cover is on the rise as well, because of forest planting and commercial plantation programs, a large protected area network, and other habitat conservation schemes. Despite these increases, however, the nation's net carbon dioxide emissions have risen since

1990 as a result of increasing fossil fuel use associated with economic growth and changing forest growth rates associated with age structure. Scientists caution that the forests of New Zealand will not be able to maintain their current 50 percent absorption ratio unless reductions are made in actual carbon dioxide emissions. Without such reductions, the government will also have less freedom to sell "carbon sink credits" at a lucrative price to other countries unable to meet their Kyoto treaty obligations.

In addition, in 2002 New Zealand announced its intention to impose a carbon tax to encourage conservation in fossil fuel consumption, and thus reduce emissions of carbon dioxide and other chemicals responsible for climate change. The tax of up to NZ$25 a ton of carbon dioxide equivalent will be levied sometime after 2007—and will be imposed only if the Kyoto Protocol comes into force internationally. It would raise retail gasoline prices by up to 6 percent, diesel by 12 percent, and gas and electricity prices by 8 to 9 percent. The tax's biggest target, however, would be coal users, who would see fuel costs jump by nearly 20 percent. Still, some constituencies—such as farmers—are exempt from the tax.

If global climate change does wash over the planet in the twenty-first century as predicted, the repercussions for New Zealand are likely to eclipse weather changes associated with more familiar climatic patterns such as the El Niño-Southern Oscillation (ENSO) phenomenon, a recurring pattern that periodically makes the country cooler, drier, and more prone to cyclone activity. This event, triggered by changes in surface air pressure over the Pacific Ocean, is capable of altering ocean currents, precipitation patterns, winds, and temperatures around the world, and scientists candidly admit that the implications for New Zealand and other countries of interaction between global warming and ENSO remain largely a subject of conjecture and speculation. Still, climatologists do suspect that ENSO events may increase in frequency or duration as a result of human-induced climate change (ibid.).

Irrespective of ENSO, the Intergovernmental Panel on Climate Change and other scientific bodies predict significant changes for New Zealand in a warming world. For example, some scenarios suggest that the frost-free season in New Zealand would be some 40 to 60 days longer, the snowline would creep 100 to 400 meters (325 to 1,300 feet) higher in mountainous areas, and the sea would be 20 to 600 higher. Westerly winds would decline by 10 percent, bringing fewer rainy days to western regions. However, rain would be heavier than at present, so that the west and north would be about 10 to 15 percent wetter and the east and south 5 to 10 percent drier (New Zealand Ministry for the Environment, 2002).

These climate changes would permanently transform New Zealand, dramatically altering patterns of agriculture, reshaping human settlement and migration patterns, and wreaking major changes on land, freshwater, and marine habitat quality and species survival rates. Indeed, all natural areas, from coral reefs to rain forests will undergo substantive changes to their character, and no human demographic group—from young professionals living and working in modern urban and residential centers to indigenous Maori communities that depend on fisheries and other elements of the natural world for their livelihoods—will be exempt from the ripple effects of climate change.

In some cases, the net impact of climate change may be beneficial, at least in the short term. For example, in the realm of agriculture, some farming enterprises may benefit from elevated carbon dioxide concentrations, which could in turn produce improvements in growth rates and water-use efficiency. In addition, warmer conditions and lengthened growing seasons could provide greater agricultural opportunities in the south, where climate currently limits certain crops and related industries from taking hold (New Zealand Ministry for the Environment, 2002). But increases in the frequency and severity of drought and flood events could batter some agricultural enterprises, and temperature changes could preclude future cultivation of some traditional high-value crops. In addition, outbreaks of disease, insects, and invasive species could spread in range and severity, and the suitability of pasture lands for cattle and sheep is likely to change, with unpredictable outcomes for animal productivity and health.

A similar allotment of benefits and drawbacks associated with climate change is likely to play out in other economic sectors and geographic regions across the country's North and South Islands over the course of the twenty-first century. "It is already becoming clear that there will be temporary winners and losers in New Zealand," summarized one government study. But the report also reiterated New Zealand's support for international measures to reduce greenhouse gas emissions and its conviction that "in the long term, if climate change continues unabated, there is little question that the global economy and human welfare would be put under substantial threat" (ibid.).

Climate Change—A Threat to the Existence of Oceania?

Gradual warming of the atmosphere associated with rising concentrations of carbon dioxide and other greenhouse gases generated by human activity is of particular concern to the island states of Oceania. These Pacific Island countries rank among the most endangered nations on earth if predicted levels of climate change come to pass. Small in stature, surrounded by ocean, and in many cases perched only a few feet above sea level, these Oceanic states are acutely vulnerable to manifestations of global climate change such as rising sea levels and increased frequency of cyclones and other extreme weather events.

Islands at Muri Beach, Rarotonga, Cook Islands. COREL

Already, evidence of climate change in Oceania is multiplying. Some atolls in the region have already been lost to rising seas, and extreme weather events (such as cyclones) are appearing with more regularity. These trends, coupled with the recurring ENSO weather phenomenon, have also produced severe drought and water shortages across the region, including Papua New Guinea, Marshall Islands, the Federated States of Micronesia, American Samoa, Samoa, and Fiji. Moreover, changes in general climatic conditions have also been reported since the mid-1970s by organizations such as New Zealand's National Institute of Water and Atmospheric Research. For example, Kiribati, the northern Cook Islands, Tokelau and the northern parts of French Polynesia have all become wetter, while New Caledonia, Fiji, and Tonga have become drier. Similarly, cloud cover has increased in places like Tokelau, Samoa, and northeast French Polynesia, while locales such as New Caledonia, Tonga, southwest French Polynesia, and Tuvalu are all becoming sunnier over time. These changes alone—even without rising sea levels, increased vulnerability to storm surges and cyclones, and drought—have major implications for agricultural productivity and ecosystem functions (UN Environment Programme, 1999).

Specific changes to small island states as a direct result of global warming include profound coastal erosion and associated loss of land and property, forced dislocation of people and communities, increased risk from storm surges, reduced resilience and health of coastal ecosystems (including coral reefs, mangroves, and seagrasses), and wrenching changes to subsistence livelihoods based on reef fishing and domestic and commercial crop production. Tourism, which has become an integral part of many island economies, would also be damaged or destroyed by any combination of these events. Finally, infectious tropical and subtropical diseases, especially mosquito-borne pathogens such as malaria, filariasis, dengue fever, and yellow fever, are expected to become more widespread. "Adaptive capacity of human systems is generally low in small island states, and vulnerability high," summarized the IPCC. "Small island states are likely to be among the countries most seriously impacted by climate change" (Intergovernmental Panel on Climate Change, *Climate Change 2001: Mitigation, Impacts, Adaptation, and Vulnerability,* 2001).

Of all the impacts of global warming on Oceania, however, the most dreaded is the prospect of outright submersion of islands by rising sea levels. The IPCC has issued estimates that sea levels are likely to rise 50 centimeters (19 inches) by the year 2100, with some scenarios placing the increase as high as 95 centimeters (37 inches, or 3 feet) by the end of the century. These are sobering prognostications for citizens of island states such as Tuvalu, where the highest point of land is only 5 meters (16 feet) above sea level. Moreover, studies indicate that sea level rise is already occurring, and that further encroachment is likely even if the provisions of the Kyoto Protocol are adhered to and the world eventually ends all anthropogenic greenhouse gas emissions after 2020 (Jones, 1998, 1999; Intergovernmental Panel on Climate Change, 2000).

The island states of Oceania are responsible for virtually none of the greenhouse gas emissions that are warming the earth's atmosphere. But they also have only modest political and economic power that they can use as leverage in convincing major producers of anthropogenic greenhouse gases (such as the United States, Japan, Russia, Canada, and Australia) to curtail their emissions. This has given rise to feelings of bitterness and helplessness in some Pacific Island states. As one observer noted in a discussion of Tuvalu's plight, "What does a country do when it knows it is of no concern to the rest of the world, has no natural resources to sell, occupies a location so exposed to the elements that is seems geography has played a bitter joke, and emerges from colonial dependency into the warming-up postmodern world?" (Levine, 2002).

Nonetheless, experts have encouraged Pacific Island countries to take some measures to prepare for the climate changes that seem inevitable. The UN Environment Programme, for example, states that local preparations could limit or minimize the negative fallout of climate change. "Improving the management of natural coastal systems such as coastal forests, mangroves, beaches, reefs, and lagoons, the careful planning of coastal zone developments, and the construction of coastal defenses such as seawalls to protect particularly valuable and vulnerable sites, are all actions that can be implemented now. Adaptation strategies will not be cost-free . . . [but] an adaptation strategy that is planned for implementation over 30–50 years [in conjunction with other investments and environmental objectives] will impose lower costs than one that has to be handled [absorbed] in a five-year period" (UN Environment Programme, 1999). Some authorities in Oceania are also exploring immigration programs to Australia and New Zealand should rising sea levels and heightened vulnerability to storms render some islands uninhabitable.

Sources:

Anderson, Stephan, and K. Madhava Sarma. 2003. *Protecting the Ozone Layer.* London: Earthscan.

Austin, D., and R. Repetto. 1997. *The Costs of Climate Protection: A Guide for the Perplexed.* Washington, DC: World Resources Institute.

Australian Bureau of Resource Economics. 1999. *Getting Energy and Greenhouse Gases into Perspective.* Canberra: ABARE.

Australian Bureau of Statistics. 2001. *Australia's Environment: Issues and Trends 2001.* Canberra: ABS.

Australian State of the Environment Committee. 2001. *Australia State of the Environment Report 2001.* Canberra: Commonwealth of Australia.

Buamert, Kevin A., et al. 2002. *Building on the Kyoto Protocol: Options for Protecting the Climate.* Washington, DC: World Resources Institute.

Carbon Dioxide Information Analysis Center. 2000. *Trends: A Compendium of Data on Global Change.* Oak Ridge, TN: Oak Ridge National Library, DOE.

Chiswell, Stephen, Melissa Bowen, and Brett Mullan. 2001. "New Zealand in a Warming World." *Water and Atmosphere* 9 (December).

Christoff, Peter. 1998. "From Global Citizen to Renegade State: Australia at Kyoto." *Arena Journal* 10.

———. 2002. "Australia: A Continent in Reverse." Report prepared for nineteen environmental and conservation groups in response to *WSSD-Australian Assessment Report.* Australia.

Downie, David. 1995. "Road Map or False Trail: Evaluating the Precedence of the Ozone Regime as Model and Strategy for Global Climate Change." *International Environmental Affairs* 7 (fall).

———. 1999. "The Power to Destroy: Understanding Stratospheric Ozone Politics as a Common Pool Resource Problem." In *Anarchy and the Environment: The International Relations of Common Pool Resources.* Edited by J. Samuel Barkin and George Shambaugh. Albany: State University of New York Press.

Environment Australia. 2002. *WSSD–Australian National Assessment Report.* Canberra: Environment Australia.

Environmental Protection Authority, Victoria. 2000. *Melbourne Mortality Study: Effects of Ambient Air Pollution on Daily Mortality in Melbourne 1991–1996.* Publication 709. Victoria: EPAV.

Fisher, G., and R. Thompson. 1996. "Air Quality Monitoring in New Zealand." Paper presented at the Clean Air Society Conference, Adelaide, October.

Hales, S., P. Weinstein, and A. Woodward. 1996. "Dengue Fever Epidemics in the South Pacific: Driven by El Nino Southern Oscillation?" *Lancet* 348.

Intergovernmental Panel on Climate Change. 2000. *The Regional Impacts of Climate Change: An Assessment of Vulnerability.* Geneva: IPCC.

———. 2001. *Climate Change 2001: Mitigation, Impacts, Adaptation, and Vulnerability: Summaries for Policymakers.* Geneva: IPCC.

———. 2001. *Climate Change 2001: The Scientific Basis.* Geneva: IPCC.

Jones, R. 1998. "An Analysis of the Impacts of the Kyoto Protocol on Pacific Island Countries. Part One: Identification of Latent Sea-level Rise within the Climate System at 1995 and 2020." Report presented to the South Pacific Regional Environmental Programme, Apia, Western Samoa.

Jones, R., et al. 1999. "An Analysis of the Impacts of the Kyoto Protocol on Pacific Island Countries. Part Two: Regional Climate Change Scenarios and Risk Assessment Methods." Report presented to the South Pacific Regional Environmental Programme, Apia, Western Samoa.

Kuschel, G., and G. Fisher. 1996. *Proceedings of the 1996 National Workshop Series on Air Quality Issues: Motor Vehicle Emissions (Christchurch, 30 April 1996).* Auckland: National Institute for Water and Atmospheric Research.

Leggett, Jeremy. 2001. *The Carbon War: Global Warming and the End of the Oil Era.* London: Routledge.

Levine, Mark. 2002. "Tuvalu Toodle-oo." *Outside* 27 (December).

Loughran, Robert J., Paul J. Tranter, and Guy M. Robinson. 2000. *Australia and New Zealand: Economy, Society and Environment.* London: Edward Arnold.

New Zealand Ministry for the Environment. 1997. *Climate Change, the New Zealand Response: New Zealand's Second National Communication under the Framework Convention on Climate Change.* Wellington: Ministry for the Environment.

———. 1997. *The State of New Zealand's Environment.* Wellington: Ministry for the Environment.

———. 2002. *Climate Change Impacts on New Zealand.* Wellington: Ministry for the Environment.

Stone, R. 1995. "If the Mercury Soars, So May the Health Hazards." *Science* 267.

Turton, Hal, and Clive Hamilton. 2002. *Updating Per Capita Emissions for Industrialised Countries.* Canberra: Australian Institute.

UN Environment Programme. 1998. *Production and Consumption of Ozone Depleting Substances 1986–1996.* Nairobi, Kenya: UNEP Ozone Secretariat.

———. 1999. *Global Environment Outlook 2000.* London: Earthscan.

———. 2000. *Action on Ozone.* Nairobi, Kenya: UNEP Ozone Secretariat.

UN Framework Convention on Climate Change. 2003. *Greenhouse Gas Inventory Database.* Available at http://ghg.unfccc.int/ (accessed January 2003).

Weinstein, P. 1996. "When Will the Mosquitos Strike?" *New Zealand Science Monthly* 7, no. 3.

Woodward, A. 1995. "An Overview of the Consequences for Human Health of Rapid Climate Change." In *Health Effects of Climate Change in New Zealand and the South Pacific—Conference.* Wellington: Wellington School of Medicine.

World Bank. 1999. *World Development Indicators 1999.* Washington, DC: World Bank.

World Meteorological Organization and UN Environment Programme. 1998. *WMO/UNEP Scientific Assessment of Ozone Depletion.* Geneva: WMO/UNEP.

World Resources Institute. 2000. *World Resources 2000–2001, People and Ecosystems: The Fraying Web of Life.* Washington, DC: World Resources Institute.

Environmental Activism

—Kathryn Miles

The history of all colonized countries is a dichotomous one: Indigenous peoples and their colonizers often existed at great cultural odds with one another. At no time is this more apparent than when examining human ecology—the relationship between these various peoples and their environment. The role of the land for indigenous peoples, who often practice pantheistic religions, and their white colonizers, who sought to claim and develop that same land, is hugely varied and often proved violently incompatible. This great ecological divide is brilliantly pronounced in the history of Australia and Oceania. Explored and settled largely by the Dutch, French, and English in the eighteenth century, these islands have witnessed great conflict over the handling of their lands and native peoples for more than two centuries.

Although the colonial births of these countries is not significantly different from those found in much of the Americas, the relative newness of their development brings the great cultural divides of their populations into stark relief, and it has left an indelible mark on the consciousness of these people. Nationhood has been a recent phenomenon for most of the islands of Oceania, with Australia abolishing the last of its constitutional ties to Great Britain in 1968; New Zealand declared its independence in 1907, Fiji in 1970, and Papua New Guinea as late as 1974. Palau, meanwhile, only gained independence in 1994. Some of the islands in the region still remain under the jurisdiction of the British, French, and U.S. governments.

Because of these strong political and social ties to Europe and America, the rise of the modern environmental movement on the islands of Oceania has been largely tied to the environmental movements of Great Britain and the United States. The Oceanic environmental movement, particularly in Australia and New Zealand, first found rooting in the nineteenth century (as

Australia's aboriginal peoples have been described as the continent's first conservationists. COREL

did the nascent labor, women's, and peace movements), but it remained in a largely quiescent mode until the 1960s. From that time forward it grew rapidly, and the environmental movement is now a potent political force in both countries (Hutton and Connors, 1999).

Roots of Modern Environmentalism

Precolonial cultures established on these islands by Polynesian settlers were steeped in respect for and understanding of the natural environment. But the modern "environmental movement," as the phrase is understood today, is grounded in the mid to late nineteenth century, when European exploration of the region intensified. Much of the initial Western exploration of the region was undertaken by Captain James Cook, a Royal Navyman and the first Western explorer of the South Pacific. "When Captain James Cook first set sail for the South Seas on board the *Endeavor* in 1768 he knew there was a large landmass—known only as *Terra Australis Incognita*—which, as the name suggests, was largely unexplored by Europeans. Dutch and English sailors had started to map the west coast of this 'unknown' continent; enough to know that it was a very large land mass. But they were not impressed with the arid landscapes they encountered" (Mulligan and Hill, 2001).

Cook's expedition nevertheless undertook extensive documentation of the flora and fauna of the region. This endeavor was spearheaded by Joseph Banks, the chief naturalist aboard the *Endeavor*. Through Banks's use of Linnaean taxonomy (a system of classification using formal Latinate genus and species names), the Western world first became familiar with the varied and rich environment of Oceania. It was also in Banks's work that the long conflict between native and Western environmentalism had its genesis. Banks "initiated the concept of *terra nullis* to suggest that the land was open for claim, and he extended this concept to Australian plants and animals because he saw little commercial potential in them. . . . Banks had quickly reached the conclusion that the new land had little to excite the interest of Europeans. The animals were exotic and the plants very unusual but there seemed little that could be eaten or even used by humans. Despite his close encounters with Aborigines, he thought they held 'a rank little superior to that of monkeys.' He suggested that the land was essentially unoccupied, thus coining the notion of *terra nullis*" (ibid.).

Banks's characterization of the Aboriginal peoples as "little superior" to monkeys was a common one throughout much of the eighteenth and nineteenth centuries. Although by this time many—but by no means all—scientists were prepared to acknowledge that humankind belonged to one species, most still touted the belief that there were levels of human development evinced by various races. The lowest or most animal-like level of humanity was termed savagery, and the aboriginal peoples of Oceania were held up as examples of this stunted level of development (Head, 2000).

These aboriginal peoples—a patriarchal and nature-worshipping culture of hunters and gatherers—exercised their own unique version of conservation, based largely on a naturalistic religion and sense that identity is tied to the earth, as well as a keen understanding that their welfare was inextricably tied to the health of the environment around them. What this meant in terms of environmentalism was a severe schism in which the native and colonial settlers would undertake two very distinct approaches to early environmentalism. Both the aboriginal and colonial people perceived Oceania as a land of plenty for humankind; however, the aboriginal peoples assimilated with the natural world and "became conservationists," while white settlers continued to exploit the land with no awareness of "ecological reality" (ibid.).

The British Invasion: European Settlement and Scientific Exploration (1820–1880)

Although the early nineteenth century witnessed early glimmers of environmental concern, such as P. E. D. Strzelecki's *Physical Description of New South Wales and Van Diemen's Land* (1845), which warned of soil erosion at the hands of Western crop practices, the nascent environmental movement at this time was defined largely through colonial art and biological inquiry. Indeed, Oceania had become something of a hotbed of colonization by the mid-1900s, as British people flocked to areas such as Tasmania and the Swan River Colony. Although colonial law allowed the Aborigines to continue to own property, a rising form of ethno-geography pioneered by Griffith Taylor suggested that certain regions or zones of the region were particularly suited for various races. This allowed white settlers, particularly in Australia, to justify removing Aborigines to the desertlike interior of the continent while they enjoyed the biological diversity of the coastal areas.

The first task of European scientists in Oceania was twofold: remove the shroud of mystery—the *terra incognita* aspect—surrounding the region, and begin establishing a coherent classification system to account for the myriad new and potentially valuable forms of life. The most famous of these endeavors is, of course, Charles Darwin's scientific inquiry while serving as chief naturalist aboard the *HMS Beagle* in the mid-1830s. Darwin's travel journal, which was later published as *The Voyage of the Beagle,* lay the foundation for his later theories of evolution and natural selection.

But Darwin was not alone in his work. One of the most notable environmental scientists of this era was Georgiana Molloy, the wife of a Swan River

Colony settler who became an expert in Australian botany and did much to raise awareness of Oceanic flora throughout Europe. Initially homesick for her English gardens, Molloy struck a close relationship with British horticulturalist Captain James Mangles, who sent her a box of seeds common in British gardens. "What was unusual about the gift was that it came with a note asking Molloy to return the box filled with Australian seeds and pressed flowers. . . . The trip [to fill this box] became a daily event and her knowledge about the diversity of life grew enormously. Captain Mangles was delighted by the collection he received, and he and Molloy maintained an active correspondence" (Mulligan and Hill, 2001). Through Molloy's work, England and the rest of Europe not only became familiar with the lush vegetation of Australia, they also learned to value this new world of plant life through its strategic placement in many of the continent's botanical gardens.

Oceania's numerous and exotic species of flora also piqued the interested of environmental artists. John Glover, a painter famous for his romantic depictions of the natural landscape, sailed to Tasmania and quickly became a lifelong student and admirer of the Tasmanian environment and its native inhabitants. Art became a vehicle for early conservation as well. Eugene von Guérard, another transplanted landscape painter, helped to launch one of the first formal acts of conservation in the region. His 1857 painting set in a forest at Ferntree Gully in the Dandenong Ranges east of Melbourne sparked a public campaign against a proposal to log the area in 1861. The literary world also did much to raise awareness about the Oceanic environment. Along with Glover, Adam Lindsay Gordon—a romantic poet deeply influenced by Coleridge, Byron, and Wordsworth—moved to South Australia to experience the beauty of this new and largely unsullied wilderness. His subsequent works, which touted the beauty of the Australian landscape, earned him widespread recognition as the "National Poet of Australia" (ibid.).

Through the work of these early pioneers, the rest of the world caught a glimmer of the rich biodiversity and natural resources offered by Oceania. Although the taxonomic systems of collection and classification used by these first scientists and artists may seem primitive to our contemporary sense of environmentalism, they nevertheless paved the way for later appreciation and eventual protection of the Oceanic wildlife.

The Birth of Conservation (1880–1960)

Spurred on by the work of writers and artists, the colonial cultures of Oceania began to assert their own identities independent of European rule. The first such movement to this end was the school of Heidelberg painters, the first Australian school of art. Although influenced largely by French impressionism, members of this school—Tom Roberts, Frederick McCubbin, Arthur Streeton, Charles Conder, and Louis Abrahams—created a style very much their own that was dictated largely by the unique landscape of the Australian coast. This tendency was shared by writers of the day as well. With the emergence and success of the periodical *The Bulletin* came a new voice for the Australian people. The writers of *The Bulletin* "were determined to tackle the cultural cringe toward all things English in order to assert a new and proud Australian identity. For both the Heidelberg painters and *The Bulletin* writers, the emerging Australian identity was rooted in the experience of distinctive and challenging landscapes. While trying to take a fresh look at the relationship between Australian identity and the land, the *Bulletin* writers maintained the dominating *terra nullis* attitude toward the indigenous people" (ibid.).

The late nineteenth century brought with it a desire for organized action concerning the environment. Much of this action was directed toward social recreation; however, there was also an important element—albeit modest in size—of environmental activism and habitat protection as well. Indeed, many historians cite the decades of the 1860s, 1870s, and 1880s as the real nexus of early environmentalism among white communities in Australia and New Zealand. During this period the Melbourne-based *Argus* newspaper emerged as an ardent supporter of preservation of areas of natural beauty, especially forests being targeted by loggers. In addition, a variety of organizations and societies devoted to scientific exploration of the natural world were created, including the Zoological Society of Victoria, the Australian Association for the Advancement of Science, the Field Naturalists Club, the Western Australian Natural History Society, and the New Zealand Society, a national scientific group with a membership constituted of imported British gentry. In 1880, meanwhile, the founding of the Victorian Field Naturalists Club heralded the beginning of an era in which organizations devoted to enjoying and protecting the outdoors proliferated (ibid.; Hutton and Connors, 1999).

The face of environmentalism in Oceania began to change dramatically during this era. In Australia and New Zealand in particular, economic stability had created a white middle class with time for leisure and recreation. The creation of this middle class allowed for the development of four streams of environmentalism. These branches of environmentalism included the creation and support of a national parks system, the conservation of flora and fauna, the protest against millinery use of plumage, and the nascent bushwalking conservation movement. "There was no mass mobilization to bring the four streams together. . . . [E]arly environmentalists defined themselves narrowly by their own specific causes. Within the four streams, however, there were patterns of growth, consolidation, resolution of demands or failure" (Hutton and Connors, 1999).

The first of these movements, the campaign to create a national park system, began officially in 1879 with the creation of the Royal National Park, just south of Sydney. The first national park in Oceania, the Royal National was also the second national park in the world, created just after the unveiling of Yellowstone Park in the United States and six years before Canada's Banff National Park came into being. The creation of the Royal National Park and subsequent parks was deeply indebted to these efforts in North America. But unlike the United States and Canada, where management of national parks and national forests is the responsibility of the federal government, Australia determined to place responsibility for its protected areas in the hands of the states, rather than the commonwealth.

The creation of the Northern District Forest Conservation League in 1888 ensured that development of a national park system would continue into the twentieth century. But the ultimate shape and character of this system—and wildlands conservation efforts in general—can be traced in great measure to Ros Garnet and Myle Dunphy. Garnet, a leading figure in the Field Naturalists Club of Victoria, also helped in the publication of *The Victorian Naturalist*, a catalog of botanical discoveries, and he was integral in raising public awareness and political support needed to sustain the early parks. Myles Dunphy also became a great advocate of national parks, especially those primarily aimed at preserving wilderness. In 1932 he formed the National Parks and Primitive Areas Council, which has been called Australia's first wilderness society, and he doggedly worked to shift public perceptions about the value of wilderness. Moreover, Dunphy's writings convinced a large contingent of the environmental movement to abandon its long-time reliance on harvesting, collecting, and displaying of exotic species. "For Dunphy, wilderness was a source of infinite variety and personal inspiration and he sought to share his excitement about wild country in his writings" (Mulligan and Hill, 2001). Fourteen major parks were eventually established as a direct result of the council's campaigns to preserve them as wilderness for backpacking and other recreational purposes (McNeely et al., 1994).

Another watershed moment in the history of the Australian environmental movement was the millinery craze of the early twentieth century. In addition to recreation, the growing middle class of white Oceania demanded the latest in haute fashion as a way of demonstrating their commitment to leisure. For many, that meant adorning themselves with feathers and furs. This trend led to the massive extermination of Oceanic birds and marsupials and created an immediate crisis for the blossoming environmental movement. In response to the slaughter, concerned individuals formed a variety of conservation groups in Tasmania, South Australia, and other parts of the country. For example, the massive harvest of birds was a factor in the 1909 founding of Australia's

Wildlife Preservation Society, which eventually developed into an organization of significant political clout and national presence.

The millinery issue also compelled people and organizations that had previously limited themselves to scientific inquiry to adopt more of an advocacy position in behalf of threatened natural landscapes and species. A particularly telling example of this shift toward conservation was evident within the Linnean Society of South Wales, an organization devoted to plant and animal biology and taxonomy and natural history. In 1908, the society's president, A. H. S. Lucas, publicly joined the movement to force Australia to begin protecting its birds, a decidedly different and more political decision than any previously made by the Linnean Society. Meanwhile, the Australian Ornithologists Union pointed to species protective legislation enacted by the United States and Britain and argued for the need for similar laws in Australia.

By the early 1900s the pressure exerted by these groups convinced a number of states to pass legislation extending greater protections to some native birds. "The campaign against Australia's bird and feather trade was probably the first organized environmental activity to pierce the Australian consciousness about a particular environmental threat," concluded one analysis. "It was also significant, for this campaign was not based on preserving potential recreation areas, nor was it of direct utilitarian benefit to most Australians: it was about the imminent loss of native species, some of which had become national icons" (Hutton and Connors, 1999). Similar events took place in New Zealand as well. In 1914, several members of Parliament organized the New Zealand Forest and Bird Protection Society. It soon disbanded, but was replaced in 1923 with the Native Bird Protection Society, which was similarly dedicated to the preservation of the country's bird species and the habitat upon which they depended.

Even the Australian Bushwalkers, originally a group of landed Westerners desiring to conquer the remaining uncolonized land in Australia, joined in the burgeoning conservation movement. The Bushwalkers became deeply committed to the idea of preserving and protecting Australian land for its own sake. This shift in group identity occurred in 1931, when a group of Bushwalkers led by Alan Rigby discovered that a tract of land near the Grose River was leased and being cleared. Rigby approached the Mountain Trails Club and the Bush Walkers Club with the idea of buying, and thus preserving, this land. Rigby and the Bushwalkers were successful in their endeavor, and the tract of land became known as the Blue Gum Conservation area. This initiative was the first such action taken by conservation groups in Australia (ibid.).

The early decades of the twentieth century also witnessed the first popular attention to the plight of the Aboriginal peoples of Oceania. Literary circles led the way in this endeavor. In the 1910s, children's literature author May Gibbs wrote a series of books introducing children to the forests of Oceania and its native occupants. Her most widely known works—*Gum-Nut Babies, Gum-Blossom Babies,* and *The Magic Pudding: Being the Adventures of Bunyip Bluegum and His friends Bill Barnacle and Sam Sawnoff*—all depict mythical Aboriginal youngsters in an exotified but compassionate light. What seems most significant about these depictions is Gibbs's ability to capture the connection between these peoples and their environment as well as their respect and awe for the natural world.

Adult literature was making similar strides. In the 1930s, a group of writers dedicated to celebrating Aboriginal influence formed the Jindyworobak school. Much of their philosophy is encapsulated in the poetry of Judith Wright, who urged:

> *Listen, listen*
>
> *Latecomers to my country*
>
> *Eat of wild manna*
>
> *There is*
>
> *There was*
>
> *A country*
>
> *That spoke in the language of the leaves*
>
> — (QUOTED IN POLLAK AND MacNABB, 2000)

Like Gibbs, Wright and the other members of the Jindyworobak school saw and celebrated the connection between Aboriginal people and the environment—the ability to recognize the "manna" of the earth and its voice.

In the meantime, Aboriginal communities that had long suffered from the discriminatory policies and racist attitudes of white Australians became increasingly agitated over the changes that intensive mining, logging, cattle grazing, and farming activities were wreaking on the continent's rivers, forests, and plains. Those Aborigines employed by white Australia were often relegated to difficult jobs mining and developing the earth. Not only were these workers asked to do work antithetical to their view of nature, but they were also told to do so on land that had once been their own. This crisis of consciousness reached a head in 1946, when a group of Aboriginal stockmen in the Pilbara district of Western Australia went on strike. Although the strike did little to change the immediate conditions of the workers, it did set a tone for Aboriginal rights that would become most significant in the following decades as modern environmentalism took root throughout Oceania.

The Face of Modern Environmentalism: 1960–2000

The public presence of the environmental movement lessened during World War II and immediately thereafter in Australia and New Zealand. But both governments did institute important environmental measures during this period. Actions such as the 1948 passage of the Fauna Protection Act in New South Wales and the 1948 creation of the New Zealand "Native Birds Preservation Committee," a branch of the Department of Internal Affairs, were important milestones in habitat and species protection. Similarly, the 1951 creation of the National Resources Conservation League, an Australian nonprofit group dedicated to resource management, came about because of heavy government support. The league prospered from the outset, and it eventually grew to become one of the largest and most influential of Victoria's conservation groups (Hutton and Connors, 1999).

But it was not until the following decade that environmental activism, fueled in no small measure by increased nongovernmental organization (NGO) participation, really flourished in Oceania. "A second wave of environmentalism took shape in Australia in the late 1960s as the conservation movement began to tackle a broader agenda and adopted more radical campaigning methods," recalled one account of the continent's environmental history. "The movement was also enriched by the arrival of organizations that began life in other parts of the world, such as Friends of the Earth and Greenpeace, who brought with them a concern for global issues like the environmental threats of the nuclear industry and the loss of biodiversity on a global scale. However, even as it changed direction, the environmental movement in Australia still carried the legacy of the frontier mentality that fostered the hyperseparation of people and 'the bush'" (Mulligan and Hill, 2001).

The Little Desert Campaign

One early landmark in the development of the modern environmental movement was the 1963 Little Desert Campaign, in which the government of Victoria and local activists became deadlocked over the handling of a tract of land in the Little Desert Wilderness. This conflict arose when the Victorian government hired local developers to convert 40,000 hectares of Little Desert Wilderness into a combination of farms and single-family housing. Local residents, heavily supported by various private environmental groups, favored the conversion of this land to a national park, where it would remain protected. In 1968–1969, Sir William McDonald, the new minister for lands, disregarded environmental protests and reported that the Little Desert Land was questionable farmland; he then introduced a special Land Act to subdivide the land into fifty farms and a National Park of 32,000 hectares. This solution pleased neither side, and amidst great debate the government eventually resolved to reduce the number of farms to twelve and add an additional 500 to 600 hectares to the proposed national park. What was most significant about this action was not only the willingness of the Victorian government to work with environmental groups but also the fact that various factions of the developing environmental movement banded together over a single cause for the first time in Oceania's modern history (Hutton and Connors, 1999).

This sort of moral protest intensified in the wake of the publication of A. J. Marshall's *The Great Extermination* in 1966. Like Rachel Carson's *Silent Spring*, published four years previously in the United States, Marshall's warning about the destruction of fauna throughout Australia created something of a public sensation, for it was the first publication of its kind to use quantifiable scientific data to register grave concerns about the future of the environment in Australia.

The year 1966 proved a crucial one for Oceanic environmentalism in other respects as well. In addition to the publication of Marshall's seminal work, a growing list of legislation and direct action made environmentalism the focus for many of the region's inhabitants. During this year, the founding of the Australian Conservation League, an influential NGO, became official. In Papua New Guinea, the government passed the Fauna Protection and Control Act of 1966, one of the first environmental conservation acts for the new country. This statute provided for the creation of wildlife sanctuaries and protected areas, and forbade all hunting of threatened species except by indigenous Papua New Guineans using traditional methods for customary noncommercial purposes (Stevens, 1997). The creation of these reserves represented an attempt by the Papua New Guinea government to reinstate many aspects of the land tenure system used by its native peoples before colonialization.

Similar actions began to take shape in Australia as well. With the 1960s came the emergence of the modern Aboriginal land rights movement in the country. Originally based in the Northern Territory, this movement soon began to encompass much of Australia. It gained international attention on May 1, 1966, when a group of Aboriginal Water Stockmen in Newcastle went on strike for better working conditions and a more sustainable use of the landscape, and was quickly succeeded by the Wave Hill Strike, a similar action by Aboriginal workers. Both actions brought the Aboriginal land rights issue to the forefront of Australian political concerns, and in 1968, nearly two hundred years after the first Westerners arrived on the shores of Australia, Aborigines were granted citizenship and the right to vote.

Meanwhile, a series of development proposals by the Australian government once again galvanized the fast-growing environmental movement. In 1967, a proposal by the Hydro-Electric Commission to dam the Gordon River and flood Lake Pedder in Tasmania elicited strong protests from the environmental community, fronted by the modern Bushwalkers. The group was led by Brenda Hean, a charismatic environmentalist and devoted bushwalker who quickly took leadership of the group fighting to save Lake Pedder. Hean died later that year in a suspicious plane crash.

As significant as the fight to save the Gordon and Lake Pedder was, it paled in comparison to the fight to save the Great Barrier Reef, Australia's coastal treasure. This battle began in 1957, when Judith Wright, one of Australia's best-loved modern environmentalists, learned that water sewage discharge and other pollutants were threatening to destroy the great reef. Her fight picked up new allies and momentum in 1967 when the government received proposals to mine the reef and engage in offshore oil exploration. Wright and her allies effectively rallied widespread public support against the energy industry's plans, and the conservation campaign eventually resulted in the creation of the Great Barrier Reef National Park in 1975. This triumph has been cited as the Australian environmental movement's crowning achievement of the twentieth century (Dunlap, 1999).

Environmentalism Goes Mainstream

The "mainstreaming" of environmentalism during the 1970s was greatly aided by the written word. A series of publications, both literary and periodical, popularized the work of environmental groups. For example, writer and folk artist Meg Miller launched the hugely successful magazine *Grass Roots*, a periodical devoted to self-sufficiency and ecologically sensitive lifestyles, in 1973. Shortly thereafter, the equally successful publication *Wild* popularized the wilderness for many of Australia's younger generation, blending coverage of the booming outdoor recreation and adventure industry with the conservation mission of environmental groups. The literary world followed suit. Author Patrick White published a series of novels between 1955 and 1976 devoted to Oceanic wilderness and human ecology, and his Nobel Prize of 1963 was described as "partly a recognition of an emerging and distinct Australian literature that was drawing inspirations from Australian landscapes" (Pollak and MacNabb, 2000). White's success was shared by writers such as Xavier Herbert, who also combined depictions of the Australian landscape and an environmental mission in their work. Herbert, who was formally trained as a botanist and pharmacist, spent much of his time in the Australian bush during the 1950s and 1960s. This experience is brought to light in his 1975 novel *Poor Fellow My Country,* which exults in the Australian wilderness and champions the need for greater protection.

The rest of academia shared in this trend. Ecology and conservation biology had both arrived on the scene sometime earlier, and ecophilosophy soon followed. This school of theory was based on the deep ecology of Norwegian Arne Naess, which advocated removing environmentalism from any anthropomorphic attachments and focusing, instead, on land ethics and an ecocentric view of the world that privileges nature over humanity. Ecophilosophy shared in this commitment to ecocentricism, and scholars such as Richard Routley, Val Plumwood, Ariel Salley, and Warwick Fox allowed the movement to gain traction in Australia and the rest of the world.

Outside of academe, the environmental movement found a strong ally in the mid-1970s when the Gough Whitlam government took office. Whitlam had run on a campaign that emphasized a strong environmental focus and commitment to political and social justice. In 1973, under Whitlam's leadership, the federal government of Australia awarded $100,000 in grants to environmental centers throughout the country, the first action of its kind in Australia (Hutton and Connors, 1999). The Whitlam government followed up in 1974 with the passage of the Australian Environmental Protection Act. A year later, the government passed the Australian National Parks and Wildlife Conservation Act, which also allowed for the creation of the Australian National Parks and Wildlife Service, renamed the Australian Nature Conservation Agency in the early 1990s.

Action continued in the private sector as well. One of the most pivotal events for the growing environmental movement of Australia was the so-called Anti-Uranium Movement of the 1970s. Although uranium had been mined since the 1940s in Queensland and the Northern Territory, this practice became of new concern in 1974 when the Australian government proposed expanding mining operations into the Kakadu area. Environmental groups such as Friends of the Earth as well as various trade unions and Aboriginal groups came together to fight this proposal specifically and uranium mining more generally. "The anti-uranium campaign, as a significant component of the environment movement, reflected all of the characteristics of a successful social movement," observed one account of the struggle. "It had expanded horizontally to form umbrella groups, and these in turn had linked with other movements, such as the trade unions and indigenous groups. It had challenged principal institutional norms and sociopolitical patterns by its predication of the authoritarianism implicit in a state dependent on nuclear industry, its critique of centralized technology, and its espousal of renewable energy. It had also connected with political power by directing its message to significant sections of the trade union movement and the Labor Party" (ibid.).

Midnight Oil lead singer Peter Garrett. RUNE HELLESTAD/CORBIS

Peter Garrett: Environmental Activist and International Rock Star

Peter Garrett was born around 1953 and grew up in Sydney, Australia. His parents encouraged him "to express opinions and talk about things," he recalled. "We didn't spend our life in front of the television set" (Small, 1990). Garrett attended private schools and went on to earn a law degree from the University of New South Wales. The summer before he graduated, however, he answered a newspaper advertisement placed by a rock band looking for a lead singer. He joined the group Midnight Oil in 1977, the same year that he passed the bar exam.

Midnight Oil started out as a local band and gradually expanded its popularity across Australia. Throughout its twenty-five-year history, the group was known for its social conscience and activism in behalf of various causes, including Aboriginal rights and environmental protection. In 1986, Midnight Oil embarked on its "Black Fella White Fella" tour, traveling across Australia to remote Aboriginal settlements with the indigenous Warumpi Band. This experience had a strong effect on Garrett, as the band visited native communities devastated by poverty, disease, and discrimination. It also influenced many songs on the 1987 album *Diesel and Dust*, which brought Midnight Oil to worldwide attention. The critically acclaimed *Blue Sky Mining* followed in 1989, along with a world concert tour.

In 1990, Midnight Oil performed a lunchtime concert outside the Exxon Building in New York City to protest the *Exxon Valdez* oil spill in Alaska's Prince William Sound. The concert attracted 10,000 spectators and was turned into a documentary video, *Black Rain Falls*, with proceeds from its sale going to the environmental group Greenpeace. The group performed many other benefit concerts during the 1990s, prompting Garrett to call Midnight Oil "a terminally serious band appearing at the right places for the right things" (*Contemporary Musicians*, 1994).

Midnight Oil released more than a dozen albums over the years and earned international acclaim. One critic noted that the group "combined an acute awareness of political, social, and environmental issues with an aggressive rock sound to create one of the most distinctive voices in current popular music" (ibid.). Garrett's focus in his music was to encourage fellow Australians to examine their priorities and stimulate young people to think critically about the world around them. He retired from Midnight Oil in December 2002, following the release of the album *Capricornia* and accompanying world tour.

Throughout his career as lead singer of Midnight Oil, Garrett used his celebrity to voice his opinion on many environmental issues. In 1984 he ran for the Australian Senate on the Nuclear

(continues)

Disarmament Party ticket. His candidacy drew 200,000 votes, which nearly earned him a victory, but he later claimed that he was relieved to have lost the election. He had achieved his goal in running—which was to send a message about nuclear weapons—and was not ready to leave the band.

In 1989, Garrett was elected president of the Australian Conservation Foundation (ACF), the continent's largest environmental group. ACF is a membership-based organization that seeks to form partnerships with communities and businesses to work together toward protecting Australia's natural heritage and promoting ecological sustainability. Some of the issues ACF tackles include water resource management, endangered species, uranium mining policies, and global warming. During Garrett's tenure as president, ACF achieved results in protecting Tasmanian forests and Coronation Hill in Kakadu National Park, as well as in stopping construction of a naval base at Jervis Bay in New South Wales.

Garrett resigned from ACF in 1993 to take a position on the international board of directors for Greenpeace. He resumed his presidency of ACF in 1998, however, after deciding that he preferred to focus on Australian issues. Some of his recent work has concerned genetic engineering, coastal development, and expansion of the nuclear industry in Australia. "I don't need to wheel out a thousand scientists to sense what's happening on the planet," he once said. "I can taste the air. I can feel the wind. And I know I have to be part of the healing process" (Small, 1990).

Garrett lives in the southern highlands of New South Wales with his wife and three daughters. He has received several awards for his environmental activism. In 1997 he was named to the National Trust List of Living Treasures, and in 2000 he received the Australian Humanitarian Foundation Award in the environmental category. Garrett says that the most satisfying thing he has done in his life is "helping to raise people's awareness that the natural world is our only home to live in and take fair dinkum care of" ("Peter Garrett Talks," 2000).

Sources:

"Midnight Oil." 1994. In *Contemporary Musicians*, vol. 11. Detroit: Gale.

"Peter Garrett: ACF President." 2001. *Australian Conservation Foundation.* January. Available at http://www. acfonline.org.au/asp/pages/documen t.asp?IdDoc=20.

"Peter Garrett: Biography." Available at http://www.petergarrett.com.au/ biography.html.

"Peter Garrett Talks about His Heroes." 2000. *Heroism: Stories and Biographies.* Available at http://library.thinkquest. org/C001515/heroism/peterg.htm.

Ray, Louise. 1998. "Peter Garrett: From the Top." *Habitat Australia* 26 (August).

Small, Michael. 1990. "Environmentalist Peter Garrett, Lead Singer for Midnight Oil, Looks Like Mr. Clean and Sounds Like Mr. Cleanup." *People* (August 20).

Indeed, trade unions and the Labor Party became important players in the Australian environmental movement of the 1970s. In the third year of that decade, Jack Mundey, secretary of the New South Wales Builders Laborers Federation, coined the term "green ban." Operating under the belief that all people of Australia, regardless of income, color, or place of residence, were entitled to green space and natural environment, Mundey and the workers he represented utilized "green bans"—in essence a focused strike whereby union workers would refuse to participate in any construction project that might compromise previously undeveloped or otherwise historic space—to great effect. Over the next several years, these bans helped to preserve a variety of open spaces and historic buildings. These green bans "were so successful because they combined three important factors: widespread community mobilizations; supportive trade unions that could exert economic power to counter the developers; and ideological coherence that was contributed especially by the Communist leadership of the Builders Laborers Federation" (ibid.).

In terms of the larger environmental movement of Oceania, green bans also helped environmentalists broaden the focus of their attentions to include spaces like historic buildings and other remnants of past culture. The "environment" became not just the unsullied bush and lush shores of Oceania but the stories told by aging and unique buildings as well. To this end, Australia signed the World Heritage Convention and passed the Australian Heritage Commission Act in 1975, thereby ensuring the further protection of these places. New Zealand would follow suit with the inclusion of historic space in the Department of Conservation and National Parks office.

Of course, the wilderness of Oceania remained very much in the forefront during these changes, and organizations such as the Wilderness Society of Australia continued to focus most of their energy on enlisting public support in protecting Australia's remaining wild spaces. "We have to try to sell not the wilderness experience—that is, wilderness as a recreational resource—but the right of the wilderness to exist . . . for its own sake," declared Kevin Kiernan, a cofounder of the organization and its first director (quoted in ibid.).

Environmentalism and Race Relations

Race relations continued to be a vexing problem for the Australian environmental movement. Although many environmental groups strove to work with Aboriginal peoples, many native peoples—and white environmentalists as well—felt that too often, the efforts were cursory in nature and did not reflect sufficient appreciation for Aboriginal history and perspectives. Activists such as Judith Wright came to feel that environmentalists too often saw the interests of Aboriginal people as an obstacle to the protection of "pristine nature."

In 1990 she publicly condemned the policy of the Wilderness Society on Aboriginal land rights, describing their position as a "confirmation and endorsement of the *terra nullis* judgement," and one year later she resigned from the organization she had helped to create, the Wildlife Preservation Society of Queensland (WPSQ), because she felt that it had adopted a "weak" position on Aboriginal land rights (Mulligan and Hill, 2001).

Australian Aborigines, environmental activists, and the commonwealth government did register some notable successes during the 1970s, however. The most important of these was a commitment to the joint management of several of Australia's national parks. In 1979, the Australian government, working with Aborigines in the Northern Territory, established Kakadu National Park. What made the establishment of this park so significant was that it existed on lands owned by the Aborigines and was managed both by the Gagaudju tribe of traditional owners and the Australian Conservation Agency. Both groups characterized the formation and subsequent management of the park as a great success, and its creation signaled a victory in the quest to mend the great environmental schism between the races in the region. Since then, three more Aboriginal-owned national parks have been created in the same area—Gurig and Nitmiluk under Northern Territory legislation, and Uluru-Kata Tjuta under commonwealth legislation—and the joint management-model in place at these parks has been studied at the international level (Stevens, 1997).

Aboriginal environmentalists again led the way during the summer of 1982, when another dam was proposed for the Franklin and Gordon rivers in southwestern Tasmania. Working with white environmental organizations such as the Australian National Wilderness Society, which played a critical role in many of the continent's major wilderness disputes during the 1980s and 1990s, Aborigines used legal arguments concerning ancient land rights to defeat the proposed hydroelectric development. Relations between the groups became strained shortly thereafter, however, when the Kuku-Yalanji people who inhabited that area supported the creation of a road through the forest. Although the decision to support the road was a difficult one for many white environmentalists to understand, it has been suggested that it demonstrates the development of Aboriginal environmentalism and the complexity of their belief system. Rather than disavow all development, Aboriginal groups had begun to view the environment as a part of a larger political system that had a direct impact on their well-being (Head, 2000).

Entering the twenty-first century, Aboriginal perspectives on environmental protection and land use issues will undoubtedly remain an essential element in determining the future quality and character of Australian wilderness, biodiversity, and other aspects of the environment. In 1992 the High Court of Australia delivered its landmark Mabo decision, in which it formally recognized the legitimacy of Aboriginal land rights, called "native title." This ruling effectively rewrote the Australian common law that had long held that when Australia was "discovered" by Captain Cook in the eighteenth century, it was an empty and uncivilized land—*terra nullis.* It also gave land conservation advocates—whether Aboriginal or white—a potent weapon in the struggle to keep mining, pastoral, and logging interests out of still-intact natural areas, though opponents have energetically sought to whittle away the practical application of the judgment (Brennan, 1995; Aplin, 1998).

Australian Environmental Organizations in the 1980s and 1990s

Environmental activism in Australia continued to evolve during the 1980s and 1990s, reaching a stature and power that sparked envy and admiration among environmentalists in most other countries. "In the late 1980s, environment movement organizations claimed to have 300,000 members Australia-wide—more than all the members of political parties combined. The environment movement could probably have claimed, as the peace movement in the mid-1980s did, to be larger on a *per capita* basis than its counterparts in the rest of the Western world (Hutton and Connors, 1999).

During this period, major international conservation organizations such as the Wilderness Society, Friends of the Earth, Greenpeace, and World Wide Fund for Nature became firmly established on the continent, employing researchers, lobbyists, and public advocates who influenced public policy in ways that only industrial or trade union groups had previously been able to do. In addition, some groups, such as Greenpeace and Friends of the Earth, engaged in more radical forms of activism—from peaceful demonstrations to harassment of visiting nuclear-armed warships—on behalf of the environment. The Australian Conservation Foundation (ACF), founded in 1965, became the most prominent of Australia's national environmental organizations during this time as well, engaging in activities ranging from public education and publishing to research and lobbying (ibid.).

A host of environmental groups also formed at the state and regional level, usually organizing around regional issues in such realms as forest conservation, coastal protection, or watershed health. Most of these groups remain heavily reliant on an urban membership that is nonetheless deeply concerned about protected areas, biodiversity, air quality, and other issues. Toxic contamination and other urban "brown" issues, meanwhile, are most often tackled by local city-based volunteer groups, often in alliance with local government councils and agencies. Finally, the national land management program known as Landcare, which has sparked the creation of several similar volunteer land stewardship programs such as Dune Care, RiverWatch, Bushcare, and Coastcare, is carried out in large part by local organizations. But the Australian Conservation Foundation has been heavily involved in the Landcare movement from its inception, and it remains a heavyweight supporter of the program in all of its incarnations (Aplin, 1998).

In the political arena, Australia's dominant electoral systems present formidable hurdles for candidates from minority parties—such as the Green Party, which is a significant player in some European countries—hoping to reach elected office. Moreover, the historical single-issue emphasis of Australia's Green Party has contributed to its marginal presence on the legislative floor at the state and commonwealth level. But the Greens have broadened their vision to encompass a greater range of issues in recent years, and they have been a part of coalition governments in Tasmania and elsewhere in the 1990s. In addition, environmentalists have constituted an important constituency of the Australian Democrats, an emergent and influential "third force" in the nation's politics, which have traditionally been dominated by the Australian Labor Party (ALP) and the Liberal-National Coalition (LNC) (ibid.).

Environmental Activism on the Pacific Islands

Australia is by far the largest of the countries in Oceania, accounting for more than 90 percent of the region's total land area. It is also the most heavily populated and commercially developed of the nations of the South Pacific. As a result of these factors, the country's history of environmental activism is particularly noteworthy. But environmental activism is also present in most other Pacific Island states, and in some cases conservation organizations have emerged as significant players in efforts to address overpopulation, water pollution, habitat loss and degradation, and other environmental issues.

New Zealand has a strong legacy of environmental protection and conservation, and it is home to numerous environmental organizations. International environmental groups such as Greenpeace and World Wide Fund for Nature have a strong presence in the country, and a multitude of local and regional groups have been formed to address issues affecting particular communities and wilderness areas. The country's tradition of conservation advocacy is reflected in several landmark pieces of legislation passed by the government over the past few decades, from the 1980 National Parks Act, which eventually allowed one-third of all New Zealand land to receive formal protection within its protected area system, to the Conservation Reform Act (1990) and the Resource Management Act (1991), which outlines initiatives for sustainable use of the country's natural resources. "The sustainable management in the RMA emphasizes managing the environmental effects of human activities by promoting biophysical sustainability but also facilitating project development by rationalizing the maze of preceding environmental regulation. As such it has been a focus that both business and environmentalists have been able to support" (Yencken et al., 2000).

The remaining countries of Oceania do not have the advanced economies and financial resources of Australia and New Zealand, and with the exception of Papua New Guinea, none have land resources approaching those of New Zealand, let alone Australia. But for the people who live on these small island nations, environmental issues are also a pressing concern. Some of these problems can be addressed at the local level, such as population growth rates that are overwhelming extremely finite natural resources. Other threats, such as global climate changes that could result in the submersion of entire island nations, originate in distant lands, leaving Oceania-based advocacy groups with few options other than lobbying the global community to reduce their greenhouse gas emissions.

Oceania boasts a growing array of dedicated and articulate grassroots organizations intent on addressing various social, economic, and environmental problems. Their capacity to meet these challenges has been greatly facilitated by NGOs that have provided funding and guidance while at the same time "encouraging and empowering the disadvantaged to play a greater role in improving their own well-being" (UN Environment Programme, 1999). International environmental organizations that have played meaningful roles in this regard include the Nature Conservancy, Greenpeace, and the World Wide Fund for Nature.

These and other environment-oriented NGOs operating in Oceania have been especially active in the realms of forest conservation and preservation of indigenous cultures. During the 1980s, concerns about worldwide depletion of rain forest prompted NGOs to examine ways to halt deforestation in the Pacific Islands, where many rare and endemic species of flora and fauna exist. Steps taken ranged from heavily publicized antilogging campaigns to education programs designed to encourage increased investment in ecotourism and sustainable logging activities. "Over the same period, and sometimes with support from offshore NGOs, the local movement became more active, especially in [Papua New Guinea] and the Solomon Islands. This local thrust was partly towards non-wood forest products as a means of providing income for the forest-owning community, but it also took up the theme of sustainable management. . . . NGOs have also been strongly supportive of policy measures to protect the use of traditional and indigenous knowledge, as in the Suva

Declaration of 1995" (ibid.). Since the mid-1990s, local, national, and international environmental groups have also pursued conservation and public education programs designed to protect coral reefs, estuaries, sea turtles, and other marine resources that are essential to the livelihoods of numerous Oceanic communities.

Sources:

Aplin, Graeme. 1998. *Australians and Their Environment: An Introduction to Environmental Studies.* Melbourne: Oxford University Press.

Australia National Land and Water Resources Audit. 2001. *Australian Agriculture Assessment 2001.* Canberra: National Land and Water Resources Audit.

———. 2001. *Australia's Native Vegetation.* Canberra: National Land and Water Resources Audit.

Australian State of the Environment Committee. 2001. *Australia State of the Environment Report 2001.* Canberra: Commonwealth of Australia.

Brennan, F. 1995. *One Land, One Nation: Mabo—Towards 2001.* Brisbane: University of Queensland Press.

Crosby, Alfred. 1986. *Ecological Imperialism.* Oxford: Cambridge University Press.

Doyle, Timothy. 2000. *Green Power: The Environmental Movement in Australia.* Kensington: University of South Wales.

Dunlap, Thomas R. 1999. *Nature and the English Diaspora: Environment and History in the United States, Canada, Australia, and New Zealand.* Oxford: Cambridge University Press.

Environment Australia. 2000. "Collaborative Australian Protected Areas Database (CAPAD) 2000." Available at www.ea.gov.au/parks/nrs/capad/2000 (accessed January 9, 2003).

———. "Indigenous Protected Areas." Available at www.ea.gov.au/indigenous (accessed January 9, 2003).

———. "Parks and Reserves." Available at www.ea.gov.au/parks (accessed January 9, 2003).

Head, Lesley. 2000. *Second Nature: The History and Implications of Australia as Aboriginal Landscape.* Syracuse, NY: Syracuse University Press.

Hutton, Drew, and Libby Connors. 1999. *A History of the Australian Environment Movement.* Melbourne: Cambridge University Press.

McCormick, J. 1992. *The Global Environmental Movement: Reclaiming Paradise.* London: Belhaven.

McNeely, J. A., J. Harrison, and P. Dingwall, eds. 1994. *Protecting Nature: Regional Reviews of Protected Areas.* Gland, Switzerland, and Cambridge, U.K.: IUCN-World Conservation Union.

Miller, Char, and Hal Rothman. 1997. *Out of the Woods: Essays in Environmental History.* Pittsburgh: University of Pittsburgh Press.

Mulligan, Martin, and Stuart Hill. 2001. *Ecological Pioneers: A Social History of Australian Ecological Thought and Action.* Melbourne: Cambridge University Press.

New Zealand Department of Conservation. "About Us," http://www.doc.govt.nz (accessed January 5, 2003).

Pollak, Michael, and Margaret MacNabb. 2000. *Hearts and Minds: Creative Australians and the Environment.* Sydney: Hale and Iremonger.

Rootes, Christopher, ed. 1999. *Environmental Movements: Local, National, and Global.* London: Frank Cass.

Stevens, Stan. 1997. *Conservation through Cultural Survival: Indigenous Peoples and Protected Areas.* Washington, DC: Island Press.

UN Environment Programme. 1999. *Pacific Islands Environmental Outlook.* Available at www.unep.org, 1999 (accessed December 4, 2002).

White, Richard. 1981. *Inventing Australia.* St. Leonards, NSW: Allen and Unwin.

Yencken, David, et al. 2000. *Environment, Education and Society in the Asia-Pacific: Local Traditions and Global Discourses.* London: Routledge.

Antarctica

With an area of about 14 million square kilometers (5.5 million square miles), Antarctica is the world's fifth-largest continent. Larger than Europe and nearly twice the size of Australia, it covers about one-tenth of the earth's land surface. The continent's name, which means "opposite to the Arctic," reflects its position as the earth's southernmost region. Antarctica is surrounded by the Southern Ocean, a 28-million-square-kilometer (10.8-square-mile) body of water formed through the convergence of the southernmost portions of the Atlantic, Pacific, and Indian Oceans. The boundary between these major oceans and the Southern Ocean, known as the Antarctic Convergence or Polar Front, is often considered the boundary of the Antarctic region. Antarctica is located about 1,000 kilometers (600 miles) from South America, 2,500 kilometers (1,600 miles) from Australia, and 4,000 kilometers (2,500 miles) from Africa. It was first sighted by explorers in the early nineteenth century, making it the last continent to be discovered.

Nearly all of the Antarctic continent is covered with ice. The volume of the Antarctic ice sheet has been estimated at 30 million cubic kilometers, which accounts for 90 percent of the world's ice. About 11 percent of the ice sheet consists of permanent floating ice shelves along the coastline. The largest of these, the Ross Ice Shelf, is about the size of France. In addition, Antarctica is surrounded by floating sea ice that forms and melts seasonally. Ice floes cover about 20 million square kilometers (7.7 million square miles) of the Southern Ocean in the winter, and about 4 million square kilometers (1.5 million square miles) in the summer. Only about 2 percent of the Antarctic continent, or about 280,000 square kilometers (108,000 square miles), is free of ice. These ice-free areas occur mostly along the coastline, particularly on the Antarctic Peninsula, but they also include a few exposed mountain peaks and glacier-carved "dry valleys." Most of the sub-Antarctic and cool temperate islands of the region also remain free of ice. Although small, these ice-free areas

The Ross Ice Shelf at the Bay of Whales. This is the southern-most navigable point on the planet and the point where Norwegian explorer Roald Amundsen started his successful trek to the South Pole in 1911.
MICHAEL VAN WOERT/NOAA

are the site of most of the biological activity in the Antarctic region, from bird and seal colonies to human scientific research bases.

Antarctica is widely recognized as having the least hospitable climate on earth. It is the coldest of the world's continents, with an average annual temperature of −30 degrees Celsius. The lowest temperature ever recorded on earth, −89.6 Celsius, occurred at Russia's Vostok research station in Antarctica in 1983. Antarctica is also the driest continent: the 5-centimeter (2-inch) average annual precipitation on the polar plateau is comparable to the level found in the world's hot deserts. It also holds the distinction of being the highest continent: its average elevation of 2,300 meters (7,520 feet) is more than twice the average elevation of Asia, the second-highest continent (Australian Antarctic Division, "Information about Antarctica," 2002). Finally, Antarctica is the world's windiest continent, with an average wind speed of 67 kilometers per hour (42 mph) and high speeds in the neighborhood of 320 kilometers per hour (200 mph). Even daylight in Antarctica comes in extremes: the continent's interior experiences almost continuous darkness during the winter months and nearly continuous daylight during the summer months.

Thanks to its remote location and forbidding climate, Antarctica remains clean and unspoiled compared with the other continents. It has no permanent human population, and human activities there are currently limited to exploration, scientific investigation, and tourism. Antarctica's relatively pristine environment makes it tremendously valuable to researchers studying the effects of pollution on global ecosystems. "The Antarctic is special because it has less pollution than anywhere else in the world—it doesn't have any smokestack industry, agricultural activity, or permanent human population," explained David Walton of the British Antarctic Survey. "We can use it as the baseline against which pollution levels in other parts of the world can be measured, to tell us whether or not the situation is getting worse. From this point of view, the Antarctic will only remain scientifically valuable if it is managed properly today" (Walton, 1999).

Antarctica's icy mantle has proven particularly useful in studying the effects of long-range pollutants, such as heavy metals, radioactive debris, and persistent organic pollutants (POPs). Pollutants from industrialized regions of the world are carried to Antarctica in the upper atmosphere or on ocean currents, then deposited on the continent in the form of snow. This snow and the air trapped within it becomes part of the Antarctic ice sheet, which preserves a historical record of changes in the global climate and environment stretching back 200,000 years (Australian Antarctic Division, "Information about Antarctica," 2002).

Despite its apparent barrenness, Antarctica supports diverse ecosystems of plants and animals uniquely adapted to survive its harsh environment. Yet the high level of specialization found among Antarctic species makes them vulnerable to changes in their environment, whether caused by the effects of global warming or localized disturbances. "Antarctica is one of the most fragile and—so far—unspoiled areas on earth," said Beth Clark, executive director of the Antarctica Project, based in Washington, DC. "The choices we make now will go a long way to deciding whether Antarctica remains the last wilderness or becomes just the latest resource" (Mulvaney, 1997).

Development of the Antarctic Treaty

The Antarctic region became the target of a series of European explorers during the late eighteenth century. In a historic voyage lasting from 1772 to 1775, British navigator James Cook became the first person to cross the Antarctic Circle and circumnavigate the continent of Antarctica. Cook and others took note of the large populations of whales and seals that cruised the Southern Ocean, and their reports attracted an influx of hunters hoping to exploit the wealth of the Antarctic waters in the early nineteenth century. The population of fur seals suffered significantly during this time. In fact, fur seals were eliminated from several sub-Antarctic islands by the 1820s.

The first national expeditions to Antarctica took place in the mid-nineteenth century, and Norwegian explorer Roald Amundsen succeeded in reaching the South Pole in 1911. Yet the first year-round scientific research stations were not established until the 1940s, around the same time that the first mapping of the continent was completed. Over the next two decades, various nations raced to establish bases in order to solidify territorial claims. By the mid-1950s, seven nations held sovereignty claims to portions of Antarctica: Argentina, Australia, Chile, France, New Zealand, Norway, and the United Kingdom. Three of these claims—those of Argentina, Chile, and the U.K.—overlap and are contested. The United States and the Russian Federation reserved the right to make future sovereignty claims. Most other nations do not recognize any claims on the Antarctic continent. In contrast, most of the sub-Antarctic islands surrounding the continent are subject to widely recognized national sovereignty.

In 1957, amid fears that the rivalry between the various nations claiming territory in Antarctica would escalate into direct conflict, twelve nations agreed to participate in a series of coordinated worldwide scientific research efforts as part of the International Geophysical Year (IGY). Research conducted in Antarctica during the eighteen-month IGY yielded impressive results and helped begin the process of resolving political disputes over the continent. At the conclusion of the IGY, the participating nations established the Scientific Committee on Antarctic Research (SCAR) to continue coordinated research projects. In 1959 the twelve countries (Argentina, Australia, Belgium, Chile, France, Japan, New Zealand, Norway, South Africa, United Kingdom, United States, and USSR) signed the Antarctic Treaty.

The Antarctic Treaty was a groundbreaking agreement that ensured continued scientific cooperation between the signatory parties. It also marked a significant shift in thinking about Antarctica—away from resource exploitation and toward conservation. Rather than attempting to deal with the questions of sovereignty, the Antarctic Treaty froze the positions of various nations. It also demilitarized the Antarctic region and prohibited nuclear explosions and the disposal of radioactive wastes. The treaty guaranteed freedom of access to the continent and established it as a "natural reserve, devoted to peace and science." The number of parties to the Antarctic Treaty increased from the original twelve in 1959 to forty-four by 1999. These forty-four nations represent 70 percent of the world's population. Those countries that conduct substantial research in Antarctica are known as consultative parties to the treaty, and those that simply agree to honor its terms are nonconsultative parties.

Several conventions were added to the Antarctic Treaty over the years to address particular conservation issues. Taken together, the original treaty and the added conventions are known as the Antarctic Treaty System (ATS). The

Convention for the Conservation of Antarctic Seals (CCAS), passed in 1972, established regulations for commercial sealing in and around Antarctica. Four species of seals were protected from hunting under the convention, and strict limits were placed on the others. The CCAS also tracks the number of seals that are killed for the purpose of scientific research.

The Convention for the Conservation of Antarctic Marine Living Resources (CCAMLR), passed in 1980, was intended to address the problem of overfishing in the Southern Ocean. "Exploitation of the Southern Ocean's marine-based species has . . . had a major effect on ecosystems through the reduction in size of the populations of the targeted species, the indirect effects of harvesting such as bycatch, and the removal of so many predators from the ecosystems. Commercial harvesting has been the greatest documented human effect on the Antarctic" (Australian Antarctic Division, "Information about Antarctica," 2002). The provisions of CCAMLR identified protected species, set catch limits, established fishing regions, regulated fishing seasons and methods, and collected data on the annual catch (UN Environment Programme, 1999).

Protocol on Environmental Protection

The most wide-reaching addition to the Antarctic Treaty was the Protocol on Environmental Protection of 1991 (also known as the Madrid Protocol, after the city in which it was signed). The movement toward stricter environmental protection for Antarctica began in the 1970s, when various nations began expressing interest in the continent's mineral wealth. Although little of Antarctica's land mass has been surveyed for minerals, scientists predict that it holds large supplies of gold, copper, lead, zinc, silver, tin, iron ore, chromium, platinum, nickel, uranium, coal, and petroleum. The parties to the Antarctic Treaty began negotiating a mining convention in the early 1980s. Although the continent's remote location and forbidding climate made mineral exploitation seem impractical at that time, several additional nations rushed to establish bases in Antarctica in order to participate in the talks.

In the mid-1980s, the international environmental group Greenpeace became the first nongovernmental organization (NGO) to establish a research station in Antarctica. Greenpeace scientists monitored the impact that the national scientific bases were having on the continent's environment and wildlife. They found evidence of localized pollution and habitat destruction around many bases, including some significant problems caused by the dumping of wastes, road and airstrip construction, and vehicle pollution (Mulvaney, 1997). By 1988, when the ATS parties developed guidelines for mineral exploration in Antarctica, Greenpeace and other environmental groups had joined in opposition to the measures. Public concern about environmental protection in the polar regions grew in 1989, following the *Exxon Valdez* oil spill in the Arctic and the sinking of the Argentine supply and tourist ship *Bahia Paraiso* off Antarctica, which released 600,000 liters of diesel fuel into the Southern Ocean.

The convention on mining required the agreement of all twenty-six parties to the ATS in order to pass. Under pressure from citizens and NGOs, France and Australia refused to allow the rules to be adopted. At this point, the ATS nations changed their focus to developing an environmental protocol, which they passed in 1991. The Environmental Protocol to the Antarctic Treaty forbids mineral extraction (except for scientific purposes) for a minimum of fifty years, after which the ban remains in place unless all parties to the treaty agree to revisit the question. The protocol also sets forth strict standards for pollution prevention, waste management and disposal, and the conservation of plants and animals. Finally, the protocol requires all parties to conduct thorough environmental impact assessments for any activity undertaken in Antarctica.

The wording of the protocol stated: "The protection of the Antarctic environment and dependent and associated ecosystems and the intrinsic value of Antarctica, including its wilderness and aesthetic values and its value as an area for the conduct of scientific research, in particular research essential to understanding the global environment, shall be fundamental considerations in the planning and conduct of all activities in the Antarctic Treaty area" (UN Environment Programme, 1996). The standards set forth in this landmark convention are among the most stringent conservation rules to be established anywhere in the world. In fact, it cost the U.S. government $30 million to clean up American research stations and bring them into compliance with the protocol (Walton, 1999).

Through the addition of the Madrid Protocol and other conventions, the Antarctic Treaty System gradually expanded its role from scientific oversight to regional governance. Proponents of the ATS claim that it provides an effective system for governing Antarctica in the interests of the international community. The arrangement has come under occasional criticism over the years, however, from developing countries and NGOs that wish to have greater say in the Antarctic region's affairs. Some critics claim that Antarctica should be governed by the United Nations to ensure the widest possible international input. They note that the Antarctic Treaty is binding only upon signatory nations, so other countries are free to exploit the continent if they can overcome the inherent economic and technological barriers (Australian Antarctic Division, "Information about Antarctica," 2002). Some NGOs have proposed designating Antarctica as a World Park—a status similar to U.S. national parks, which would give it stronger protection from mining, military activities, and human settlement—but the treaty parties have thus far rejected such efforts (Puri, 1997).

McMurdo Station in Antarctica attracts scientists from all over the world. NATIONAL OCEANIC AND
ATMOSPHERIC ADMINISTRATION

In addition to the ATS, Antarctica is covered under a number of international environmental treaties dealing with such global issues as depletion of the ozone layer, marine pollution, and endangered species. Whaling regulations for the Southern Ocean fall under the jurisdiction of the International Whaling Commission (IWC). Furthermore, independent groups such as SCAR and the Council of Managers of National Antarctic Programmes (COMNAP) help establish guidelines for their members.

Human Impacts

The main focus of human activity in Antarctica is scientific investigation. By the late 1990s, scientists from seventeen nations operated thirty-six stations for year-round research in Antarctica. The total annual number of scientists on the continent increased gradually until it peaked at around 9,000 in 1990, after which it leveled off or declined slightly. Only about 1,000 researchers remain in Antarctica through the winter months each year (UN Environment Programme, 1996). The largest scientific base in Antarctica is McMurdo Station on Ross Island. Established in 1956, it has grown into a small city with more than a hundred structures, including stores, offices, laboratories, living quarters, powerhouses, and its own harbor and airport. McMurdo's summer population exceeds 1,100, though only about 250 scientists and support staff remain over the winter, when they are often isolated from March through October.

Antarctica's relatively pristine environment provides scientists with a valuable baseline against which to compare the effects of pollution in the rest of the world. Ice-core studies provide scientists with information about past glaciations, sea levels, and atmospheric composition. In addition, scientists have found that Antarctica plays an important role in regulating the earth's climate and atmosphere, as well as in determining the composition and flow of the world's oceans. Research in the Antarctic region has increasingly shifted toward global issues, such as ozone depletion and global climate change. Other major areas of study include plate tectonics, movement of the ice sheet, sea-ice dynamics, oceanic circulation, and the biology of the region's plants and animals. Finally, some researchers study the effects of the Antarctic environment on the health of scientists who live and work there.

Most scientific bases are clustered in Antarctica's few ice-free regions, which are also home to most of the continent's fragile plant and animal life. The early research stations created some environmental damage, including pollution from waste disposal and oil spills, habitat destruction from construction and terrain modification, and introduction of exotic organisms. Observers note that the damage has been extensive in a few localized areas. "Without doubt, the worst-affected place on Antarctica has to be the Fildes Peninsula [an area on King George Island in the Antarctic Peninsula where several nations maintain research stations]," said one Greenpeace representative. "There are bases built on moss beds, fuel and chemical drums spilling over onto plant life, there's an airstrip, a lake being used as a landfill—it's appalling. Large moss beds of the kind that were found at Fildes are incredibly rare in Antarctica; this was a special place, but now it is a mess" (Mulvaney, 1997). Although some abuses continue, most Antarctic research is now conducted under the strict guidelines of the Madrid Protocol.

Tourism is a rapidly growing human use of the Antarctic region. The number of tourists in Antarctica increased from 4,700 in 1990 to a record 14,700 ten years later (IAATO, 1999). Most tourists arrive on shipboard cruises that stop at ice-free areas along the Antarctic Peninsula or on sub-Antarctic islands. Although most tours feature only brief sightseeing stops on land, some are broadening the scope of their offerings to include camping, skiing, climbing, sea kayaking, and helicopter flights inland (UN Environment Programme, 1996).

Some environmentalists are concerned about the impact of tourism on Antarctica, particularly since tourist activity tends to be concentrated in wildlife-intensive areas during the four-month summer season. They claim that tourism places stress on the continent's fragile ecosystems. For example, non-native species of grasses have been introduced to several sites in the Antarctic region, and critics claim that they were likely carried on the clothing of human visitors. "It is important to remember that the Antarctic environment is tremendously sensitive. The conditions are incredibly harsh, and plant life in particular can take many hundreds of years to become established, so that what might appear to be minimal damage in temperate zones can have very serious effects," explained one expert. "Some moss beds on the Antarctic Peninsula have taken three to four hundred years to grow; a single human footprint can cause tremendous damage and remain there as a permanent record" (Mulvaney, 1997).

The International Association of Antarctica Tour Operators (IAATO) was formed in 1991 to help minimize the environmental impact of Antarctic tourism. The association, which handles the majority of Antarctic tours, includes thirty-five member organizations in ten countries. The IAATO requires its members to evaluate the environmental impact of all proposed activities in the region. It also establishes guidelines for tour organizers and promotes a code of behavior for tourists designed to minimize environmental impact. For example, tourists are required to scrub the penguin feces off the bottoms of their boots after each landing as a means of preventing cross-colony contamination. They are also asked to avoid leaving any waste behind, which includes a prohibition against emptying their bladders on shore (Donelly, 2002).

Proponents of Antarctic tourism argue that it plays an important role in ensuring the conservation of the region. They claim that visiting the continent creates a constituency of thousands of people who take a personal interest in working to preserve its ecological integrity (Mulvaney, 1997). In support of this view, they point out that some Antarctic tours are sponsored by environmental or scientific organizations such as the World Wildlife Fund and the Smithsonian Institution.

Global Climate Change

Thanks to the complex interactions that take place between the continent's ice and the atmosphere, Antarctica plays an important role in global environment dynamics. In fact, many experts believe that the Antarctic region provides strong, early indications of global climate change. Supporters of this theory note that the concentration of greenhouse gases in the earth's atmosphere, especially carbon dioxide, has increased over the past several decades, largely because of human consumption of fossil fuels and deforestation. They claim that these atmospheric changes will result in an increase in global temperatures of between 1 and 4 degrees Celsius by the end of the twenty-first century (Australian Antarctic Division, "Information about Antarctica," 2002).

If global warming occurs as these scientists predict, the polar regions are expected to show the most extreme changes. The ice that covers Antarctica's land mass and large areas of the Southern Ocean will begin to melt, which will expose more land and water to the sun. This in turn will increase the absorption of solar energy from the atmosphere (sea ice reflects between 50 and 97 percent of the radiation that hits it, while open water reflects only 10 percent), thus creating even warmer temperatures and more melting of ice (ibid.). Some experts claim that this cycle has already begun. As evidence, they point to the fact that Antarctica has shown an increase in average annual temperatures of 2.5 degrees Celsius (4.5 degrees Fahrenheit) over the past fifty years— a much faster rate of change than has been experienced in other parts of the world ("The Melting Continent," 2002). If this situation were to continue indefinitely, the eventual results could include melting of the polar ice sheets, retreat of sea ice, thawing of permafrost, and a global rise in sea levels. "Polar regions contain important drivers of climate change," said one observer. "Once triggered, they may continue for centuries, long after greenhouse gas concentrations are stabilized, and cause irreversible impacts on ice sheets, global ocean circulation, and sea-level rise" (Intergovernmental Panel on Climate Change, 1997).

If the earth's climate continues to grow warmer, experts predict that the Antarctic will suffer more serious effects than even the Arctic. One reason is

The reduction of Antarctica's winter sea ice may be one cause of the declining Adelie penguin population.
COREL

that Antarctic sea ice tends to be thinner and more mobile, with more open water interspersed with it, than Arctic sea ice. This means that global warming could have a considerable impact on the extent and characteristics of sea ice in the Southern Ocean. If the sea ice were to diminish significantly, it would reduce the habitat available to seabirds and marine mammals, affect the composition and structure of the world's oceans, and perhaps exacerbate the problem of global warming.

A wide variety of Antarctic life forms depend on sea ice for their survival. Algae form colonies on the ice floes, and when the ice melts in the springtime the algae bloom in the water. Algae blooms provide food for a number of small creatures, including crustaceans like krill, which in turn nourish fish, seabirds, and marine mammals. In addition, many marine species rely on the sea ice to provide breeding grounds or resting places where they will be safe from predators. The mobility of the ice floes makes it difficult to take accurate measurements of sea ice, but scientists suspect that several species are already suffering from a reduction in the extent of the ice. For example, the populations of Adelie penguins on the Antarctic peninsula have declined in recent years, probably because of the loss of habitat and food resulting from the retreat of sea ice. Some experts predict that global warming may cause Adelies to be replaced with less ice dependent penguin species, such as Gentoo and Chinstrap penguins (Gosnell, 1998).

The increase in average annual temperatures in the Antarctic region has already caused some notable disintegration of the continent's ice shelves, particularly in the northern and western parts of the Antarctic Peninsula. As the ice begins to melt, water seeps into tiny cracks and causes them to widen, weakening the structure of the ice. The best-known result of this process was the collapse of the Larsen Ice Shelf on the Antarctic Peninsula. This spectacular event removed a chunk of ice the size of Rhode Island from the outline of the continent. A small section of the shelf, known as Larsen A, broke off in 1995, leading scientists to predict the eventual collapse of the remainder of the shelf. But many observers were surprised at the rapid disintegration of the 3,250-square-kilometer (1,250-square-mile) Larsen B Ice Shelf over the course of a few weeks in 2002. The collapse of the 200-meter-thick (650-feet-thick) ice released approximately 720 million tons of floating ice into the Weddell Sea (Larson, 2002). This ice will not affect global sea levels, however, since the shelf was already floating.

Like these ice shelves, the glaciers on several sub-Antarctic islands have retreated in recent years. For example, Brown Glacier on Heard Island has decreased in area by 33 percent and in volume by 38 percent over the past half-century (UN Environment Programme, 1996). Global warming also has the potential to affect the ice sheet covering the Antarctic continent. Scientists believe that the East Antarctic Ice Sheet, which is mainly grounded above sea level, will remain relatively stable. But they feel that the marine-based West Antarctic Ice Sheet is inherently unstable, making it highly vulnerable to the effects of warming.

The Hole in the Ozone Layer

Antarctica is at the forefront of research and debate over the depletion of the ozone layer in the earth's atmosphere. Ozone, a naturally occurring substance that forms part of the lower stratosphere, absorbs harmful ultraviolet radiation from the sun. Humans have contributed to the loss of atmospheric ozone through the release of chemicals like chlorofluorocarbons (CFCs) and halons. These chemicals undergo reactions on clouds in the stratosphere in which they are converted into forms that destroy ozone in the presence of sunlight.

Scientists first became aware of the extent of damage to the ozone layer in the 1970s, when they discovered a hole in the ozone layer above Antarctica. The hole has appeared every year since it was first noticed, and it increased in size between 1978 and the mid-1990s. By 1998 it covered an estimated 67 million square kilometers (26 million square miles) above Antarctica. It has decreased in size slightly since then, partly as a result of reductions in human emissions of ozone-depleting chemicals. The ozone hole tends to be largest in the early spring following a cold winter; the effect generally disappears in summertime, when warming of the atmosphere causes the clouds to dissipate.

The hole in the ozone layer above Antarctica creates an increase in the ultraviolet (UV) radiation that reaches the earth's surface, which poses a potential threat to the region's ecosystems. For example, scientists have found that phytoplankton in waters outside the extent of the ozone hole show higher productivity than those inside it. One implication may be that UV-tolerant species of plants and animals eventually replace UV-sensitive ones in the Antarctic region (ibid.). On the other hand, some scientists feel that the loss of ozone from the atmosphere above the continent has helped offset some of the effects of global warming on the Antarctic environment by acting to cool the lower atmosphere (Australian Antarctic Division, "Information about Antarctica," 2002).

Biodiversity

Antarctica does not support a large variety of species of flora and fauna. There are no trees on the continent, for example, and no land mammals, reptiles, or amphibians make their homes there. But Antarctica still makes a significant contribution to the world's biodiversity because its life forms have developed unique adaptations to enable them to survive in its harsh environment. For example, the blood of some species of Antarctic fish includes chemical compounds similar to antifreeze. The region also features single-celled plants that produce their own form of sunscreen as an adaptation to the hole in the ozone layer above Antarctica. As a result of such adaptations, many Antarctic species are found nowhere else in the world (ibid.). The high level of specialization found among Antarctic species also tends to make them more sensitive to human impacts on the environment, in the form of bioaccumulation of pollutants, global climate change, and increased levels of solar radiation caused by atmospheric ozone depletion.

At first glance, the Antarctic continent appears barren; in fact, its lack of vegetation forces the region's wildlife to depend on the ocean for its food (ibid.). A number of factors work against plant life hoping to gain a foothold: all but 2 percent of the land is covered with ice; the continent's isolation makes it difficult for new species to spread to Antarctica; and the climate is characterized by low temperatures, high winds, little precipitation, and seasonal darkness. Still, Antarctica supports a variety of tiny, hardy plants that have been found growing on all known rocky outcrops as well as on and under snow and ice.

Most of the continent's terrestrial flora consists of simple organisms. There are 500 species of algae, 125 species of lichens, 30 species of mosses, and only 2 species of flowering plants. Most of this vegetation is extremely slow growing; some species of lichens may grow a millimeter every 100 years. Although scientists continue to conduct ecological studies of Antarctica's flora, they do not yet have enough information to identify endangered species. The sub-Antarctic islands, many of which are free of ice, support a greater diversity of flora than is found on the continent. Some sub-Antarctic islands contain 30 to 40 species of vascular plants, while some of the cool temperate islands of the region may support up to 150 species. The plant species of both Antarctica and the surrounding islands show high levels of endemism.

Because of Antarctica's harsh climate and limited vegetation, the region's land animals consist of microscopic organisms and primitive insects. Fauna on the continent includes protozoans, nematodes, rotifers, tardigrades, springtails, mites, collembola, and two species of midge. The largest species, the wingless midge, is only about 12 millimeters (0.5 inch) long. These organisms can be found in exposed soil, within rocks and ice, in dry streambeds, and in the water of underground lakes. Their ability to withstand extreme conditions has attracted the interest of scientists, who are investigating whether the biochemical compounds they produce may have applications in human pharmaceuticals.

The sub-Antarctic islands contain a greater diversity of fauna than the continent itself, including many rare and endemic species. Several of these islands are relatively pristine, while others have suffered significant degradation resulting from human activity. The most damaging problem for some islands was the introduction—whether deliberate or accidental—of alien species, such as rodents, cats, sheep, cattle, and reindeer. These species often had a detrimental effect on the seabirds and seals that used the islands as breeding grounds. Some of the nonindigenous species have been eradicated in recent years.

Antarctica and the sub-Antarctic islands provide an important feeding and breeding ground for a variety of seabirds and marine mammals. The region is home to forty species of seabirds, including three species of penguins, four species of albatross, and twenty species of petrels, as well as cormorants, skuas, gulls, and terns. More than 100 million birds breed along the coastline of the continent, on the surrounding islands, or on the sea ice each year. Unfortunately, several species have shown declines in recent years. For example, Adelie penguins have experienced a long-term decline in population of around 43 percent (ibid.). Some experts have attributed the drop in Adelie penguin numbers to the effects of global warming, which may be responsible for a reduction in the winter sea ice that the species uses as breeding grounds.

Furthermore, some albatross populations have declined at an unsustainable rate of 7 percent per year, largely because of unintended mortality from longline fishing in the Southern Ocean. In the early 1990s, annual albatross deaths through fishing operations were estimated at 44,000 (Brothers, 1991). As a result, several species were given unfavorable conservation status under Appendix II of the Convention on the Conservation of Migratory Species of Wild Animals, while the Amsterdam albatross was placed on the list of endangered species under Appendix I of the convention.

The marine mammals of the Antarctic region include seven species of whales, eight species of dolphins, and seven species of seals. Crabeater seals, which breed in and around Antarctica, have an estimated population of 15 million, making them the most numerous large mammals surviving in the wild (Australian Antarctic Division, "Information about Antarctica," 2002). Antarctica's marine mammals were heavily exploited by humans in the nineteenth century. In fact, fur seals were eliminated from many sub-Antarctic islands by the 1820s. Most species have recovered from overexploitation under the protection of the CCAS, however, and no extinctions are known to have occurred because of hunting.

About 1.3 million great whales—including blue, fin, humpback, and sperm species—were harvested in the Antarctic region during the twentieth century. Exploitation of these marine mammals had a significant impact on the biological makeup of the Southern Ocean. The International Whaling Commission voted for an indefinite global moratorium on whaling in the Southern Ocean in 1982. In 1994 the IWC established the Southern Ocean Whale Sanctuary, in which commercial whaling was prohibited. Despite such protection, which was afforded over the objections of Japan, the populations of several species have been slow to recover. In 2001, however, IWC proposals to create new whale sanctuaries in the South Pacific and South Atlantic were defeated by Japan, Norway, and other prowhaling nations.

Scientists have limited knowledge of the deep sea around Antarctica, but they know that the continental shelves and slopes of the Southern Ocean support a variety of fish species. Some taxonomic groups are poorly represented in the Southern Ocean, including mollusks and bottom-dwelling fish. But other groups are well represented, including crustaceans and sponges. One of the most important species in the Southern Ocean is krill—small, shrimplike, free-swimming crustaceans that provide a key food source for most Antarctic seabirds and marine mammals, including whales, seals, and penguins (UN Environment Programme, 1996). Krill holds the distinction of being the multicellular animal with the greatest biomass on earth, at an estimated 500 million tons. Overfishing is the main threat facing the Southern Ocean. Several heavily exploited species are protected under CCAMLR, but abuses continue.

Freshwater

The Antarctic ice sheet contains between 60 and 70 percent of the world's freshwater (ibid.). For the most part this water remains inaccessible, though Saudi Arabia and some other nations have investigated the possibility of transporting icebergs north out of the Southern Ocean in order to claim the freshwater locked inside them. The continent also features a number of freshwater and saline lakes in coastal areas and ice-free regions, such as the Larsemann Hills, Bunger Hills, Vestfold Hills, and Schirmacher Oasis. The freshwater lakes are generally fed by glacier melt streams, and their bottom waters can sometimes reach temperatures of 35 degrees Celsius due to warming from the sun (UN Environment Programme, 1999). Small lakes formed from melt water can occasionally be found inland on the surface of the Antarctic ice sheet. There are also several large lakes located deep beneath the ice sheet in the central part of the continent. These lakes are of particular interest to scientists because they have not been exposed to the atmosphere for half a million years (ibid.).

The lakes in Antarctica's ice-free areas are environmentally fragile, yet they are often at the center of human activities. This situation has led to contamination of several lakes over the years. For example, one lake in the Larsemann Hills suffered severe degradation when a nearby research station used it for waste disposal and generator cooling. Similarly, Lake Glubokoye on Schirmacher Oasis now contains high levels of phosphorus on account of dumping of wastewater by a nearby Russian station. ATS parties have attempted to address such problems by developing an environmental code of conduct specific to research operations in ice-free areas. Meanwhile, some lakes have suffered degradation resulting from natural processes. For example, some lakes on the islands of the Antarctic Peninsula have undergone eutrophication as a result of increasing populations of seals transferring marine nutrients to their waters.

Oceans and Coastal Areas

Antarctica is surrounded by the Southern Ocean, which is formed through the convergence of the southernmost parts of the Atlantic, Pacific, and Indian oceans. Although it could be considered an extension of these major oceans, most scientists designate the Southern Ocean as a separate body of water because of its marked differences in temperature and salinity. At 28 million

Nearly seven times the amount of ice covers the Southern Ocean in the winter than in the summer months.
COREL

square kilometers (11 million square miles), the Southern Ocean accounts for 10 percent of the world's oceans.

The oceanographic boundary dividing the Southern Ocean from its northern counterparts is the Antarctic Convergence, or Polar Front. This boundary—which is a few kilometers wide and ranges from 47 to 62 degrees south latitude—marks the zone where cold, dense, northward-drifting Antarctic surface waters sink below warmer, southward-drifting sub-Antarctic waters. The Antarctic Circumpolar Current, which has four times the volume of the Gulf Stream, flows from west to east between the continent and the Antarctic Convergence. This current drives a gradual exchange of heat, oxygen, carbon dioxide, and nutrients between the oceans (Australian Antarctic Division, "Information about Antarctica," 2002).

Although little of its surface is permanently covered by ice, the Southern Ocean undergoes extreme seasonal fluctuations in ice cover. Antarctic sea ice extends over an area of around 4 million square kilometers (1.5 million square miles) in the summer, but increases its coverage to nearly 20 million square kilometers (7.7 million square miles) in winter (Allison, 1997). Scientists have discovered that sea ice plays an important role in global oceanic composition and circulation. When ice covers the Southern Ocean during the winter months, salt is extruded from the ice into the water below. This water becomes very dense as a result of its high saline content and sinks to the ocean floor. It eventually spreads throughout the world's oceans, helping to create vertical circulation and driving major currents (Australian Antarctic Division, "Information about Antarctica," 2002). When the ice melts, it deposits freshwater on the surface of the ocean, further changing the composition of the water. Furthermore, sea ice has an effect on global climate: the ice reflects more solar radiation than the underlying water, thus inhibiting the exchange of heat and energy between the ocean and the atmosphere.

The continent of Antarctica features more than 23,000 kilometers (8,900 square miles) of coastline. Around 40 percent of this coastline is composed of ice sheets. Ice formed in the middle of the continent gradually creeps outward toward the coasts, where it breaks off to form icebergs. Although the calving of icebergs is a natural process, some of Antarctica's floating ice shelves—particularly in the northern and western parts of the Antarctic Peninsula—have disintegrated at an unprecedented rate in recent years. Scientists have associated this phenomenon with a regional increase in average annual temperatures of 2.5 degrees Celsius (4.5 degrees Fahrenheit) over the past fifty years, which in turn may be related to global climate change.

Probably the most serious threat facing Antarctica's marine resources is overharvesting of a few key commercially valuable species, including the Patagonian and Antarctic toothfish, mackerel icefish, krill, and squid. Finfish harvesting in the Antarctic region began in 1969, and more than 3 million tons were reported caught over the next twenty years (UN Environment Programme, 1996). The fishery began to decline in the late 1980s, however, on account of overharvesting. Krill harvesting began in 1972, and the total take through the end of the century was estimated at over 5 million tons. By the early years of the new millennium, economic factors had reduced the market for krill, which was used for human consumption as well as to feed farmed fish, and the annual krill catch averaged around 90,000 tons per year. This amount was less than 10 percent of the annual catch allowed under CCAMLR, which is set at 10 percent of the estimated total krill biomass. Squid was harvested by the United Kingdom through 1989, but the species has not been actively pursued in the Antarctic region since that time (ibid.).

The annual takes of these species are regulated under the CCAMLR, which entered into force in 1982 and was updated in 1989 to include more stringent rules intended to halt the decline of fish stocks. But critics claim that some of the catch limits were set without taking biological data into account. Furthermore, illegal and unreported fishing is a problem. For example, the reported legal catch of Patagonian toothfish for 1997 was 10,245 tons, but the illegal catch for the same year was estimated at more than 107,000 tons in the

Indian Ocean section of the Southern Ocean alone (CCAMLR, 1998). In fact, some nations are suspected of reflagging their fishing fleets in countries that are not parties to CCAMLR in order to circumvent the rules.

Environmentalists are also concerned about the problem of bycatch, particularly the deaths of albatrosses and petrels from longline fishing operations. In addition, scientists are monitoring the effects of bottom trawling on the Southern Ocean. Bottom trawling, which is the primary method used in finfishing, involves dragging fishing gear along the seafloor, which disturbs sediments and may harm slow-growing communities of bottom-dwelling organisms. In recent years, measures have also been put in place to reduce the amount of debris left behind by fishing vessels in order to protect Antarctic species. For example, boats are forbidden to use plastic packaging bands to secure bait boxes, since these bands can be hazardous to seabirds (UN Environment Programme, 1996).

"The Antarctic has suffered a great deal of exploitation, particularly in the Southern Ocean," said Beth Clark of the Antarctic Project. "Despite that, the continent at least still remains essentially pristine. The big question is whether it's going to be allowed to stay that way. Nobody's saying that Antarctica should be completely off-limits to human activity. Not many are arguing that there should be no commercial fishing in the Southern Ocean. Right now, we have a choice: we can continue the way we are going, exploiting resources throughout the world and moving into the Antarctic when nowhere else is left. Or we can decide that one part of the world, at least, is going to be treated differently, left largely alone and allowed to remain the way it has been for millions and millions of years" (Mulvaney, 1997).

Sources

Allison, I. 1997. "Physical Processes Determining the Antarctic Sea Ice Environment." *Australian Journal of Physics* 50.

———. 2002. "Antarctic Ice and the Global Climate System," *Australian Antarctic Magazine* 3 (autumn).

Australian Antarctic Division (AAD). 2002. "Antarctica, Planet Earth: Looking after the Antarctic Environment." *Australian Antarctic Magazine* 3.

———. "Information about Antarctica." Available at http://www.antdiv.gov.au/information/ (accessed November 2002).

Brothers, N. 1991. "Albatross Mortality and Associated Bait Loss in the Japanese Longline Fishery in the Southern Ocean." *Biological Conservation* 55.

Convention for the Conservation of Antarctic Marine Living Resources (CCAMLR). 1998. "Report of the CCAMLR Observer to ATCM." Information Paper No. 64. Lima, Peru: Antarctic Treaty Consultative Meeting.

Donelly, Joanne. 2002. "Crowd Control: More People than Ever Are Heading to Antarctica to Get Away from It All. But Should They Really Be Allowed to Holiday on this Pristine Land?" *Geographical* (January).

Gosnell, Mariana. 1998. "Meltdown? Sea Ice May Be Thawing, Which Could Mean Disruption of Life at Earth's Polar Ends." *International Wildlife* (July–August).

Intergovernmental Panel on Climate Change (IPCC). 1997. *The Regional Impacts of Climate Change: An Assessment of Vulnerability.* Geneva: IPCC.

International Association of Antarctica Tour Operators (IAATO). 1999. "Overview of Antarctic Activities." Information Paper No. 98. Lima, Peru: Antarctic Treaty Consultative Meeting.

Larson, Vanessa. 2002. "Larsen B Ice Shelf Breaks off from Antarctic Peninsula." *World Watch* (July–August).

2002. "The Melting Continent." *Environment* (May).

Monastersky, Richard. 1998. "Antarctic Ozone Hole Reaches Record Size." *Science News* (October 17).

Mulvaney, Kieran. 1997. "The Last Wild Place." *E* (November–December).

Puri, Rama. 1997. *Antarctica: A Natural Reserve.* Shimla, India: Indian Institute of Advanced Study.

Simpson, Sarah. 2002. "Melting Away: The Shrinking of an Immense Swath of Antarctic Ice Threatens to Raise Sea Level—and There May Be No Stopping It." *Scientific American* (January).

UN Environment Programme (UNEP). 1996. *Question of Antarctica: State of the Environment in Antarctica.* Report of the Secretary General to the 51st Session of the UN General Assembly, September 20, Christchurch, NZ.

———. *Global Environmental Outlook 2000.* 1999. London: Earthscan.

Walton, David. 1999. "Antarctica's Tainted Horizons." *UNESCO Courier* (May).

Appendix

African-Eurasian Migratory Waterbird
Agreement (AEWA)
http://www.unep-wcmc.org/
AEWA/index2.html

Albertine Rift Conservation
Society (ARCOS)
http://www.unep-wcmc.org/arcos/

Association of Southeast
Asian Nations (ASEAN)
http://www.asean.or.id/

Biodiversity Planning Support
Programme (BPSP)
http://www.undp.org/bpsp/

BirdLife International (BI)
http://www.birdlife.net

Botanic Gardens Conservation
International (BGCI)
http://www.bgci.org.uk/

CAB International (CABI)
http://www.cabi.org/

Centre for International
Forestry Research (CIFOR)
http://www.cifor.org/

Circumpolar Protected Areas
Network (CPAN)
http://www.grida.no/caff/
cpanstratplan.htm

Commission for Environment
Cooperation (CEC) (North
American Agreement on
Environmental Cooperation)
http://www.cec.org/

Commission on Genetic Resources
for Food and Agriculture (CGRFA)
http://www.fao.org/ag/cgrfa/
default.htm

Commission for Sustainable
Development (CSD)
http://www.un.org/esa/sustdev/csd.htm

Committee on Trade and Environment
(CTE), World Trade Organization
http://www.wto.org/english/
tratop_e/envir_e/envir_e.htm

Conservation International (CI)
http://www.conservation.org/

Consultative Group on International
Agricultural Research (CGIAR)
http://www.cgiar.org/

Convention on Biological
Diversity (CBD)
http://www.biodiv.org/

Convention on International Trade in
Endangered Species of Wild Fauna
and Flora (CITES)
http://www.cites.org/

Convention on Migratory
Species of Wild Animals (CMS)
http://www.unep-wcmc.org/cms

European Centre for Nature
Conservation (ECNC)
http://www.ecnc.nl/

European Community (EC)
http://europa.eu.int/

European Environment
Agency (EEA)
http://www.eea.eu.int/

Forest Stewardship Council (FSC)
http://www.fscoax.org/index.html

Foundation for International
Environmental Law and
Development (FIELD)
http://www.field.org.uk/

Global Assessment of Soil
Degradation (GLASOD)
http://www.gsf.de/UNEP/glasod.html

Global Biodiversity
Information Facility (GBIF)
http://www.gbif.org

Global Coral Reef
Monitoring Network (GCRMN)
http://coral.aoml.noaa.gov/gcrmn/

Global Forest Resources Assessment
2000 (FRA 2000), UN Food and
Agriculture Organization
http://www.fao.org/forestry/fo/fra/
index.jsp

Global International Waters Assessment
(GIWA), UN Environment Programme
http://www.giwa.net/

Global Invasive Species
Programme (GISP)
http://globalecology.stanford.edu/DGE/
Gisp/index.html

Global Resource Information Database
(GRID), UN Environment Programme
http://www.grid.no

Inter-American Biodiversity
Information Network (IABIN)
http://www.iabin.org/

Intergovernmental Oceanographic
Commission (IOC), UN Educational,
Scientific, and Cultural Organization
http://ioc.unesco.org/iocweb/

Intergovernmental Panel on
Climate Change (IPCC)
http://www.ipcc.ch/index.html

International Center for Agricultural
Research in the Dry Areas (ICARDA)
http://www.icarda.cgiar.org/

International Centre for Living Aquatic
Resources Management (ICLARM)
http://www.cgiar.org/iclarm/

International Centre for Research in
Agroforestry (ICRAF)
http://www.icraf.cgiar.org/

International Cooperative
Biodiversity Groups (ICBG)
http://www.nih.gov/fic/programs/icbg.
html

International Coral Reef
Action Network (ICRAN)
http://www.icran.org

International Coral Reef
Information Network (ICRIN)
http://www.environnement.gouv.fr/
icri/index.html

International Council for the
Exploration of the Sea (ICES)
http://www.ices.dk/

International Council for Science (ICSU)
http://www.icsu.org/

International Food Policy Research
Institute (IFPRI)
http://www.ifpri.org/

International Fund for
Agricultural Development (IFAD)
http://www.ifad.org/

International Geosphere-
Biosphere Programme (IGBP)
http://www.igbp.kva.se/

International Institute of
Tropical Agriculture (IITA)
http://www.iita.org

International Maritime
Organization (IMO)
http://www.imo.org/

International Rivers Network (IRN)
http://www.irn.org/

International Union of
Biological Sciences (IUBS)
http://www.iubs.org/

Man and the Biosphere Program MAB),
UN Educational, Scientific, and
Cultural Organization
http://www.unesco.org/mab/index.htm

Marine Stewardship Council (MSC)
http://www.msc.org/

Organization of African Unity (OAU)
http://www.oau-oau.org/

Organization for
Economic Cooperation
and Development (OECD)
http://www.oecd.org/

Ozone Secretariat Homepage
http://www.unep.ch/ozone/

Pan-European Biological and Landscape
Diversity Strategy (PEBLDS)
http://www.strategyguide.org/

Program for the Conservation of
Arctic Flora and Fauna (CAFF),
Arctic Council
http://www.grida.no/caff/

Protocol Concerning Specially
Protected Areas and Wildlife (SPAW)
http://www.cep.unep.org/law/
cartnut.html

Ramsar Convention on Wetlands of
International Importance (RAMSAR)
http://www.ramsar.org/

South African Development
Community (SADC)
http://www.sadc.int/

South Pacific Regional
Environmental Programme (SPREP)
http://www.sprep.org.ws/

Species Survival Commission (SSC),
World Conservation Union
http://iucn.org/themes/ssc/index.htm

TRAFFIC (the joint wildlife trade
monitoring programme of World
Wide Fund for Nature and World
Conservation Union)
http://www.traffic.org

United Nations Centre for
Human Settlements (UNCHS)
http://www.unchs.org

United Nations
Children's Fund (UNICEF)
http://www.unicef.org

United Nations Conference on
Environment and Development
(UNCED), Rio de Janeiro, June 1992
http://www.un.org/esa/sustdev/
agenda21.htm

United Nations Conference on Trade
and Development (UNCTAD)
http://www.unctad.org/

United Nations Convention to Combat
 Desertification (UNCCD)
 http://www.unccd.int/main.php

United Nations Convention
 on the Law of the Sea (UNCLOS)
 http://www.un.org/Depts/los/
 index.htm

United Nations Development
 Programme (UNDP)
 http://www.undp.org/

United Nations Educational, Scientific,
 and Cultural Organization (UNESCO)
 http://www.unesco.org/

United Nations Environment
 Programme (UNEP)
 http://www.unep.org/

United Nations Food and
 Agriculture Organization (FAO)
 http://www.fao.org/

United Nations
 Forum on Forests (UNFF)
 http://www.un.org/esa/sustdev/
 forests.htm

United Nations Framework Convention
 on Climate Change (UNFCCC)
 http://www.unfccc.de/index.html

United Nations Industrial
 Development Organization (UNIDO)
 http://www.unido.org/

World Agricultural Information Centre
 (WAIC), UN Food and Agriculture
 Organization
 http://www.fao.org/waicent/search/
 default.htm

World Bank (WB)
 http://www.worldbank.org

World Commission
 on Dams (WCD)
 http://www.dams.org/

World Commission on Protected Areas
 (WCPA), World Conservation Union
 http://www.wcpa.iucn.org/

World Conservation
 Monitoring Centre (WCMC)
 http://www.unep-wcmc.org

World Conservation
 Union (IUCN)
 http://www.iucn.org/

World Health Organization (WHO)
 http://www.who.int

World Heritage Convention (WHC)
 http://www.unesco.org/whc/index.htm

World Resources Institute (WRI)
 http://www.wri.org/wri/

World Summit on Sustainable
 Development (WSSD),
 Johannesburg, South Africa,
 September 2002
 http://www.johannesburgsummit.org/

World Trade Organization (WTO)
 http://www.wto.org/

World Water Council (WWC)
 http://www.worldwatercouncil.org/

World Wide Fund
 for Nature (WWF)
 http://www.panda.org/

WorldWatch Institute
 http://www.worldwatch.org/

Index